FROMMER'S TOURING GUIDE TO EGYPT

Author
Denise Basdevant

Translation
Eric Inglefield

Adaptation
Times Editions, Singapore and Hachette, Paris

Production
Times Editions, Singapore

This edition published in the United States and Canada in 1987
by Prentice Hall Press
A division of Simon & Schuster, Inc.
Gulf+Western Building
One Gulf+Western Plaza
New York, New York 10023

PRENTICE HALL PRESS is a trademark of Simon & Schuster, Inc.

This guide is adapted from *En Egypte, la Vallée du Nil* published
by Hachette Guides Bleus, Paris, 1986.

Library of Congress Cataloging-in-Publication Data

Basdevant, Denise.
  Frommer's touring guide to Egypt.
  Translation of: En Egypte, la vallée du Nil.
  Includes index.
  1. Egypt — Description and travel — 1945– —
Guide-books. I. Title.
DT45.B29313   1987   916.2'044   86-30361
ISBN 0-13-331299-2

Printed in Singapore

FROMMER'S TOURING GUIDE TO EGYPT

PRENTICE HALL PRESS

NEW YORK

HOW TO USE YOUR GUIDE

Before leaving, consult the information given in the chapter 'Planning your trip' (p.9). On arrival, use addresses and practical information from the chapter 'Amenities in Egypt' (p.56). Names of the main sites, monuments and hotels are followed by grid references to help you locate them on the maps (see below). At the end of the guide, you will find an index of places, sites and monuments.

SYMBOLS USED

Sites, monuments, museums, works of art
* ★ interesting
* ★★ remarkable
* ★★★ exceptional

Hotel classification
* ▲ tourist and economy
* ▲▲ medium class
* ▲▲▲ first class hotel
* ▲▲▲▲ delux hotel

MAPS

▬ CONTENTS

Photo credits: A. Barbey, pp. 14, 95, 138–139, 150 – D. Basdevant,
pp. 119, 134 – M. Guillet, pp. 26, 75 – J. Marthelot, pp. 18, 30, 42, 47,
62, 70, 74, 79, 91, 102, 111, 115, 130, 146 – M.-L. Varin, p. 147.

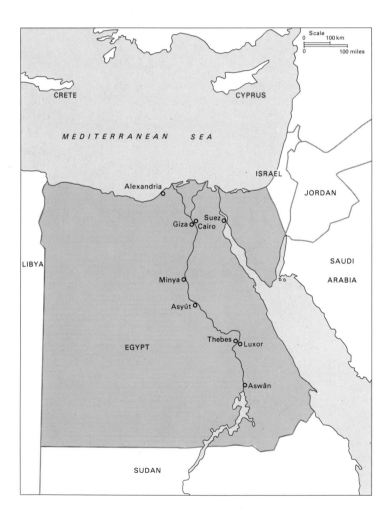

INTRODUCING EGYPT

To explore Egypt is to take a journey back in time to the age of the pharaohs. It is also to explore the city of Cairo at the entrance to the Nile Delta, a great Muslim capital, the largest metropolis on the African continent and an acknowledged center of the Third World. Getting to know Egypt also means plunging into the hustle and bustle of Alexandria, one of the biggest ports in the eastern Mediterranean and a city that has kept its name and fame intact for over 2300 years. The history of Egypt stretches back 5000 years into the past of a narrow ribbon of fertile land, about 670 miles/1080 kilometres long, the valley of the Nile. The Nile Valley was the first area in the world to provide the right conditions for human life and commerce — that is to say, civilization — and, as a result, Egypt has the longest continuous known history prior to the emergence of the great civilization of China. In the course of time, the country has been subjected to many foreign masters; yet along the banks of the Nile, the *fellahin* still preserve the same way of life, impervious to political change. The figures you see working in their fields today seem to have stepped straight from the great Egyptian paintings created more than 2000 years before the time of Christ.

In Cairo, however, you can follow the slow progress of Egyptian history from the ancient kingdom of the pharaohs right up to the republic of today. You will discover the earliest evidence of Christianity in Egypt in the first centuries A.D. It was then that the great innovator St. Anthony of Thebes established the first Christian monastery in the Egyptian desert; his followers, the Copts, still make up nearly 15 percent of the Egyptian population. Islamic civilization blossomed in Egypt between A.D. 639, when the Caliph Omar brought the country under his rule, and 1524, when Suleiman the Magnificent reduced it to the status of a Turkish province. Splendid mosques still bear witness to this glorious era.

In Cairo, too, you will be able to trace the rise of modern Egypt, which Nasser dated from Napoleon's military expedition of 1798. It is generally agreed that the credit for this must go to Mehemet Ali, an officer in the Turkish army and one of Napoleon's most fervent admirers, who seized power in 1804. To a land that had barely emerged from feudalism, he had the courage to give an effective structure along the lines of the western nations. Although Egypt, under his leadership, was to become conscious of its role as a Muslim power and to regain its pride in the historic achievements of the pharaohs, it still had to undergo a period of western colonialist domination before being able to forge its own destiny. A large part of the Cairo city center still bears evidence of this, with its middle-class housing built to accommodate the European engineers and specialists who came to modernize the Egyptian army and economy, followed by the brokers who invested large sums in the country's development. In fact, the Suez Canal was to become a combined French and British venture and, in 1882, Britain made Egypt a protectorate, a state of affairs that would last, whether by law or de facto, until Nasser's revolution of 1952. An intensely nationalistic army officer, Nasser gave Egypt back to its people and restored its independence.

Cairo's vitality reflects the leading role of Egypt in the modern international community, particularly in the Middle East. It is also a city of dramatic over-population and widespread poverty. The magnitude of Egypt's development problems and their complexity are all the more difficult to comprehend because this is a nation which has inherited one of the richest civilizations on earth, and is certainly the oldest.

Upon the death of Nasser in 1970, his successor, Anwar Sadat, set out to apply pragmatic remedies to his country's problems. After Sadat's assassination in October 1981, President Hosni Mubarak, his successor, continued with similar policies, particularly in social and cultural matters. The huge University of Cairo is today the scene of intense activity, and vast construction projects are under way in various parts of the city, from the modern hospital on the banks of the Nile to the new public housing estates on the outskirts. Many modern factories now surround the city, and across the silver-speckled cottonfields of the delta, you find them again around Alexandria.

Alexandria itself is a lively, airy, seaside city, but it is a long way from the Nile Valley. There are few reminders of past glories here. Yet the fine buildings along its superb coast roads remind us that Alexandria has always been a place where dreams and ambitions could be realized. Jewish craftsmen and merchants, and Greek and Levantine ship-owners found wealth here. As a center of trade and culture, it once attracted all the great figures of the Orient; today it beckons Arab oil potentates. Alexandria's busy port is often referred to as the 'commercial lung' of the country, and it is destined to remain a key factor in the nation's future.

PLANNING YOUR TRIP

This section covers practical information on the weather, means of travel, official formalities, useful addresses and currency.

▬ WHEN TO GO

Egypt is essentially a country for winter holidays, although given the dryness of the climate, even the hottest periods are bearable. Nevertheless, visits during the summer are the most testing. In spring there is a chance that the windy squalls of the *khamsin*, laden with sand and dust, may spoil your stay. If you are traveling on business, avoid the busy late-spring period of Ramadan, which lasts about 12 days on dates that vary from year to year.

Average temperatures

	Degrees	Jan. min.	max.	Mar. min	max.	May min.	max.
CAIRO	°F	47.5	66.4	52.3	74.6	63.3	90.3
	°C	8.6	19.1	11.3	23.7	17.4	32.4
ALEXANDRIA	°F	48.7	64.9	52.2	69.8	62	79.7
	°C	9.3	18.3	11.2	21	16.7	26.5
PORT SAÏD	°F	52.3	64.4	56.3	68.3	67.3	78.4
	°C	11.3	18	13.5	20.2	19.6	25.8
LUXOR	°F	41.7	73.2	51.2	84.2	69.2	102.9
	°C	5.4	22.9	10.7	29	20.7	39.4
ASWÂN	°F	49.1	76.5	57.2	87.1	74.3	104.5
	°C	9.5	24.2	14	30.6	23.5	40.3

	Degrees	July min.	max.	Sept. min.	max.	Nov. min.	max.
CAIRO	°F	70.7	95.7	67.8	90.1	57	77.2
	°C	21.5	35.4	19.9	32.3	13.9	25.1
ALEXANDRIA	°F	72.8	85.3	70.3	84.9	58.6	75.9
	°C	22.7	29.6	21.3	29.4	14.8	24.4
PORT SAÏD	°F	75.4	86.7	75	84.5	65.1	75.2
	°C	24.1	30.4	23.9	29.2	18.4	24
LUXOR	°F	74.6	105.4	70.7	91.2	54.1	84
	°C	23.7	40.8	21.5	32.9	12.3	28.9
ASWÂN	°F	79	107.4	75.2	105.8	61.7	88.5
	°C	26.1	41.9	24	41	16.5	31.4

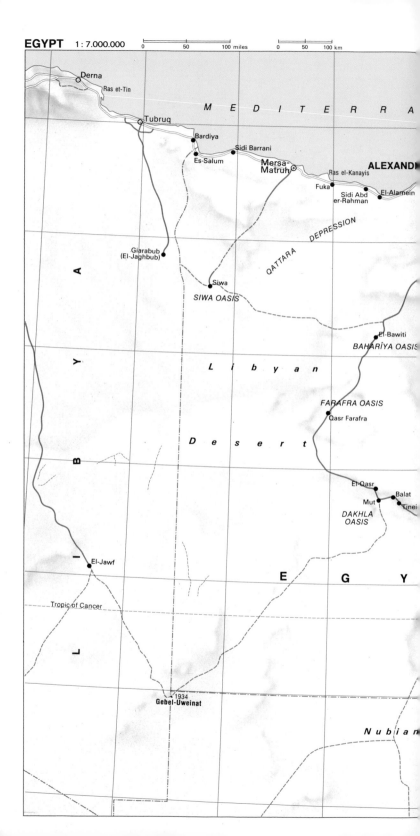

EGYPT   1 : 7.000.000

0   50   100 miles

0   50   100 km

Derna

Ras et-Tin

M E D I T E R R A

Tubruq

Bardiya

Sidi Barrani

Es-Salum

Mersa-
Matruh

Ras el-Kanayis

ALEXAND

Fuka

Sidi Abd
er-Rahman

El-Alamein

DEPRESSION

Giarabub
(El-Jaghbub)

QATTARA

Siwa

SIWA OASIS

A

El-Bawiti

BAHARĪYA OASIS

Y

L i b y a n

FARAFRA OASIS

Qasr Farafra

D e s e r t

B

El-Qasr

Balat

Mut

Tinei

DAKHLA
OASIS

El-Jawf

I

E

G

Y

Tropic of Cancer

L

1934
Gebel-Uweinat

N u b i a n

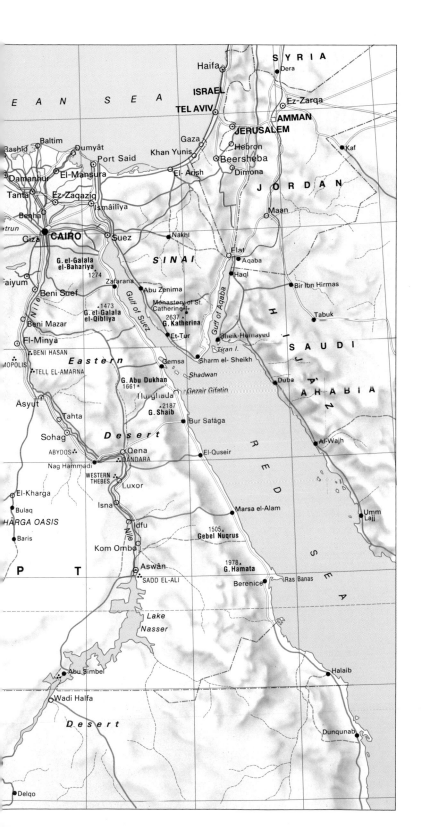

The average temperature varies from 65°F (15°C) in winter (December, January, February) to 90°F (30°C) in summer (June, July, August). There is virtually no rain at all, but there are constant clouds of sand and dust.

WHAT TO TAKE

Clothing

In winter, you will need fairly light clothes and some woolens, perhaps even a wrap or jacket for evening wear or trips in a *felucca*. In summer, avoid synthetic fabrics, but do not forget to take (as in all desert countries) a sweater for *son et lumière* displays. In addition, go equipped with sandals, comfortable shoes, sunglasses, and swimwear for a brisk dip in one of the pools provided by nearly all the hotels and cruise-boats. Wide-brimmed hats can be bought when you arrive.

Finally, do not forget the following items: an alarm clock, because you will want to get up early; a flashlight powerful enough for visiting the tombs; a number of good books to read; and anti-mosquito lotion for use when dining out-of-doors.

Cameras and photographic equipment

Although there are no restrictions on the taking of non-commercial photographs and amateur video films by visitors and Egyptology students at temples, mosques, churches and other open-air monuments and sites, fees are payable for taking photographs and video films inside the pyramids, tombs and museums at varying rates between L.E. 5 and 25 per day. Fees for commercial photography and filming for television and cinema purposes are, of course, much higher, and strict regulations are enforced. Consult your travel agent for details.

As a general rule, out of consideration for others, you should avoid taking 'picturesque' scenes of poor districts in Cairo or the countryside. You are, therefore, left mainly with the natural scenery and the monuments. In order to get good pictures with shadows or relief effects in the constant sunshine, take a sun-shade, a yellow filter for monochrome films and an ultra-violet filter for color films. Finally, don't forget an air-brush to remove dust and sand. For taking pictures inside the tombs you will also need a flash attachment and possibly a wide-angle lens.

Health

Egypt has a healthy climate. There is no danger of contracting malaria, but do not put your feet in the Nile or in the canals, where there is a risk of catching bilharzia, a disease caused by a parasitic worm and very difficult to cure. As in all hot countries, pay strict attention to food hygiene, take any medical products you need to ward off risks of infection, avoid drinking alcohol before going in the sun, and be wary about salads and any raw foods that may not have been properly washed. Finally, always carry a few Band-aids with you for cuts or blisters.

OFFICIAL FORMALITIES AND INFORMATION

Passports and visas

All visitors to Egypt must hold a passport or equivalent travel document valid for at least six months and a visa. Visas are obtainable from any Egyptian consulate and, if applying in person, are issued within 24 hours of completing the official application form and submitting it with your passport, a passport-size photograph and the appropriate fee. Different rates are payable from country to country, depending on whether the application is for a tourist or business visa and for either one or three visits. When applying by mail, a self-addressed envelope, stamped for return by registered or recorded mail, should be included. Mail applications take at least two weeks to process. Visas for a single visit are valid for three months from the date of issue and permit a stay of one month from the date of arrival. Visas for three visits are valid for six months. Travelers in transit do not require a visa.

Egyptian consulates where applications for visas can be made include:

United Kingdom: London: 19 Kensington Palace Gardens Mews, London W8, tel. (01) 229 8818/9.

United States: Chicago: 505 North Lake Shore Drive, Suite 6502, Chicago, Ill 60611, tel. (312) 670–2633/4, (312) 670–2693.
Houston: 2000 West Loop South, Suite 1750, Control Data Building, Houston, TX 77027, tel. (713) 961–4915/6.
New York: 1110 Second Avenue, New York, NY 10022, tel. (212) 759–7120.
San Francisco: 3001 Pacific Avenue, San Francisco, CA 94115, tel. (415) 346–9700, (415) 346–9702.
Washington D.C.: 2310 Decatur Pl., NW, Washington DC 20008, tel. (202) 232–5400.

Canada: Montreal: 3754 Côte de Neiges, Montreal, Quebec H38 1V6, tel. (514) 937–7781.
Ottawa: 454 Laurier Avenue E, Ottawa, Ontario K1N 6R3, tel. (613) 234–4931.

REGISTRATION

All visitors to Egypt must register with the Ministry of the Interior within seven days of arrival. The hotel normally does this for you. However, if you are staying privately with friends you must present yourself at the first floor of the Government Building in Midan el-Tahrir (Liberation Square) in Cairo, or at any police station. Applications for extensions of visas can also be made at Midan el-Tahrir.

HEALTH REGULATIONS AND VACCINATIONS

Vaccinations are not required for visitors traveling directly from western countries. However, certificates of vaccination against cholera and yellow fever are compulsory for travelers arriving from countries where these diseases are endemic or where there is an outbreak. Check the current regulations with your travel agent well before your date of departure.

CUSTOMS

General entrance regulations are the same as those in force in most countries. A warning: declare binoculars, musical instruments, cassette recorders, cameras, video cameras and any other expensive item of equipment, and keep a copy of your declaration to present to customs officers if required on your departure from Egypt. See also the currency regulations referred to below.

There are no restrictions on taking souvenirs and gifts bought in Egypt out of the country, provided their total value does not exceed the total amount of money you took into the country and declared on your arrival. You will not, however, be permitted to take out any archaeological object without proper authorization, and this is very difficult to obtain.

CURRENCY REGULATIONS AND BANKING

There is no restriction on the importation of foreign currency into Egypt, but visitors are not allowed to bring in or take out more than 20 Egyptian pounds (L.E. 20). On arrival you must declare all the money you are carrying

in the form of cash and travelers checks, and any gold worth more than L.E. 500. You should also declare what credit cards you are carrying. Foreign currency or travelers checks equivalent in value to U.S. $150 (approximately U.K. £100) or more must be exchanged into Egyptian pounds on arrival in Egypt for spending in the country. However, visitors traveling with organized tours and transit travelers are exempt from this requirement.

You should not, of course, have more money in your possession on your departure than you had on arrival. Keep records of all currency transactions for presentation at customs if required. Facilities for changing money are generally available in hotels, airports and travel agencies.

In banks you will be asked for your passport number when changing currency. Be sure to make a note of this and carry it with you, because your hotel will probably keep your passport until your departure. Banks are open from 8.30 am to 2.30 pm every day except Fridays and Saturdays. Almost all are open on Sundays.

The rate of exchange of the Egyptian pound varies considerably. Despite the advantage tourists enjoy, you will probably spend more than you thought. You will find there are a surprising number of extra costs you did not expect during your stay, let alone the money you spend on the souvenirs you are constantly being offered.

The Egyptian pound is made up of 100 piastres (pt), and prices are almost always shown in piastres. There are notes in denominations of L.E. 20, 10, 5 and 1, and of 50, 25, 10 and 5 piastres.

GETTING THERE

Many tour operators and travel organizations in western countries provide package tours to Egypt of varying length, and you are advised to consult your local branch to see which tour suits your interests and is available, and the cost involved. Going as a member of an organized group eliminates all the separate bookings you would have to make for travel and accommodation if you were traveling on an individual basis.

By air

Egypt's own national airline, Egypt Air, and most major western airlines operate regular services to Cairo. Flights from Britain are direct, but some U.S. flights involve a change of plane or a stop at a European capital on the way. Early booking is essential for visitors planning their own trips, especially during the height of the tourist season in the winter months. Tours to the Nile Valley mostly begin in Cairo, and flights arrive at Heliopolis International Airport, some 10 miles/16 kilometres from the city center. There are also new direct charter flights from Britain to Luxor, Aswân and the Red Sea resort of Hurghada. Luxor has a brand-new airport with six terminals designed to receive over two million passengers every year.

Travelers arriving at the Cairo airport can use the regular coach service provided to get to the city center. First-time visitors may, however, prefer to take one of the limousines that normally provide a shuttle service to the big hotels, or, if these are not at the waiting-point, a taxi. The fare for the ride varies according to your destination, and will probably be between L.E. 10 and 15, but don't be afraid to bargain. Negotiate the price first, and go with plenty of change in your pocket because drivers do not always have change for big notes.

By sea

Although the most practical way to get to Egypt is by air, it is possible to take a ship to Alexandria from Venice or Greece. It is best to let your travel agent work out the details.

Using the shaduf to draw water.

By car

It is also possible to take a car into Egypt, either by sea from Europe or across the land frontier with Israel at Rafah and Taba. This applies only to private cars and not to solar or diesel vehicles. Passengers must not exceed seven, plus the driver, and the owner or a member of his family must be in the car. Documents required include a valid driving license and International License, together with official documentation from a motoring organization in the country of origin.

Although traveling by car in Egypt is not impossible, it is not recommended except for the most experienced and hardy explorers. Apart from long and tedious customs formalities at the port or frontiers, there are the constant worries of finding accommodation for the night, navigating carefully under desert conditions, and keeping the car in good working order in a country where garages are hard to find. Egypt holds a 1863-mile/3000-kilometre car rally every year, the Pharaohs Rally, that takes in difficult road conditions.

Organized tours

As you would expect, a trip to Egypt is, more than anything else, a fantastic archaeological adventure but it is also an opportunity to get to know one of the most engaging and fascinating nations on earth.

Egypt is able to come up to expectations and to satisfy the curiosity of all kinds of travelers. People flock there from all directions and, despite the efforts made by the Egyptian government to receive them, there are always more than the hotels and transport system can cope with. It often happens that the traveler who takes the chance of organizing his or her own stay in Egypt finds the hotel room or airline seat he or she had booked has been snatched away by some last-minute foreign delegation or political congress. Under such circumstances, you are only likely to get satisfaction on your arrival in Egypt if you made your booking by telex and can present a copy of it with the confirmation made in Egypt. Nevertheless, all your plans, carefully worked out in advance, may be ruined. It is wise, therefore, to entrust the planning of your trip to one of the organizations that are used to doing so and are aware of the problems. In addition to group tours, the major travel companies now provide one-week stays in the hotel of their choice for people traveling separately in either Cairo or Luxor. In this way, excursions can be arranged to suit individual preferences. Your local travel agent will be able to provide you with the brochures of appropriate companies.

▬ *USEFUL ADDRESSES*

For more information to help you plan your trip to Egypt, contact any of the following national tourist offices:

London: 168 Piccadilly, London W1, tel. (01) 493 5282.
Montreal: 40 Place Bonaventure, Frontenac, P.O. Box 304, Montreal, P.Q., Canada H5A 1VA, tel. (514) 861–4420.
New York: 630 Fifth Avenue, New York, NY 10020, tel. (212) 246–6960.
San Francisco: 323 Geary Street, San Francisco, CA 94102, tel. (415) 433–7562/3.

The Egyptian government also runs its own official tour organization known as *Misr Travel*, which has offices in many countries and can help with the planning and arrangement of your trip. They can be contacted at the following addresses:

London: Misr Travel, 40 Great Marlborough Street, London W1, tel. (01) 734 0238, (01) 437–5119.
New York: Misr Travel, 630 Fifth Avenue, Suite 555, New York, NY 10111, tel. (212) 582–9210.
Sydney: Misr Travel, Suite 5, Tang House, 630 George Street, P.O. Box K 118, Sydney, N.S.W. 2000, Australia, tel. (2) 676–979.

EGYPT TODAY

According to the constitution of 1971, Egypt is a democratic socialist, Arab state. Islam is the official religion, and Koranic law is the basis for the legislation. Egypt is, however, a tolerant country that recognizes freedom of thought and worship, as well as of the press, publishing and information media.

CONSTITUTION AND GOVERNMENT

The President of the Republic, who is also Prime Minister, controls all civil and military power in Egypt. He is the head of the executive branch. Legislative power rests with the People's Assembly. This is elected by universal suffrage and has a membership of 350, of whom nearly half must be selected from among ordinary working people and peasants. Four political parties dispute the favor of the electorate; the center party, the National Democratic Party, traditionally has a very large majority. The country is split up into 25 administrative districts. Each of these is administered by a representative of the president — a governor — assisted by a governing council, some of whose members are elected, others chosen for their abilities. Councils based on the same model manage the towns and villages.

ECONOMY

Egypt's economic life is totally dominated by the Nile. It was because of the river's annual floods that the country became the granary of the ancient world. On the other hand, crop yields were highly variable, with cycles of abundance and famine. The construction of dams on the Nile has made production more consistent by guaranteeing permanent irrigation of the fields. Water from the Aswân Dam has even enabled land to be won from the desert and has enlarged the 12½-mile/20-kilometre arable belt along the valley.

These colossal undertakings are evidence of the importance Egypt attaches to the productivity and the expansion of its farmlands. They must be made to feed a population that is increasing by more than a million every year, and to supply the raw materials needed for industry and export.

In recent years, wheat has lost its primacy as a food crop, both to rice grown on the delta and to maize. Cotton is by far the most

important agricultural product both in quality — the world's best — and in quantity; Egypt's textile industry is booming. Sugar cane also produces high yields and has made Egypt a major exporter of sugar.

Egypt also owes to the Nile and its dams its ability to produce the electricity it needs for general public consumption and for industry. The country today is a net exporter of electricity, although this has not prevented it from launching an important nuclear energy program. In the sphere of industry, Egypt is moving towards greater diversification, with a view to decreasing imports of consumer goods. In addition to the established textile and food-manufacturing companies, cement works and fertilizer factories, there are now enterprises producing cars and refrigerators. Nonetheless, the equipment needed for improving the standard of living remains a burden on the national budget; for example, many of the new construction sites in Cairo have had to be undertaken in partnership with foreign contractors. Fortunately, oil and natural gas are in ample supply for the country's needs and possibilities are now opening up for their export.

Tourism remains a major source of foreign currency earnings and employment. The government is also improving traffic conditions in the country and developing new hotel facilities in Cairo and the Nile Valley.

THE POPULATION

Today, Egypt has more than 50 million inhabitants. A century ago, its population was estimated at six million. This astonishing growth, which is continuing at the rate of a million a year, has caused massive poverty and unemployment. In theory, Egypt is self-sufficient in food but, although nobody starves, most are undernourished. When unemployed peasants come to the towns to look for jobs — which they do not find — they encounter appalling living conditions. In some districts of Cairo and the suburbs, as many as 260,000 people per square mile (100,000 people per square kilometre) have been counted; many new arrivals are forced to seek shelter in the cemeteries and set up home there. President Nasser tried to promote a policy of birth-control but ran up against much Muslim resistance, especially in the rural districts. Nevertheless, the birth-rate is tending to fall.

In order to cope with the situation, the government is investing heavily in environmental projects. New communities are being built outside the towns on the edge of the desert. Running water and sewage systems are being installed in the Cairo slum districts, which are also being provided with schools and health centers.

Egypt's cultural and social problems are formidable and urgent. Poverty and unemployment can only encourage the spread of Muslim extremist tendencies throughout the country. However, the visitor will find that Egyptians are basically tolerant people. More than 80 percent of them are Sunnites, followers of the orthodox branch of Islam, but they respect those among their fellow countrymen, the Copts, who have remained loyal to Christianity. Some problems have arisen out of the desire of the Copts, who

Young **fellahin** *from Upper Egypt.*

represent 15 percent of the population, to play a greater political role but their demands have never jeopardized national unity. The Egyptian elite, whatever its creed, has assimilated western culture, and, thus, the country is guaranteed a supply of teachers, lawyers, doctors, engineers and other professional people who can compete with their foreign counterparts on an equal footing.

GEOGRAPHY

For people living at the time of the pharaohs, the Nile had no beginning and no end. It existed only from the Elephantine rapids (Aswân) as far as the delta, where it became lost in its seven branches and thousands of smaller channels. The Nile was one of the primary elements, like the earth and the sky, by which their lives were ruled.

THE WORLD OF THE NILE

Although this cosmological view of natural phenomena cannot apply in our own times, it illustrates wonderfully the originality of thought that the ancient Egyptian civilization derived from the geographical framework which protected it from foreign attack. To the south, the first cataract marked the boundary of black Africa, or Nubia, the route to the 'land of Kush', which the early pharaohs strove to annex in order to ensure the security of their own territory. To the north, the almost impassable region of marshes forming the delta insulated the country from Mediterranean influences. Between the two deserts, one stretching westward as far as the Atlantic, the other eastward to the Red Sea, Egypt naturally established its civilization along the Nile. Its prosperity was due to the fertile silt, deposited by the river along its banks from June to September, and to the miracle that made it possible for life to flourish along its 560-mile/900-kilometre course.

The Egyptians attributed this miracle to the ram-headed god Khnum, the guardian of the vast underground caverns from which the Nile waters were supposed to originate; by lifting his sandal, he released the life-giving flood. These endless reserves of water were situated in the area of the first cataract. Thanks to the explorers of Africa, we have known since the end of the 19th century that the powerful, slow-moving Nile which crosses Egypt below the first cataract is the result of the meeting of the White Nile and Blue Nile at Khartoum, in the Sudan. The White Nile flows out of Lake Victoria, fed by the snows of the mountain ranges of equatorial Africa, and has a comparatively regular flow. The Blue Nile rises in the mountains of Ethiopia, where it is periodically swollen by spring torrents. Hence the Blue Nile is the main source of the floodwater.

'Egypt is the gift of the Nile,' wrote the Greek historian, Herodotus, some five centuries before the birth of Christ. Today, we might add that the Nile is the gift of Africa. It is a river that is quite appropriate to this continent, the natural forces of which mankind has not yet managed to control. Its floods, which cause the annual rate of flow to vary between 1700 and 5300 billion cubic feet (48 and 150 billion cubic metres), have always held Egypt in their power. When they are too small, they condemn the land to drought and famine, and when they are too great, they drown the fields and livestock in a dreadful catastrophe. Since the beginning of time, men have struggled to manage the Nile's waters to make the land fertile. The founding of Memphis, the first capital of ancient Egypt, was connected with the first great engineering works undertaken to control the river's flow. A whole history of Egypt could be written taking as its sole theme the irrigation policies adopted by its rulers, from the digging of the waterways of El Fayyum during the Middle Kingdom (2060–1785 B.C.) to the construction of the high dam at Aswân, begun under President Nasser in 1960.

We may wonder whether, with the help of modern technology, Egypt will finally succeed, after 5000 years of effort, in controlling the Nile, in bending this natural giant to the will of mankind. Only time will tell. Along its famous valley, bounded on the west by the cliffs of the Libyan plateau and on the east by the Arabian mountains, life still goes on in the old, familiar way.

AN AGE-OLD WAY OF LIFE

The fields, edged with lines of palm trees, are no longer quite the same as in the past. Wheat has largely given way to cotton and, over the years, to sugar cane and maize. But in the villages, filled with children's cries, laughter, animal sounds and other noises, earth-colored mud houses that blend with the soil still survive, simple boxes hand-built by the people who live in them. Some distance away, clouds of birds indicate the presence of one of the traditional pigeon-houses that look like fantastic pottery and clay termite-hills.

The landscape is crossed by high-tension cables which run to the electric power stations at the dams marking the course of the river.

On market-day, the roads vanish beneath the dust raised by the carts and the ramshackle taxis piled high with people. The markets should not be missed, with their sacks of maize and spices, their towers of round hats, their artisans and open-air butchers' stands, where urchins fan the meat with fly-swatters under weighing scales that hang from the trees.

Round about, life follows its ancient rhythm. Men sitting astride little donkeys and caravans of heavily-laden camels pass by along the river. Women in voluminous black robes descend to the water's edge to fill the jars that they carry sideways on their heads. Little ducks and geese that are the living image of those in the tomb paintings from Medum, now on display in the Cairo Museum, splash about in the muddy water. Oxen go on turning the waterwheels, the ancient *sakia*, as if nothing had changed in Egypt for a thousand years. In the dry air that gives them a special delicacy of tone, you can see the kaleidoscope of yellows, blues, greens and mauves that play across this timeless land as far as the horizon, just as they do on the walls on pharaonic tombs.

THE DELTA

In the delta, everything is different. Under heavy skies, the Nile leaves Cairo behind and opens out into countless channels to unload its silt into the Mediterranean along 125 miles/200 kilometres of coastline. With its fields of cotton, wheat, maize, green clover and rice, this whole river-fertilized region stretches to the horizon, broken here and there by clusters of palm-trees or rows of eucalyptus, and crossed by the sails of *feluccas* that glide along invisible channels. In places, the land is cultivated like a kitchen-garden. Then it disappears into swamps, those impenetrable swamps where they say the goddess Isis hid her son upon the death of Osiris, and which for so long protected the Nile Valley from raids by foreign pirates. Today, the delta is crossed by two navigable branches of the river, the Rosetta channel in the west and the Damietta channel in the east, and is one of the most fertile and densely-populated regions in the world. Some 12 million people live here, one-third of Egypt's population. There is one long succession of hamlets, villages, and even towns, some of them with more than 200,000 inhabitants. Rice and dates are the main commodities. Cotton, picked by men stripped to the waist and helped by their black-robed wives, is woven in the area, generating much wealth, as the charming balconied houses show.

The lagoons along the coast are still the preserve of herons, swans, flamingoes and pelicans but, already, the noise of the factories surrounding Alexandria is creeping closer.

EGYPT THROUGH HISTORY

Egypt was the first country in history to develop a politically organized society. From the point of view of our own times, it is easy to appreciate that, from the moment they set up home in the Nile Valley, the first settlers saw the need for a united effort to improve their agriculture with drainage and irrigation schemes — in a word, to face the problems that still confront the *fellahin* today.

It appears that, during the fourth millennium (4000–3000 B.C.), two kingdoms arose, one in the Nile Valley, the other in the delta. According to legend, a southern king named Menes brought the northen kingdom under his rule around 3000 B.C. and so laid the foundations of the combined state ruled by one pharaoh. He consecrated his victory by joining together the tall white crown of Upper Egypt and the red crown of Lower Egypt, to create the royal double crown. This also bore their combined emblems, the vulture of Upper Egypt and the cobra of Lower Egypt. For nearly 3000 years until the last pharaoh, the rulers of Egypt would remain faithful to the double crown, but to the two emblems of south and north they added a reed and a bee. The greatest of the pharaohs came from the south, but they never, it seems, thought of merging the two geographical regions into an artificial state. Yet by bringing together under the same crown the Nile Valley with its links to the mysterious continent of Africa, and the delta with its myriad river channels, they laid the basis of Egypt's future greatness and prosperity.

EGYPT UNDER THE PHARAOHS

The pharaoh, guardian of universal order

The pharaoh represented order on earth, and no one questioned this notion for over 3000 years. The Egyptians were fascinated by the harmony of the universe and lived in constant dread of its destruction. According to their myths, the sun was attacked during his nightly journey by his enemy, the serpent Apopis, and escaped only because of the intervention of his mother, Nut, the goddess of the sycamore, who swallowed him up each night, bringing him back to life next morning as young and handsome as ever. The miracle was, of course, constantly repeated, but the danger was always present. In order to counteract it and, at the same time, reinforce the beneficent power of the gods, the priests in the temples performed rites and worshipped the pharaoh, who was the incarnation of the god Horus. His links with the cosmos were then emphasized. His crowns placed him under the protection of local divinities, while his ritual titles swiftly confirmed him as the son of Ra, the sun god, and of Amun. There were five of them and they made up his official designation. The last two, inscribed in a frame or 'cartouche', represented his divine essence through magic on the walls of the temples he had had built and within his tomb. His symbol could not be defaced without mutilating the pharaoh himself. He was, in a word, a god-king. In addition, two ceremonies during the course of his reign reinforced his divine power: his coronation and, 30 years later, his *Heb Sed*, or jubilee. The pharaoh was an object of daily worship, and remained so for more than 3000 years. Such staying power is beyond our understanding. It is even more amazing when you realize that over the same period, Egyptian society itself remained fixed in its subservience to the constraining hierarchy imposed upon it from the start by religion, and its civilization as a whole remained true to established values.

Nevertheless, throughout its history, the country experienced grave crises and many times had to face the dangers of internal strife or tension caused by foreign armies along its borders.

THE OLD KINGDOM (2750–2180 B.C.)

Today, the history of Egypt under the pharaohs remains something of a mystery. However, a chronological record has come into our hands from which various historians have gleaned information given in the writings of a priest of Heliopolis, named Manetho. According to his account, it is thought that 30 ruling families, or dynasties, succeeded to the pharaoh's throne between 3000 and 300 B.C. Papyrus scrolls, details in the royal records, a carved stone tablet preserved today in Palermo — plus the whole of Egyptian art — provide the experts with additional, but scattered, information. All of this is difficult to interpret, because the Egyptians did not take note of the passage of time but dated each reign from the year 1. Nevertheless, it has been possible to identify three major periods of achievement, separated by long intervals of darkness, in this long and impressive story.

The pyramids

The Old Kingdom is regarded today as, first and foremost, the age of the pyramids. More than 80 of these were built, it is thought, on the west bank of the Nile around Memphis, the capital founded by Egypt's kings at the entrance of the delta to govern the 'Two Lands'. Not much is known about this period, which lasted from the 3rd to the end of the 6th dynasty. If the names of some of its rulers are still remembered, it is because their impressive tombs have defied the passage of time. Thus, eternal fame has been assured to Zoser by the step pyramid at Sakkara, to Sneferu by the rhomboid pyramid, and to Cheops, Chephren and Mycerinus by the three sister pyramids on the Giza plateau 1½ miles/2 kilometres from Cairo. The pyramids are proof of the indisputable power already

held by the pharaohs. Royal authority had to be on a firm footing itself if it was to mobilize the considerable manpower needed for the construction of such huge stone monuments on hilltops. This was a time, it must be remembered, when the use of the wheel for moving stone blocks was unknown, and when the only tools for cutting the slabs of granite or the polished limestone used as a finishing trim were flints and wooden wedges that would swell when water was poured over them. It is also a fact that there was never enough local labor, so the pharaohs would mount raids into Nubia and Libya to bring back slaves by the thousands. From the shores of Lebanon and Palestine, they brought the huge timber logs that their own country did not produce. To these ventures must be added expeditions to the mines of Sinai for copper and turquoise and to the land of Punt (perhaps modern Somalia) for myrrh and incense. It is clear that, by the time the veil of history was raised for the first time, Egypt was already a well-organized state with a long and prosperous past.

Hieroglyphs

The long passages of hieroglyphs carved in royal tombs from the 5th dynasty onwards can only be the culmination of a long process of refinement. Closely identified with the lands along the Nile, this form of writing represents people and things by pictures, but it is also sufficiently developed to use signs for particular sounds. This allows it to express abstract ideas in written symbols and, although it has nothing like our system of vowel sounds, it makes up for the deficiency by adopting conventions that are amazingly clear in meaning. The language recorded by this system of writing is also highly developed. The written texts, which consist of hymns, prayers and set phrases, are meant to assist the pharaoh's ascension to the heavenly spheres, and are still difficult for us to understand today. Yet they permit us to see how the different nature and destiny of the king separated him from the ordinary people over whom he ruled and formed the basis of the social structure of pharaonic Egypt.

The developed, class-structured society

The ruins of large numbers of impressive private tombs, known as *mastabas*, have been found scattered over the hills around the pyramids. They were built by high-ranking people close to the tomb of the sovereign, whom they had served all their lives. *Mastabas* have nothing in common with royal tombs. On the walls, instead of great texts condensed into a few rows of religious hieroglyphs, there are frescoes of daily life that today seem charged with strange meanings, but which the wealthy occupants saw as the continuation of this life in the next. Thus we have a picture of Egyptian society under the early pharaohs with its daily drudgery and moments of joy, its officials and scribes, and its peasants and craftsmen. In this moving tableau, repeated from one tomb to the next, a nation of anonymous people is portrayed living in tune with nature and under the direction of all-powerful and high-ranking masters. Already, we can detect the rigid class structure that was to keep pharaonic society unchanged until its final days.

The Sphinx at Memphis.

THE FIRST INTERMEDIATE PERIOD

Civilization was on the march and about to undergo its first test. At the end of the 6th dynasty, about 2180 B.C., the Old Kingdom disintegrated and sank into such anarchy that Egypt is said to have had 70 kings in 70 days. The truth is that nobody knows what happened during this First Intermediate Period. What we do know is that Egypt had lost none of its dynamic energy or creative power when it regained its unity under the Middle Kingdom.

THE MIDDLE KINGDOM (2060–1785 B.C.)

Wealth and expansion

The Middle Kingdom began with the opening, by the 11th dynasty, of a trade route to the Red Sea. It continued with the development of the Fayyum area, followed by the colonization of Nubia. Fortresses were built on the borders of the Sudan, the oases of the Sahara were developed, a campaign was mounted in Palestine, and Egypt's influence in Syria was extended to Byblos, where important Egyptian colonies were established. These were only the most important ventures in a highly successful policy of aggrandizement. Only a few vestiges remain of the enormous construction projects that were carried out at this time. The splendid buildings that once demonstrated the wealth of the rulers, have vanished almost without trace. These were clustered around Thebes, where the pharaohs founded their first capital, and then at El Fayyum, to which the government was moved in order to facilitate the administration of the 'Two Lands'. We know, however, that the most famous of these buildings, the temple of Amenemhet III, contained no fewer than 3000 rooms, and that it so impressed the Greek historian Herodotus with its open spaces, twisting passageways and false exits that he referred to it as a 'labyrinth'. Although it is no longer possible to form a clear idea of the importance of these two prosperous centuries in Egyptian civilization, we know that a tremendous expansion took place at this time.

The worship of Osiris, the god of resurrection

During the Middle Kingdom, the great myths of the past took on a human dimension that makes them more readily acceptable today. It was at this time that a creed of hope, associated with Osiris, the god of resurrection, emerged at Abydos. Bound up with the Nile, whose beneficent floods made the sun-scorched fields green again each year, the old myth of Osiris and his wife Isis, which represented the renewal of the land, went back to the dawn of time. The legend would have it that Osiris himself had been the king of Egypt after the departure of the gods. Having presented Egypt with agriculture, he enjoyed such prosperity that his brother Seth killed him and usurped his throne. In the course of a long and tearful search, aided by the jackal-god Anubis, Isis had found the pieces of her husband's dismembered body on the banks of the Nile. Binding them together with strips of cloth, and so forming the first mummy, she succeeded, thanks to the spells of the god Thoth, in restoring Osiris to life. After presenting her with a son, Osiris then went to live forever in the underworld, not far from the world of humans. Transformed into a god, he presided henceforward over the funerary rites. Although at first reserved solely for pharaohs, the promise of eternal life, which his story represented, was extended bit by bit to the high-ranking people of the kingdom, so during the Middle Kingdom all the Egyptian notables were drawn to Abydos, where the mysteries of resurrection were celebrated. There, close to the tomb of the god, they left steles that would represent them and facilitate their entry into eternity on the appointed day. Scores of these can still be found today. Such fervor is all the more astonishing because the figure of Osiris then represented values that we ourselves hold today. In fact, he allowed into his kingdom only the righteous and the good, those whose hearts, when placed on the divine scales of judgement, weighed no more than the feather of the goddess Maat.

It was also during the Middle Kingdom that Hathor, the generous, all-providing cow-goddess, took on a human face to become the goddess of love and beauty. Her lovely face began to sprout everywhere on the capitals of temple columns, framed in a heavy wig and accompanied by a *sistrum*. The sound of this percussion instrument, it is said, dispelled all grief. Of her animal origins, only two discreet cow's ears remained.

A humanistic trend?

From the ancient theological traditions and popular beliefs in which Egyptian civilization continued to develop, a genuine humanistic movement arose at the beginning of the second millennium B.C. Evidence of this may be seen in the museums, in the faces of the royal statues discovered in the ruins of temples and in the great variety of people represented in tombs. However, it is in literature, which is only accessible to experts, that the signs are most striking. The Middle Kingdom was not content to add new funerary texts connected with the worship of Osiris, but also attempted fictionalized biography, popular epics, and tales that resembled the 'Thousand and One Nights'. We can judge only those compositions that have come down to us in fragments carved on steles or written with a brush on papyrus in a difficult language. We know that these works gave Egypt a classic literary basis to which educated people would later have recourse, and that they employed a handwritten script, known as Hieratic, which was to come into wider use as culture was popularized. The very fact that such works existed at all removes any doubt about the high level of development Egypt had attained by 1785 B.C. when the Middle Kingdom came to an end.

THE SECOND INTERMEDIATE PERIOD

For some time, waves of invaders had been on the move in the lands to the east of Egypt. Emerging from the plateaux of Anatolia or out of the deserts of Arabia, these peoples had changed the historic face of Asia. In about 1730 B.C. an Asian bedouin people known as the Hyksos attacked Egypt and overthrew the 12th dynasty. Little is known about these invaders, except that they seized power and introduced the horse and chariot to the valley of the Nile, an innovation of immense importance two centuries later when Egypt itself became a conquering nation after the unification of the New Kingdom.

The temple at Dendera.

THE NEW KINGDOM (1580–1085 B.C.)

The conqueror-kings

The New Kingdom, which lasted for five centuries from 1580 to 1085 B.C., was ruled during the 17th, 19th and 20th dynasties by the most famous pharaohs in Egyptian history. Around Thebes, its capital, this period has left us some of mankind's most impressive monuments. In a word, it gave Egypt its eternal greatness. Although the course of events during this period cannot be traced exactly because records are not continuous, the great changes of fortune that took it from glory to decline are, nevertheless, known from accounts recorded in the history of the Middle East. The New Kingdom began with a victorious campaign that pushed the Hyksos invaders back as far as Palestine. It then embarked on a policy of conquest that was intended to guarantee the security of the kingdom by means of solid frontiers. Tuthmosis III (1484–1450 B.C.) pushed south as far as the fourth cataract and east to the Euphrates, on the border of the mysterious kingdom of the Mitanni, in order to stabilize the situation. All was in vain, however, because the rising power of the Hittite empire was already changing the map of the Middle East. For more than a century, the Hittites kept Egyptian rule abroad on the defensive and it was not until the 19th dynasty that the tide turned. The glory of ending this bitter struggle fell to Ramesses II (1298–1235 B.C.) at the battle of Kadesh. The battle was immortalized on all the temples the pharaoh ordered to be built, where it is made to look like a victory of divine law over the barbarians; the confrontation at Kadesh had, in fact, neither winner nor loser. Its main effect was to bring about a reconciliation between the former enemies, and Ramesses put a seal to the peace by marrying a Hittite princess. After his death, however, new dangers began to loom on the horizon. Assyrian ambitions began to grow in the east, and newcomers in the north, known as the 'Sea Peoples', now presented a formidable threat along the shores of the eastern Mediterranean. They were on the march from the Balkans, across Anatolia, to Palestine and were all the more frightening because they used iron weapons. Some of them made for Cyprus, while others settled along the coast as far west as Libya and, acting like pirates, terrorized the inhabitants of the Nile Delta. Their forays along Egypt's frontiers increased until the country once again found a ruler who was a match for them. In a tremendous naval battle portrayed in reliefs on the walls of the temple of Medinet Habu, Ramesses III, the last of the great pharaohs (1198–1167 B.C.), succeeded in halting the advance of these formidable barbarians whom nothing, according to the inscriptions, could resist.

Egypt's enemies, however, were to retain their hold over the eastern Mediterranean, and the decline of the New Kingdom was merely postponed. Its pace accelerated under the eight pharaohs who followed Ramesses III, and when the 20th dynasty came to an end with Ramesses XI in 1085 B.C., the country was plunged once more into chaos. Then, over a period of 15 centuries, interspersed with brief moments of glory, Egypt's political greatness went into a long, slow decline.

The reign of Amun, the god of Thebes

Despite its political decline after the 20th dynasty, Egypt's ancient civilization was to remain unshakably consistent, surviving all the vicissitudes of history. In taking it to its highest point of achievement, the New Kingdom ensured its own immortality.

If we are to understand how this came about, we must know something of the centuries that gave us Karnak and Luxor, the rock-cut tombs of the Valley of the Kings and the treasures of Tutankhamun, the huge private burial-grounds and funerary temples of the left bank of the Nile, and the holy sites of Nubia, the most famous of which, Abu Simbel, was saved by UNESCO from the waters of the Aswân Dam. These are only a few of the great structures built at this time, a period so absorbed in building that archaeologists are still uncovering its remains from the delta to the heart of the Sudan. Great scenes depicted on the walls of temples, recording the presentation of tributes to the pharaoh by conquered peoples or allies, clearly show the boundless wealth that brought about this incredible flowering of architecture and of art as a whole. In these scenes, Asians can be seen making offerings of gold and silver, vases and jewels, and huge tree-trunks from the forests of Palestine; they are followed by Africans with animal skins, ivory, ebony, sycamore and many other precious things. Everywhere there are crowds of men, women and children, who have been brought along the Nile to tend the lands of the god-kings and to build their temples.

There was also a superhuman or divine dimension to this, represented by pharaohs who claimed to be gods, sons of Amun, the king of the gods. The extraordinary story of Queen Hatshepsut, whose fine head can be seen in the museums, with the heavy hair-style and false beard worn by pharaohs, testifies to the power conferred by divine origins. As a royal princess, it seemed, at first, that Hatshepsut was destined merely to bring about, by marrying first one and then the other, the accession to the throne of her half-brother, Tuthmosis II, and then his illegitimate son, Tuthmosis III. However, she succeeded in doing what no other woman before her had ever attempted: she seized power and, keeping the boy confined in the temple, ruled for 15 years. She justified her *coup d'état* by claiming divine descent, and she had a scene carved in her tomb showing Amun carnally united with her mother. Despite their divinity, it seems that the pharaohs were nonetheless prey to ordinary human passions! When, after the death of the queen, Tuthmosis finally came to the throne, he indulged in a frenzy of revenge and obliterated images of the woman who had been both his mother and his wife. He also destroyed or defaced the great buildings that her favorite, the architect Senenmut, had created, from Deir el-Bahari to Karnak. The effect of repeated royal disputes such as this, involving both politics and religion, was to make Amun not only the source of all power but also the supreme judge for all those who regarded him as their authority on earth. Another effect was to give the priesthood, already fabulously rich as a result of the booty donated to it by the pharaohs after their victories, such power that it was able to question royal authority. As a result, the clergy remained the real masters of Egypt until the end of pharaonic rule.

Twenty years of revolutionary mysticism

It was against this background that the spiritual revolution of Amenophis IV (1372–1354 B.C.), the husband of the celebrated Queen Nefertiti, took place. Although this revolution lasted less than 20 years, it was, nevertheless, one of the most bizarre events in the history of the world. No sooner was Amenophis installed on the throne than he outlawed the name of Amun, closed his temples and dedicated himself to the worship of the sun-disk, Aton, the universal god who would unite all the temples under one single religion. The upheaval was total. The king changed his own name to Akhenaton, 'he who is pleasing to Aton'. He took all Amun's possessions into royal ownership and left Thebes to build a completely new capital from nothing. Named Akhetaton, 'Aton's horizon', this capital was situated on the site of present-day Tel el-Amarna, hence the name 'Amarna Revolution' given to the movement that some experts regard as the first of the world's great religious schisms and the first manifestation of monotheism. It would be foolhardy to give a modern interpretation to this politico-religious movement, over which many uncertainties still hang, and which was brought to an end by a brutal return to tradition. On the death of Akhenaton, the high priests of Amun regained power. Tutankhamun, his son-in-law and successor, was compelled to proclaim his adherence to the god of Thebes and transfer his capital, and the priests did their best to obliterate all trace of the heretic pharaoh. These traces are now re-emerging bit by bit in random excavations, and they still have much to tell us about this extraordinary period of freedom.

Ramesses II and the triumph of classical civilization

The failure of the Amarna Revolution serves to underline the unbreakable bond that Egypt maintained with ancient tradition, order and a civilization born of the land, a civilization that was to be personified forever by Ramesses II 60 years later. His reign, which might easily be compared to that of Louis XIV in France, is marked by the splendor of the buildings he erected from Nubia to the delta and by the unprecedented gigantism of Karnak and Luxor. Egyptian art was then at its zenith. Under Ramesses III, it left one final masterpiece testifying to the greatness of the New Kingdom, the temple of Medinet Habu, and then it entered a long, barren period before producing, a thousand years later, miraculous evidence of its perennial greatness with the temples of Idfu and Dendera.

FOUR CENTURIES OF CHANGING FORTUNES

During the Third Intermediate Period, a period of four centuries, Egypt was divided between local and foreign ruling families. In the north, a Libyan dynasty succeeded the pharaohs of Tanis. Then, in 950 B.C., an Ethiopian dynasty imposed its rule over the entire Nile Valley and brought a century of prosperity. In 667, Assurbanipal, the fearsome king of Assyria, took Thebes and looted the fabulous treasures of the temple of Amun. Meanwhile, Greek city-states were already emerging out of the shadows and were engaged in trading and maritime activities that heralded the flowering of their civilization.

THE ARRIVAL OF GREEK MERCHANTS

With the establishment of the 26th (Saite) dynasty, after 666, Egypt revived for a time. The new rulers came from the delta, and the age-old tradition that gave southern Egypt a dominating influence over the north was broken. The Nile Valley slumbered but, in the coastal ports, trade was growing between, on one side, the wine, oil, pottery and weapons of the Mediterranean region and, on the other, the cereals and papyrus of Egypt and the treasures of Africa brought down the Nile. To promote this activity, the pharaohs founded the town of Naucratis for the use of the Greek merchants. In 525 B.C., the Saite dynasty was overrun by the Persians; the Egyptians repeatedly tried to regain their independence and they succeeded in doing so, with the help of the Greek city-states, during the brief interval of the 30th dynasty (380–342 B.C.) and the brilliant reign of Nectanebo. This period was short-lived; they were soon to fall yet again under even harsher foreign domination. So it was as a liberator that, in 333, they welcomed Alexander the Great who, while returning from the brilliant campaigns that had taken him as far as the River Indus, made himself master of Egypt.

THE FOUNDING OF ALEXANDRIA

Alexander the Great's stay in Egypt was brief. Nevertheless, before he set off again on fresh campaigns, he determined the path the country would follow for the next five centuries. By consulting the oracle, who recognized him as the son of Amun, and offering ritual sacrifices at Memphis, he maintained the continuity of the ancient civilization of the Nile. By founding Alexandria, however, he placed the country's power and wealth in Greek hands. His successors, the dynasty of the Ptolemies, followed his example. They revived the sacred tradition of the god-kings and, like them, surrounded themselves with ceremonies going back to the dawn of time. They also made Alexandria the greatest port of the eastern Mediterranean, a cultural capital which attracted all the learned and well-educated people of the time, drawn by a library and museum that have long since passed into history.

THE PTOLEMIES

It is hard to imagine how the ancient, land-oriented civilization of the Nile Valley managed to co-exist with that of the Greek city-states, which stemmed from the far more recent culture of a nation of mariners. We know that the Greeks were impressed by the Egyptian myths and adopted them for their own use, so that Zeus became intertwined with Amun, and the mysteries of Osiris with those of Dionysos. Yet the world of the pharaohs remained unchangeable, and the religious buildings erected by the Ptolemies, who were anxious to equal the most celebrated pharaohs in history, are evidence of this.

Roman Egypt

The Ptolemies designed their buildings in the traditional style of Karnak and Luxor, and it is to them also that we owe the great classical structure at Idfu. The drastic changes that took place in Alexandria did not penetrate as far as the Nile Valley, where the ancient rites endured in the temples and, thanks to the pharaoh's intercession with the gods, assured the stability of the world. They were still being celebrated there when, after three centuries of murders, wars and palace revolutions, Cleopatra VII, the inspirational force behind Julius Caesar and Mark Antony, killed herself following Egypt's defeat by the Romans, and brought the dynasty of the Ptolemies to an end.

Before the Ptolemies, Alexander and the Persian ruler Darius had had themselves designated as pharaohs. Now Tiberius, Nero and their successors assumed the *uraeus*, insignia of divine authority awarded to the god-king in their temples of Kom Ombo and Dendera. As the principal producer of grain in the Mediterranean, Egypt was a rich source of wealth for the Empire and was not involved in its various crises.

It was not until the end of the 1st century A.D. that a decisive blow was delivered to the cult of the pharaoh. As just one among a whole group of oriental cults recognized as official religions of the Roman Empire, its importance and self-confidence were greatly diminished. Egyptian high priests were now exposed to the philosophical ideas that were shaking the Greco-Roman world, and they themselves eagerly surrendered to such ideas in the 3rd century. It was then that the spirits of ancient Egypt deserted the temples. The people, whose character the priests had helped to mould and who were used to living in close touch with the afterlife, were swift to absorb the new religious message.

In A.D. 40, the apostle Mark brought Christianity to the delta, and it swept invincibly through the Nile Valley. When the edict of Theodosius closed the 'temples of paganism' throughout the Roman Empire in 383, Egypt had already joined the Christian world.

EGYPT UNDER CHRISTIANITY

When, in the 4th century, St. Anthony retired to the desert to commune with God, Egypt witnessed the birth of monasticism. Many other religious recluses followed his example, and monastic life quickly became established. Monasteries sprang up around Thebes and then spread along the Nile Valley. By the 5th century, the city of Alexandria itself was ringed with religious foundations.

The fervor of Egypt's religious faith spread as far as Asia Minor and the lands of the eastern Mediterranean. The emperor, Theodosius, placed it under the authority of Constantinople in 395, when he divided the empire between his two sons, an arrangement that was not to Egypt's liking. The country was then caught up in the momentous dispute among the eastern churches concerning the nature of Christ; broadly, the Egyptian church took the position that Christ's divinity took precedence over His human nature, and this found itself out of step with official orthodox doctrine. Egypt thus asserted its 'monophysite' belief in the single nature of Christ. Because religious and political power were indivisible at that time, Egypt's stance strengthened its nationalistic attitudes. Differences with Constantinople became so serious that, when Caliph Omar's Arab horsemen overran the delta in 640, they were greeted as liberators.

ISLAM

The age of the caliphs

Egypt was one of the first countries to be conquered by the Arabs after the death of Muhammad in 632. It was a period of expansion that, in a single century, took the Arab nations as far as the banks of the Indus in the east and over the Pyrenees in the west as far as Poitiers. These conquests upset the balance of the Mediterranean world, but the effects were barely felt in Egypt. The Umayyed caliphs who ruled this vast empire from Damascus between 660 and 750 changed none of the traditional forms of government of the conquered territories; nor did they attempt to convert the Christians of Egypt to Islam. They were content to have Koranic law applied there through their governors and, in the 8th century, they made Arabic the official language throughout their territories.

The situation remained the same under the Abbasids, who succeeded the Umayyed dynasty and moved the capital of the empire to Baghdad.

In 868, however, a particularly enterprising governor of Egypt named Ibn Tulun succeeded in gaining independence for this province which was so fertile that it supplied the entire Arabian peninsula with wheat. (Ibn Tulun was the builder of the superb mosque in Cairo that bears his name.) Egypt's bid for freedom ended in 905, when a punitive expedition mounted by the caliph of Baghdad crushed Ibn Tulun's successors. Egypt then plunged into 60 years of anarchy, before gaining a leading place in the Muslim world under the Fatimid dynasty.

The Fatimids, who originated in the Maghreb region of North Africa, claimed to be descended from the Prophet, and aspired to destroy the Abbasid caliphs of Baghdad. About the middle of the

10th century, they embarked on a campaign to conquer the empire. In 969 they founded the city of Cairo to shelter their ruler and his entourage and turned it into a prestigious cultural capital. Through the study of astronomy, medicine and mathematics, Egypt was soon ablaze with intellectual brilliance. The mosque of Al-Azhar, which was built at this time, is still one of the crucibles in which the living doctrine of Islam is forged and leading Muslims educated. Magnificent buildings followed in rapid succession.

Egypt at this time was very wealthy. Apart from its natural fertility and abundance of skilled craftsmen, it had become one of the leading commercial centers of East-West trade. Through the Red Sea, Egypt received incense, cloves, aromatic essences, bitter aloes, cardamum and many other precious goods and spices from India, China and Ethiopia, while on the quaysides of Alexandria, Venetian merchants unloaded cloth from Flanders, silks from Italy, amber from the Baltic — everything the West could supply. At this time, Egypt was playing a leading commercial role in the eastern Mediterranean.

The country's prosperity continued through the fall of the Fatimid empire which was brought about by the Crusades and the establishment of the Frankish kingdom of Jerusalem as an outpost of western Christendom in the eastern Mediterranean. Saladin, the nephew of the caliph of Baghdad, then gained power in Cairo. His reign (1171–1193) was one of the most glorious in the history of Islam.

Saladin was a great general and a devout Muslim, who set himself the goal of driving the Christians from the eastern Mediterranean. By taking Jerusalem, he delivered a fatal blow to the Frankish kingdom. He also gave a new impetus to Sunnism, the orthodox faith of Islam, and throughout the empire, particularly in Cairo, he set up *madrasas*, great religious colleges where young men could devote themselves to the study of the Koranic law.

Saladin's successors, the Ayyubids, continued his policies, and Egypt became one of the strongholds of Islam. When King Louis IX of France decided, in 1248, to recapture the Holy Places, it was to the Nile Delta that he sent his fleet. He landed in triumph at Damietta but was later taken prisoner and had to pay a large ransom for his freedom. Meanwhile, the Ayyubid dynasty had fallen from power and the Mamluks had taken its place.

THE MAMLUKS AND TURKISH DOMINATION

The Mamluk state was original in every sense. It was ruled by an aristocracy of slave-mercenaries who came from Turkey. The first Mamluks were recruited by an Ayyubid prince to support his ambitions against his brothers but they seized power for themselves. Bound by a strict military code, they recruited their own members and chose their leader from among their own ranks through intrigues of appalling violence and cruelty. Some of the Mamluks were Mongols, others slaves, and a number of them came from Circassia.

The Mamluks behaved like an oppressive army of occupation but, all the same, the Mamluk period was one of the most outstanding in Egypt's history. A multitude of religious institutions, monasteries, *madrasas*, and public fountains were built, and the mosques in Cairo raised by the Mamluks clearly demonstrate their strict adherence to the Sunnite branch of Islam. However, in the 16th century, their wealth, based essentially on a monopoly of trade with Venice, suddenly collapsed. The discovery of the sea route around the Cape diverted a large part of the trade with the Orient through the Atlantic and dealt a fatal blow to the Mamluk state. The Ottoman Turks, who had taken Constantinople in 1453 and were then vigorously building an empire, met little resistance when they took possession of Cairo in 1517. Now transformed into a Turkish province, Egypt sank into a period of darkness. The Mamluks, however, still had a role in Egyptian politics, even though they now governed on behalf of the sultan of Constantinople.

NAPOLEON'S EXPEDITION TO EGYPT

The French expedition to Egypt in 1798 was mounted within the framework of the international conflict between revolutionary France and Britain. Napoleon's aim was to control the route to the Indies, where the British had built up a trading empire.

Napoleon had other great ambitions. 'For a long time,' he wrote, 'a band of slaves ... has maintained a tyrannical grasp on one of the jewels of the world ... because of my assistance, no Egyptian will henceforth be prevented from taking great responsibilities, and all will have the opportunity to rise to the highest ranks.' In a word, Napoleon saw himself as the bearer of the great principles of the French Revolution. The French army landed at Alexandria on July 12, 1798, but while it was winning possession of Cairo in the Battle of the Pyramids, Britain's Admiral Horatio Nelson destroyed Napoleon's fleet in the Bay of Abukir, and the French were trapped. They were unable to leave Egypt until September 1801 and so remained in occupation for three years.

This was too short a time to put into effect Napoleon's plan to set up a *diwan*, a government assembly through which Egyptians could themselves help to reorganize the government and revitalize the economy. It was, however, long enough for a sort of national consciousness to awaken and for a breath of freedom to blow through Cairo, where newspapers appeared for the first time. By the time the French army left, Egypt had emerged from the shadows. Moreover, the scholars, artists, engineers and writers whom Napoleon had brought with him, and who accompanied the French army up the Nile Valley, had discovered the country's fabulous heritage and lost no time in revealing it to the world. Thanks to the documents they brought back, especially the famous Rosetta Stone which allowed Champollion to decipher Egyptian hieroglyphic script in 1822, the science of Egyptology came into being.

MEHEMET ALI AND MODERN EGYPT

The new ambitions of the British, the expectations of the Mamluks, still obsessed with memories of past glories, and the desire of the sultan of Constantinople to restore his authority — all these conflicting motives plunged Egypt into chaos after the departure of the French.

The country was eventually saved in 1804 by a young Albanian officer in the Turkish army, Mehemet Ali, who seized power and restored order. Shortly afterwards, the sultan of Constantinople recognized him as viceroy of Egypt, and he ruled until 1849. An unusual personality, with ambitions to match, Mehemet Ali was to play a leading part for 40 years in the upheavals then shaking the Ottoman Empire. During those 40 years, he also succeeded in coaxing Egypt into the modern world.

An admirer of Napoleon, Mehemet Ali took what he needed from the Corsican's grand design but, to it, he could add a major trump-card: he was a Muslim. Consequently, he was supported by the religious authorities. He relied both on them and on the country's leading figures and strengthened Egypt's still-fragile sense of nationhood by recruiting an army from among Egyptians themselves, something that had never been done before, and organizing it on the European model.

Surrounded by scholars, engineers, technicians and artists, most of them foreigners, Mehemet Ali finally undertook the modernization of the country's institutions. He created new ministries and schools, built canals, introduced the cultivation of sugar cane and cotton and developed a textile industry, among other reforms. By the time of his death, Egypt had acquired an international standing and was attracting the attention of the western powers, even though it still belonged to the Ottoman Empire.

Mehemet Ali's successors continued what he had begun. One of their first concerns was to loosen the ties that kept them bound as vassals to the sultan of Constantinople. They first won from him the title of *khedive* for themselves, then, in 1875, they won total responsibility for the government of Egypt and for enacting legislation.

THE SUEZ CANAL AND BRITISH RULE

In 1854, the French engineer Ferdinand de Lesseps easily persuaded Mehemet Ali's son and successor to adopt his plan to cut through the isthmus of Suez. However, the building of the Suez Canal was so costly that an international fund had to be opened. The French were the only nation to respond. Forty-four percent of the shares in the Suez Canal Company went to Egypt. The opening of the canal on November 17, 1869, amid great celebrations and in the presence of the Empress Eugénie and foreign dignitaries, was a glorious day for the *khedive*, Ismael.

Six years later, financial difficulties, brought about by his ambitious modernization program, forced Ismael to sell his own interests in the canal company. They were bought by British subscribers. The following year, on the verge of bankruptcy, Ismael had to accept the setting up of an Anglo-French condominium to manage his financial affairs. Finally, Britain dispatched an expeditionary force to Egypt in 1882 to put down serious disturbances that had broken out in Alexandria. The soldiers remained and following the dismantlement of the Anglo-French condominium, Britain began exerting a dominant influence over political life in Egypt.

The rise of nationalism

The British presence did not in any way hinder Egypt's development. In Cairo and in Alexandria, larger and larger projects were undertaken with the collaboration of western businessmen. The work of French scholars who, in collaboration with Auguste Mariette, founded the Institute of Archaeology in 1880, alerted Egyptians to their ancient heritage. Cultural life experienced a new burst of activity. Eventually, the development of parliamentary politics brought into prominence the Egyptian National Party to which the name of Mustafa Kemal was inseparably linked. Egypt aspired to full independence, but events were to delay its attainment. When the First World War broke out, Britain was worried by the threat posed to the Suez Canal by the alliance between Germany and Turkey and turned the 'de facto' protectorate it already exercised over Egypt into a protectorate solidly founded on law.

In 1919, however, the international climate changed. Encouraged by ideas about the rebirth of Arab nationalism and by the political influence of the United States — Woodrow Wilson's 'fourteen points' foresaw the liberation of peoples under Turkish domination — the sultan of Egypt attempted to win his country's independence from Britain. The treaty of 1922 recognized the independence of the kingdom of Egypt, but responsibility for the country's defense and for the Suez Canal remained with Britain. Egypt, however, was given a constitution, and the Wafd, the political party that had negotiated independence, assumed the reins of government. However, the king retained considerable privileges that hampered parliamentary progress.

The domestic situation worsened along with the international situation. Fearing the intentions of Mussolini's Italy, then in control of Libya, the Egyptian ruling authorities strengthened their links with Britain. In 1936, the two countries signed the treaty that later allowed British forces to mount their North African campaign to defend Egypt and the Suez Canal and to halt the combined German and Italian advance on Suez at El-Alamein in 1942.

The signing of the Arab League pact

Immediately following the victory at El-Alamein, Egypt found the support necessary for full independence. In March 1945, the Arab states of the Middle East met in Cairo and signed a pact creating the League of Arab States, or 'Arab League'. Their principal concern was to maintain a united front in the pursuit of their claims, all of which were inspired by the same desire for independence, and to adopt common positions on the problems they faced.

The internal situation in Egypt itself at this time was deteriorating rapidly through unemployment and inflation. The monarchy had been discredited by the extravagance and corruption of King Farouk and his entourage. Public agitation, stirred up by an extreme right-wing, openly anti-British movement called the Muslim Brotherhood, was assuming dangerous proportions. Its message was clear: only the principles of Islam could bring peace to a country deprived of spiritual sustenance. Despite the Brotherhood's violent methods, it managed to recruit many members among students and the military.

The creation of the state of Israel in 1948 had the effect of destabilizing the monarchy in Egypt. The Arab armies responded to what they considered a provocation by invading Palestine. However, the Egyptians were ill-prepared for war and, in 1949, Israeli forces entered the Sinai peninsula. The Egyptian people did not forgive the king for this unfortunate episode. Riots followed in Cairo, and politicians accused of collusion with the West were murdered. The government was unable to control the situation and, on July 23, 1952, after three years of public disturbances, a 'Committee of Free Officers' led by Gamal Abdel Nasser seized power. Two days later, King Farouk was forced to abdicate. On June 18, 1953 a republic was proclaimed, and a new chapter began in Egypt's long history.

EGYPT IN TODAY'S WORLD

The republic under Nasser

Nasser's first concern was to free Egypt from the grasp of the West — from what he considered economic and military colonialism. In 1954, he began talks with London that led to the evacuation of British forces from the Canal Zone the following year. He decided to place Egyptians at the head of foreign companies operating in the country. In 1955, he asserted his political independence by taking part in the Bandung Conference, which brought together all the Third World countries that wished to present a united front towards the two super-powers, the United States and the Soviet Union. Nasser emerged as the champion of non-alignment. When the United States refused to supply the modern weapons for the Egyptian army or finance for the Aswân Dam, Nasser turned to the Soviet Union (which built the dam) and to countries of the eastern bloc, to embark upon an ambitious program of heavy industrialization.

In the meantime, on July 26, 1956, Nasser took the gamble of nationalizing the International Suez Canal Company. The armed intervention by Britain and France was halted by a U.S. ultimatum and this won Nasser tremendous prestige in the Arab world.

Eventually, in 1967, Nasser attempted an attack on Israel which proved a disaster. He then offered his resignation but crowds in Cairo, in a spectacular show of confidence, forced him to stay. The Soviet Union then began to rearm Egypt in an attempt to exploit the situation, and large numbers of Soviet experts and military advisers were installed in the country. Three years later, however, Nasser died suddenly, and Egyptian policy once again changed direction.

The years of President Sadat

At the time of the death of Nasser, Egypt found itself facing terrible poverty and under-development, exacerbated by the rapidly rising population.

Anwar Sadat, the former vice-president, now took power; he broke the treaty of alliance with the Soviet Union, expelled the Soviet technicians, and turned back to the industrialized countries of the West for aid. They responded without hesitation.

As early as 1973, the United States undertook the construction of the oil pipeline from Suez that would make Alexandria an oil port. The U.S. commitment grew, as did that of France, which shared in the building of Cairo's underground railway and hospital, the modernization of the telephone system and the development of nuclear power stations.

Sadat was aware that the long-term success of his development program depended on removing the permanent threat posed to Egypt since 1949 by the state of war with Israel. The military disaster of 1967 had left the armed forces badly bruised. Sadat brought the army up to date and gave it sophisticated equipment which, unlike his predecessor, he sought not only in the eastern bloc but also in London, Paris and Washington. Then, in October 1973, he launched his troops across the Suez Canal in a surprise assault on the Sinai. The success of this operation finally enabled Sadat to open peace talks with Israel on an advantageous basis.

Discussions took place under the auspices of the United States, the only great power likely to have an influence on Israeli political decisions. The negotiations were extremely difficult, as one of the Egyptian objectives was to have the rights of the Palestinian people recognized; they led to the 1978 Camp David agreement, later embodied in the treaty of March 26, 1979, ending 30 years of hostilities between Egypt and Israel.

President Mubarak takes office

The death of President Sadat, assassinated on October 6, 1981, brought President Hosni Mubarak to power. President Mubarak has essentially sought to continue the policies of the Sadat administration, while attempting to re-insert Egypt into the mainstream of Arab politics from which it had been almost entirely excluded since the Camp David agreement.

EGYPTIAN ART UNDER
THE PHARAOHS
The Sacred Myth

In order to understand the art of the long-vanished world of the pharaohs, we must first discard modern ways of thinking. There was nothing fixed about the ancient Egyptian view of the universe, and there are also many different modern interpretations of it. All the variations, however, are closely identified with the Nile. Broadly speaking, the Egyptians believed that the world was created from a 'primordial hill' that some mysterious force caused to emerge from a vast ocean — that is to say, out of chaos — like the spits of sand and mud that appear along a river bed as floods recede. After this apocalyptic event, the sun, the source of all creation, rose in its turn from the darkness, just as it rises in the east each morning, and the god of light, Horus, in his role as guardian of universal order, made the pharaoh his representative on earth.

For modern man, these ancient mysteries, and the roles played in them by the various gods represented in Egyptian art, are difficult to comprehend, not least because the Egyptian pantheon was a world that evolved constantly through the ages. At the beginning of history, it was ruled by Ra, the sun-god, but then a number of separate gods emerged. The most famous of these gods were Osiris, the god of renewed life and of agricultural fertility; his wife Isis; Hathor, the goddess of love and happiness; and Amun. The latter, at first an obscure god of Thebes, shared in the glorious achievements of the New Kingdom pharaohs during the second millennium B.C., particularly those of Ramesses II and, in consequence, became king of the gods. All this is straightforward. However, alongside these major divinities there were always countless deities appearing in the form of every animal in Egypt, many of them connected with the burial cult. As time passed, their personalities took on different facets and assumed new, and sometimes contradictory, roles under different names but without losing their original characters. All this is extraordinarily difficult to follow but, nonetheless, the art of ancient Egypt exercises a fascination which is independent of its religious basis.

Deir el-Medina, decorations from the tomb of Sennedjem.

ART IN CUT STONE

To modern eyes, Egyptian Pharaonic art is, first and foremost, an art of cut stone, the oldest form of art in the world. It began impressively at the beginning of the third millennium B.C. with the first of the pyramids, near the capital, Memphis. This was the step pyramid surrounded by an imposing mock-palace complex which the architect, Imhotep, built above the tomb of King Zoser. Archaeologists working on the plateau of Sakkara today are still finding trimmed and decorated pieces of the beautiful limestone that was brought from the nearby quarries of Tura for the project. This magnificent monument marked the beginning of a 3000 year period in which Egyptian art expressed a deep concern with immortality. We know nothing of Zoser, except that legend placed him among the gods and so did him justice for having created in the desert the bold structural forms for which the Nile civilization seemed to be waiting. The pyramid was an example of a type of architecture which, right to the last, was to strengthen the bonds between earth and universe. It was connected, without any doubt, to sun-worship and, throughout the Old Kingdom — that is, for five centuries — it offered a long slope above the royal tombs which would permit the pharaoh, at the moment of death, to ascend to the sky and take his place among the gods. There would never again be an architectural complex like the one built by Imhotep around his pyramid in the image of his king's earthly dwelling. Nonetheless, by interpreting in stone a form of construction used, from all the evidence, for buildings of the time (sun-dried brick, wood and woven reeds and papyrus), Zoser's architect made a decisive contribution to the future development of Egyptian art.

MAGICAL FORMS DERIVED FROM THE NILE AND ITS FLORA

From the moment you enter the vast enclosure of Zoser's funerary complex, which is more than 1640 feet/500 metres long, you are struck by the systematic way in which tried and tested patterns borrowed from nature were used. The doors were painted red to give the illusion of being made of wood, while the roofing timbers were cut and arranged like the trunks of palm trees, and the columns, almost 23 feet/7 metres tall, were made to look like bundles of reeds, following the current practice. This loyalty to ancient traditions, which Egyptian art maintained to the end, is by no means the least of its original features. What is more, it springs from something that is even more mysterious to us today: the supernatural aspect of Egyptian art. This impressive continuity of tradition demonstrates how, using its various forms as interme-diaries, Egyptian art maintains a relationship with the hidden forces of the universe. This is a dimension that is beyond our comprehen-sion and continues to puzzle archaeologists. We have to admit this fact; it occurs everywhere. In all ancient Egyptian art you will come across 'intermediate zones' that do not quite belong either to this world or the other world, but which use the magical power of their forms and images to unite myth and reality, between which the pharaonic world evolved. This applies to the pyramids, or the great rock-cut tombs (the *hypogea*) of the Valley of the Kings, that provided the pharaohs with the sacred way to the after-world. It is also the case with the temples of Upper Egypt or Nubia, which guaranteed the stability of the universe, and the vast private burial grounds, the decoration of which assured the continuity of the everyday tasks and pleasures of the people into eternity. Whether you are wandering in your imagination with the pharaohs among the gods, or delving, alongside viziers, scribes and officials, into the daily life of a society strongly divided by class, yet miraculously close to nature, do not attempt to exercise your own judgement. Modern criteria on architecture, painting or sculpture have no place here. Give yourself up to the spell cast by art, the elements of which are inseparable, and which speak of a civilization that, for 3000 years, responded satisfactorily to the questions asked by mankind about its destiny.

THE PYRAMIDS

The pyramids were, as we have seen, the first signs of existence left by the ancient Egyptians and, although they remain connected in our minds with the legendary grandeur of the Old Kingdom and ceased to be built after the second millennium B.C., they have become the very symbol of Egypt. They owe this to their wonderfully clean lines, which stand out against the sky above the tombs of Cheops, Chephren and Mycerinus in the desert 1½ miles/2 kilometres from Cairo. These very severe and imposing piles may once have been capped with gold. The four sides face the cardinal points of the compass as if ordained by some mysterious power. Yet they only attained perfection after a long period of tentative experiments. The first pyramid, that of Zoser, arose directly out of the brick *mastabas* which, until then, had constituted the royal tombs. It was, in fact, by placing six of these flat-topped structures of decreasing size one on top of the other that the architect created the pyramid, representing a wonderful giant staircase which allowed the pharaoh to ascend into the sky.

A century later, and without any evidence meantime to show how it evolved, the pyramid of Sneferu, the founder of the 4th dynasty, appeared with a smooth outer casing of fine limestone. Its 'rhomboidal' outline, however, provides evidence of successive stages of construction. We do not know whether the geometric design of the stone pile as a whole was the result of technical advances or a response to ceremonial requirements. Nor do we know whether it was used for all the tombs built around Memphis by the pharaohs of the 5th and 6th dynasties. There are too few remains. We can form some idea of this when we think of the splendid sight that 80 or so pyramids strung out for nearly 31 miles/50 kilometres along the clifftop on the western edge of the Nile Valley must have made at the end of the Old Kingdom. They bustled, we know, with intense activity. Not only did the pyramids themselves have to be built — and a king's reign was barely long enough to accomplish this — but also a whole surrounding complex of temples for the funeral ceremonies: the mortuary temple, on the east side of the enclosure around the pyramid, and the valley temple, situated on a canal with a jetty, to which the dead body was taken to be mummified. Linking these elements was a magnificent paved causeway. Along this, the mummy, placed in two or three sumptuous coffins, was carried amid great pomp on the day of the funeral to the mortuary temple, where the funerary rites were celebrated. Although the pharaoh's body then disappeared forever, walled up in the burial vault deep below the pyramid, where a heavy stone sarcophagus awaited it, the priests in the temple went on rendering the god-king the obsequies due him. Unfortunately, nothing, or almost nothing, remains today of these huge architectural complexes which were usually completed with small pyramids intended for the queens and with vast pits in which the great ships used by the god-king on his voyages through the celestial ocean were placed. To modern eyes, the pyramid is nothing more than a huge, fascinating shape isolated in the desert. It is entered, or rather penetrated, by a narrow passageway, with granite gates all along its length, flat stretches, changes of direction and broader sections; the passage descends to the heart of the pyramid, leading not to the infernal regions but to the burial chamber which no one should ever have entered. On the walls, mysterious funerary texts were often painted in long strips of blue hieroglyphs, providing the dead with the power to take wing, as a falcon or a heron, and tear themselves away from the earth. Narrow openings allowed the soul to escape from the tremendous pile of stones that imprisoned the mummy in the burial chamber. Life has no place here.

There was, however, plenty of life in the tombs that court officials and important people — all those who had served the pharaoh — built near the god-king's pyramid during the years that it was under construction.

THE MASTABAS

It is on the plateau of Sakkara that you get the best impression of the size and splendor of private Egyptian burial-grounds. This is difficult at first, because the broad, bench-like structures — the *mastabas* — that marked the site of the tombs, and to which they owe their name, have been worn down by time and buried again beneath the desert sand. You soon discover, however, that the rows of mounds are really a kind of village, complete with alleyways, and that the tombs are also dwellings that reflect the wealth and social rank of their owners. Some are simply funeral chapels; others, however, have what amount to living apartments around them. The most important are laid out around courtyards and small spaces. All have amazing pictorial decorations which, together with accompanying hieroglyphs, describe the daily lives of the people who lived along the banks of the Nile between 2500 and 2100 B.C.

The mummy itself lies out of reach at the bottom of a deep shaft, enclosed in an enormous sarcophagus and surrounded by the things it needs for survival after death. In these private tombs, as in the immense funerary complexes of their god-kings, the ancient Egyptians entrusted the eternal life of the human body to the earth. The living apartments which are being discovered by archaeologists today were intended for the dead person's spiritual double, or *ka*. It was there that he regained contact with the world of the living; an inscription on the door often invited passers-by to enter. However, if you wish to grasp what these strange funeral chapels represented, you have to leave all the usual ways of thinking behind at the threshold. You must accept that the stele directly above the burial vault and before which, on a heavy stone table, the libations, fumigation rites and food ceremonies required by the cult had taken place, was a genuine means of communication with the after-world. It is, in fact, often called the 'false door', and so it appears. You must also try to believe, as the ancient Egyptians did, in the magical

Deir el-Medina: scenes of daily life.

power of pictorial images and in their special virtue that enabled them, through cult ceremonies or sacred formulae in the hieroglyphic inscription, to restore a semblance of life to people and things. From here, it is only a short step to the belief that a statue of a dead person, hidden in the close confines of the *serdab*, acted like a genuine substitute body and could smell, through a narrow chink in the wall, the life-giving aroma of the food offered to it. In the same way, a dead person's image, painted life-size on the walls of his eternal resting-place, could continue in life, thanks to the familiar ceremonial scenes or pictures of personal experiences depicted around it.

FRESCOES OF EVERYDAY LIFE

Frescoes representing everyday existence are, by far, the most moving things to have survived from the age of the pharaohs. Inspired by a deep love for earthly things, these frescoes take the form of panoramas in finely modeled bas-relief, enhanced with bright colors. You can see them in all the *mastabas* of the Old Kingdom and in the tombs of the New Kingdom of a thousand years later cut into the hillsides on the left bank of the Nile by their rich Theban owners. They can be seen in random excavations in the ruins of private burial-grounds of all periods. Everywhere, they depict the same hard-working, rural Egypt with its animals and people, its sowing-times and harvests, and its craftsmen at their work. Enriched over the centuries by new themes supplied by an increasingly rich and refined society, these paintings give us a vivid idea of daily life in the vanished world of ancient Egypt.

Ritual scenes (such as funeral rites, embalming ceremonies, processions of hired mourners and the weighing of souls in the balance) are also depicted, reminding us of other mysterious influences in this long-dead civilization. The art in which these influences found expression, is proof enough of their presence.

SUPERNATURAL CONVENTIONS

With their huge eyes elongated with make-up and set in facial profiles in which the lips and nose are heavily emphasized; with their square torsos, their hips turned three-quarters around above their long legs, their two left hands, or two right hands ... these ancient people do not quite belong to this earth. Nor does the landscape in which they are placed, for it is a landscape that pays no regard to shadows or perspective. In order to carry human beings and things over into eternity, the Egyptians reasoned that their pictorial images had to conform to certain conventions that today escape us. The way they are arranged and the poses they strike are undoubtedly charged with obscure meanings. Their proportions pay no attention to visual appearances. Thus, a child never exceeds the height of his father's knee. Colors, too, are involved in this symbolism: red ochre is reserved for men, yellow ochre for women; green, we assume, would be associated with blossoming life, and black with resurrection. In a word, everything in this total view is connected with 'universal' order, but it is of such beauty, that at no time, do we question whether it is true to life in our sense. Without ever showing the slightest regard for aesthetics, in our sense of the word, the artists of ancient Egypt have left us true masterpieces. They were motivated by a steady desire to fulfil the mission entrusted to them, and they never ceased perfecting their means of expression without ever breaking with the traditions in which they were expected to work.

Thus, in the depths of the tombs at Thebes, we can admire whole series of pictures of increasing complexity, in which the figures become progressively more refined, supple and animated, and in which gestures, particularly those of women, become wonderfully graceful. In some of these bas-reliefs, the Egyptians even managed to convey the transparent quality of a veil, or the pleats in linen garments. The heights achieved in painting are more striking still. Previously, painting was always done in association with architecture and sculpture, but inside the tombs it was free to be itself because the stone was too soft to be carved. Artists discovered the endless possibilities of their palette, ranging from the most sumptuous to the most delicate of effects. And so, from the rich coloring of their ceremonial feasts to the play of blues and greens in their marshes, they captured some of the most vivid images of that vanished world.

MEN AND GODS DESTINED FOR IMMORTALITY

The funerary statues that provided the dead person with a substitute body and were intended to come to life in the secrecy of the tomb have themselves become part of the world's general fund of art treasures. They were made neither to be seen nor to be admired, and yet, all those which have been discovered, have found places in the world's great museums. They possess the spiritual quality of an art that was not concerned with making things appear realistic, nor even with idealizing them. The Egyptian artist sought to project people into eternity in the best possible light and, at the same time, to keep some resemblance to their real appearance, without which their spirit, or *ka*, would not recognize the body in which it had dwelt. The sculptor was caught between these unavoidable requirements and the ritual conventions that were imposed upon him — and upon everyone charged with reproducing living things — and which even determined the proportions and subjects he had to use. So, quite naturally, he tried to express the personality of his models in their poses, their faces and, especially, the look in their eyes. Sculptors applied themselves to this challenge for 3000 years and endowed even their most familiar subjects with surprising inner depth. So among the figures of scribes displayed in the world's museums, waiting with unfailing attention to perform their irreplaceable service, you will find one or two faces that are marked with a particular kind of gravity, a gravity that preceded the artist's inspiration. The great temple statues that had a religious role to play in the eternal life of the pharaohs show signs of the same development.

It is true, however, that many Egyptian religious works are cold and unapproachable. Large numbers of identical copies of the same image have been found among the ruins, as if there were only one prototype capable of performing its task. However, when we can detect a glimmer of humanity in the gaze of these stone pharaohs the effect is very powerful; and when his personal qualities shine through, what majesty! The oldest royal statue we have was discovered at Sakkara. This is the statue of Zoser (*c.* 2800 B.C.). Battered and chipped, with his eyes torn out and his nose broken off, the king is still imposing and superb. The statue of Chephren, dating from 100 years later, seems protected by the outstretched wings of the falcon-god Horus; this figure conveys the divine yet human nature of the pharaoh by the quiet gaze of the eyes. A thousand years later, sculpture incorporated the personality of this kind into its style. By the time of Queen Hatshepsut, its techniques had softened so much that they could respond to the queen's attractive face.

The reign of the revolutionary pharaoh Akhenaton, on the other hand, led to strange distortions. His own statue, with its monstrously heavy body, bears a face that has been stretched in length, while the almond eyes, slanting up to the temples, are absorbed in a sort of inner contentment. This aesthetic revolution, which produced such spiritual masterpieces as the portraits of Queen Nefertiti and her daughters, the six little princesses, barely survived the religious upheaval to which it was linked. Under the 19th dynasty, that of Ramesses II, the great classical tradition of art was to triumph anew with a marvelous series of colossal statues, vivid portraits of the pharaohs who took ancient Egypt to the peak of its glory. You will find them in the museum in Cairo or at Abu Simbel, where they appear with their mothers, wives or children, well-proportioned, powerful and, above all, human in spite of their size. Yet these are gods. You will not doubt this fact when you enter one of the mysterious tombs that the pharaohs of the New Kingdom dug for themselves in the Valley of the Kings.

THE VALLEY OF THE KINGS

The *hypogea*, or rock-cut tombs, of the Valley of the Kings were conceived as an imitation underground universe in which the sun disappeared each evening to journey through the depths of the other world until dawn. Their long, narrow passages descend into the heart of the mountain, where, beneath a blue and black vault supported on sturdy pillars and studded with imaginary astral figures, the heavy royal sarcophagus lies in state upon a rock, as if upon the 'primordial hill'. Fantastic decorations cover the walls of this stairway to the underworld. These are no less than illustrations, interspersed with hieroglyphic texts, of the numerous chapters of the 'Book of the Dead'. Through the ages, these illustrations were used as embellishments for the magic formulae inscribed inside the pyramids; their purpose was to facilitate the pharaoh's voyage across the heavens and his arrival among the gods.

The mummy was protected inside two or three magnificent coffins of human form (mummiform coffins), which were covered with numerous amulets, especially enameled pottery scarabs which, when placed over his heart, permitted the dead person to keep an untroubled conscience during the weighing of his soul. In most tombs, the mummy has disappeared, as has everything that the god-kings, confident of the outcome of their impending adventure, took with them into the depths of the earth — their furniture, weapons, jewels, even the portraits of the people who served them. Tomb-robbers preceded archaeologists into these places, which the living were forbidden to enter. In fact, the tomb of Tutankhamun is the only intact example of one of these celestial household removals, which were meant to ensure that the god-king would have everything he needed in eternity. Given the magnificence of the funerary trappings of this comparatively insignificant boy pharaoh, we can only marvel at the splendor which must have surrounded a major figure such as Ramesses. However, we must remember that the pharaohs of the New Kingdom, in building their great temples, celebrated the gods of Thebes while seeking to perpetuate their own glory.

TEMPLES WITHOUT NUMBER

The Egyptians gave the name 'temples of millions of years' to those impressive architectural complexes which, in their eyes, had a role to play in eternity, as did everything on the west bank of the Nile where the sun entered the after-world each evening. These temples are considerably less numerous today than the tombs in the Valley of the Kings would indicate. Many have disappeared, such as the famous temple of Amenophis III, which filled the Greeks and Romans with admiration. The memory of this temple is preserved only by the twin statues known as the Colossi of Memnon, towering in awesome isolation above the surrounding fields. Three of these ruins, now restored, count among Egypt's and indeed the world's great masterpieces. They are the temple of Hatshepsut, at Deir el-Bahari, the oldest and 'most sublime of the sublime'; the Ramesseum, erected by Ramesses II, which expresses a certain proud nostalgia in the colossal dimensions of its ruins; and finally, the temple of Ramesses III at Medinet Habu, where pylons covered with reliefs reflect the greatness of the last conqueror-king.

It was, however, on the right bank of the Nile that the supreme power of Thebes expressed itself at the peak of the empire. It was here that the temples of Karnak and Luxor were built. At first, nothing distinguishes these from other temples along the river. Once you are standing amid their ruins, however, you realize at once that they belong to a world that is even more imposing. The succession of pylons, courtyards and colonnades have a spiritual grandeur which defies description. Here it was no longer just a matter of building architectural complexes conceived and executed by some ruler to ensure his own immortality. Karnak and Luxor were dedicated to the cult of Amun-Ra and grew because of it; or perhaps because the conqueror-kings, on returning from their campaigns, offered the bulk of their booty to the god who had assured their success and enriched his temples with new buildings. These were dynastic temples and were constantly being altered. At Luxor, which is principally the work of two rulers, Amenophis III and Ramesses II, the development of the temple has remained clear. At Karnak, on the other hand, the architectural complexity of the building reflects its history. Its lack of order suggests the busy secular life of such colossal architecture. In addition to such amazing *tours de force* as the celebrated hypostyle hall, Karnak preserves the traces of rulers who did not hesitate to damage or destroy masterpieces of the past in order to make room for their own creations, sometimes even wreaking posthumous vengeance on their predecessors. In all the monuments of ancient Egypt, fragments of pylons, chapels or obelisks may be seen that have been destroyed then reused in the walls and foundations of the temple ruins we know today. Karnak is a mine of information for modern archaeologists who, through slow and meticulous reconstruction, can retrace the course of Egyptian history from one discovery to the next. Not surprisingly, Karnak continues to symbolize pharaonic splendor.

Egypt once had countless other great temples that have, for the most part, disappeared forever. The most famous, the temple at Heliopolis, near present-day Cairo, was dedicated to the solar cult of Ra. It went back to the dawn of history, yet so powerful was its influence that, just prior to the Christian era, the Greeks went there to establish contact with the regions of the Nile. Today we only have pictures of the courtyards and the high, open-air spaces of Heliopolis; the temple itself has vanished. Of temples with local importance, only a few vestiges remain, with the exception of the great temple built at Abydos by Seti I and the ruins of the nearby temple of Ramesses II. There were also numerous temples in Nubia. When the plans for the Aswân Dam were drawn up, these temples were threatened with inundation. Conservation efforts saved them, and the subsequent publicity drew the world's attention to Abu Simbel, one of the most original structures known to man.

Every one of the temples that ancient Egypt bequeathed to us is marked by the personality of the pharaoh who undertook its construction and of the god to whom its was dedicated. Each is unique in its own way. For example, when the Ptolemies, the successors to Alexander the Great, wished to join the long line of great pharaohs by building temples of their own, they wanted the style of their buildings to imitate those erected by Ramesses and his predecessors. They took the main features of the great classic architecture of the past for their own use in the temple of Isis at Philae, the temple of Horus at Idfu and, finally, the temple of the crocodile-god at Kom Ombo. It is to them that we owe some of the great architectural sites in the upper Nile Valley. The Romans followed their example with the temple of Hathor at Dendera and the hypostyle hall at Isna. These Late Period temples have considerable artistic and historic interest. Descriptions and explanations of the rites and ceremonies that took place in them are carved on the walls in long, narrow rows of hieroglyphs between religious figures of gods and kings. From these temples we can get an idea of what the people of the time considered to be a perfect religious building, and come to a better understanding of those that were constructed earlier.

ARCHITECTURE OF COSMIC SIGNIFICANCE

In ancient Egypt, the temple was apparently the place favored by a god for his dwelling and a structure that played a symbolic role in the cosmos through all its different parts. It was contained in an immense precinct, which was entered through a monumental gateway known as a propylon. In front of this stretched a paved causeway lined with sphinxes, because ancient myth claimed that all the entrances to the underworld were guarded by lions. These impressive structures were set out along a straight axis and ringed by a stone wall. The entrance was marked by two broad towers with inward-sloping sides, or pylons, which were separated by a narrow gateway that suggested two mountains between which the sun rose each morning. Housed in deep grooves in their walls were tall masts brought from the distant forests of Lebanon, from which fluttered banners indicating a divine dwelling-place. Before their facades, which were completely covered with reliefs of ritual scenes, there were sometimes two obelisks dedicated to the solar cult, at the top of which the pyramidion, encased in metal that was three-quarters gold, shone brightly in the sun. Next came a huge colonnaded court, in which stood two colossal statues of the king and which served as a setting for great spectacles during annual festivals. The hypostyle hall marked the beginning of the private and secret part of the temple. Its forest of sturdy columns, enclosed within low walls between the columns, concealing everything happening inside, is one of the greatest innovations of Egyptian architecture.

Unfortunately, we cannot experience its special magic today, because the roofs it supported more than 33 feet/10 metres above the ground have nearly all gone and, with them, the play of shadows created by the raised roof of the central passageway that let the light filter in. A second hypostyle hall, not so wide or high, often followed the first, then a number of rooms that were even lower and darker. Finally, amid a labyrinth of corridors and narrow, overlapping chambers lined with crypts piled one on top of the other in niches hollowed out of the walls, came the monolithic stone sanctuary where, behind closed doors, the image of the god was kept. Sometimes the sanctuary was preceded by the repository of the sacred bark, which was taken out during processions. Staircases completed the whole structure. They provided access to the walled terrace where the image of the god came several times a year to be united with the solar disk — that is to say, to be exposed to the sun's rays, which revitalized the divine presence within it. Finally, there was a sacred pool nearby, the water of which sprang, according to tradition, from the 'primordial ocean', and allowed the priests to cleanse themselves at daybreak before the first rites. Sanctuaries dedicated to minor gods were often built around the main temple. Additional buildings arose as time passed — first 'kiosks', or funerary chapels, then, during the Greco-Roman period, temples called *mammisi* in which the mystery of the birth of the god was celebrated.

The remains of these huge building complexes have become such a labyrinth that it is difficult today to find your bearings. Nonetheless, large numbers of the magnificent columns that once bore heavy ceilings are still standing under the open sky. With their stone capitals inspired by Egypt's loveliest plants — the papyrus, lotus and palm tree — and their shafts derived directly from the wooden poles or reed bundles of primitive structures, they revive for us the tremendous hidden power of the original building as a whole. Their designs are so varied that it is impossible to give examples of them all. They range from the 'proto-Doric' columns of Deir el-Bahari, which suggest tree trunks shaped with an adze, to the flowering umbels of Luxor. Until the Greco-Roman era, new forms were developed, such as the 'composite baskets' containing bunches of acacia twigs and all sorts of plants.

All this is a long way from the strict orders of Greek architecture. There is a feeling that these capitals, an intrinsic part of that spiritual world in which the temple as a whole is steeped, are not just blocks of stone but a medium through which the supernatural operates — something that escapes our understanding. In addition, it is clear that Egyptian architects preferred pillars employing mythological subjects. Such were the Osiris pillar, on which the pharaoh's image appeared as a mummified god, and the Hathor-headed, or Hathoric, column. On the latter, the lovely face of the cow-eared goddess, symbol of joy and love, appeared on 2 or 4 sides along with the *sistrum*, the sound of which dispelled grief. Whether in the form of columns or pillars, the roof supports of a pharaonic temple, like all the other structural elements, helped to create a link between sky and earth and so contributed to the stability of the universe.

PRESERVING THE STABILITY OF THE UNIVERSE

This awesome purpose of the Egyptian temples fully explains the impressive dimensions of their surrounding precincts. It also accounts for the size of the mud-brick villages that grew up around the main complexes to provide the homes, workshops and store-rooms used by the priests and servants. These ensured the continuity of the daily rites and the organization of the great ceremonial processions for which the temple served as the setting. We may imagine the daily ceremonies that provided the sacred image with the care and honor to which the pharaoh was entitled, from the rituals in which the image was sprinkled with cool water, dressed and promenaded, to the ceremony in which it was offered a meal that included dishes of real food. On the other hand, the meaning of such major ceremonies as the procession of the sacred barks, which are depicted on most pylons and chapels, remains obscure. Their interpretation is all the more hazardous because, alongside pictures of real festivals, we find symbolic scenes, such as the 'fishing expedition of the gods in the marshes', which reappear everywhere and the significance of which we do not understand. What is certain is that the decoration as a whole contributes to the general magic of the structural form and that, more often than not, we cannot attune ourselves to its mysterious signals. So it follows that the giant pharaoh who greets you from the walls of the pylons at the entrances of the temples, fearsomely whirling his arm above pleading crowds of vanquished enemies, is not, as you might think, celebrating the glory of his reign but ensuring through this ritual gesture the domination by Egypt of rebellious neighbors who happen also to be good targets for plunder. In other words, the pharaoh represents the victory of order over chaos.

Many of these scenes will seem coldly detached. They are bound to be so. Nevertheless, when the conqueror-pharaohs of the New Kingdom recount the story of their glorious exploits, even without the conventional guidelines, they manage to breathe life into the universal epic. And when you stand in front of the figure of Ramesses II, tall and serene as you see him on all his temples, and watch him hurtling along in his chariot or bending his bow at the battle of Kadesh, while beneath him, and separated from him by an invisible diagonal line, the contorted bodies of his enemies are piled in a twisted mass, you wonder for a moment whether the god-kings of ancient Egypt really were the sons of Amun, the god of the sun, and his lieutenants upon the earth.

CHRONOLOGY OF PHARAONIC EGYPT

Old Kingdom (2750–2180 B.C), capital Memphis
— Sakkara, step pyramid of Zoser, *c.* 2800.
— Giza, pyramid of Cheops, *c.* 2650.
— Giza, pyramid and sphinx of Chephren, *c.* 2620.
— Giza, pyramid of Mycerinus, *c.* 2600.
— Sakkara, pyramid with hieroglyphs of Unas, *c.* 2400.

First Intermediate Period (2180–2060 B.C.)
Internal anarchy.

Middle Kingdom (2060–1785 B.C.)
Period of trade expansion as far as Byblos and Assyria. Very few remains.
— Karnak, the white chapel of Sesostris I (1961–1928)

Second Intermediate Period (1785–1580 B.C.)
The Hyksos, Asian bedouin peoples, overrun the Nile Valley. They bring the wheel and the chariot.

New Kingdom (1580–1085 B.C.), capital Thebes
Period of conqueror-kings. Egypt extends its empire to the Mediterranean lands and Assyria in the east, and to Nubia in the south.
— Valley of the Kings, Valley of the Queens, tombs of nobles and artists.
— Deir el-Bahari, funerary temple of Hatshepsut, *c.* 1500.
— Karnak, obelisks, between 1500 and 1450.
— Karnak, festival chamber of Tuthmosis III, *c.* 1480.
— Luxor, temple of Amenophis III (1408–1372); Colossi of Memnon.
— Tel el-Amarna, ruins of capital of the revolutionary pharaoh Akhenaton (1372–1354), husband of Nefertiti.
— Abydos, temple of Seti I (1312–1298).
— Luxor, first pylon, Ramesses II (1298–1235).
— Karnak, hypostyle hall, Ramesses II.
— Thebes, Ramesseum, the funerary temple of Ramesses II.
— Abydos, ruins of the temple of Ramesses II.
— Abu Simbel, rock-cut temples of Ramesses II.
— Karnak, temple of Seti II (*c.* 1200)
— Medinet Habu, funerary temple of Ramesses III (1198–1166).

Seven centuries of decline (1085–332 B.C.)

Anarchy. Ethiopian pharaohs (751–656). Appearance of Greek traders under the Saite pharaohs (663–525). Changing fortunes under the Persian occupation (525–332).

Alexander and the Ptolemies (332-30 B.C.)

Conquest by Alexander (332), who is created pharaoh by the high-priest of Amun. He founds Alexandria. On his death, his lieutenant, Ptolemy, is given Egypt as his share of the empire. His descendants succeed him until Egypt becomes a Roman province on the death of Cleopatra. The Ptolemies and the Romans build the temples of Dendera, Idfu, Kom Ombo and Philae.

AMENITIES IN EGYPT

TRAVEL WITHIN EGYPT

Depending on the trips you will be taking, you will travel by air, train, coach, minibus, taxi, donkey or camel, boat, carriage or bicycle.

Air travel

Internal air services are good. There are three flights a day in both directions between Cairo and Luxor, and then on to Aswân, and two flights between Aswân and Abu Simbel. Additional flights are provided whenever required by the number of passengers. However, timetables are somewhat confusing. Departures in the middle of the night are frequent, as are uncertain waits in crowded airport lounges. You will be sure of leaving only when you have fastened your safety belt. Individual travelers should check their reservations and flight times the day before departure with Egypt Air, either at their main office (Map pp.66–67 C–3) 6 Shari Adly, tel. 92–09–99 in Cairo, or at their agencies in the main hotels.

Train

Travel by train is comparatively cheap. There are air-conditioned sleeping-cars between Cairo and Luxor (a 12-hour journey) and on to Aswân (16 hours altogether). Standards of comfort are much improved and will enable you to avoid the congested airports. The service is good and there is often dancing at the bar until the early hours of the morning. The train is also used mainly for the return leg of a tour after the outward journey up the valley by bus — or vice-versa. Train travel is extremely attractive for students, who get a 50 percent reduction by presenting their international student card, and on the short-distance daytime trains, they can mix with a colorful and friendly crowd and even get to sites that are unknown to the general public.

Bus

The comfort of long-distance buses in Egypt has greatly improved since American coaches that had been tried and tested crossing the United States were put into service by the travel organizations. Beware of travel fatigue if you go by the older-established bus companies, whose buses are not air-conditioned but have the windows wide open most of the time. It is better to use these only in the winter months. Buses for the Nile Valley leave from Shari Shubra, behind the station; coaches for Alexandria from Midan el-Tahrir (Liberation Square).

Taxis

These can be used in the smaller towns and for one-day trips. The normal return fare for a trip to the pyramids is L.E. 4. For individual tours the fare is L.E. 5 per hour. Be sure to keep your taxi when making trips around town because it is always very difficult to get another. You can also hire a minibus from certain agencies. To book a taxi for a trip, call Limousine Misr (Map pp.66–67 C–3) Shari Talaat Harb, tel. 75–00–10.

At Luxor you will find it difficult to resist a ride in a carriage, or, when you are in the desert, a ride on a donkey or camel. Again, settle the price beforehand!

Nile cruises

A cruise on the Nile is very appealing. It allows you to become, for a brief moment, a part of the life of the river and of the peasants who carry on their traditional activities along its banks. In a country where, at certain times of the year, there is a chronic shortage of hotel rooms, a cruise is a good way of providing them. A cruise is therefore included in most organized itineraries. The big hotels, such as the Hilton or Sheraton, have their own fleet of boats, as do the major tour operators. At peak periods, such as Christmas or Easter, there are boats calling nonstop, one after the other, at the landing-stages. Standards of comfort and service range from the luxury of the largest boats to the reasonable comfort of the smallest, and generally reflect the category of the hotel in whose itinerary they appear. Whichever boat you take, a cruise will be for four or seven days. It starts at Luxor and ends at Aswân, or vice-versa. It always includes tours of the temples of Isna, Idfu and Kom Ombo, but rarely, unfortunately, those of Abydos and Dendera. It is advisable not to take the Cairo–Aswân cruise, which is long and tiring.

Certain agencies will organize cruises for eight people on small boats to meet clients' special requests. The main ones in Cairo are:
— *Eastmar Services* (Map pp.66–67 C–3; tel. 75–32–16 and 97–04–45; telex 93743), 13 Shari Qasr en-Nil.
— *Trans Egypt Travel* (Map pp.66–67 C–3; tel. 74–43–13 and 97–79–13); 37 Shari Qasr en-Nil.

▬ *YOUR STAY IN EGYPT*

Egypt is a country to which you have to return. Your first visit will just give you a taste. Travel organizations plan visits of 9 to 15 days, and they are experienced. If you are making your own arrangements, consider the reductions offered by airline companies on tickets valid for a stay of 10 to 14 days and 10 to 35 days. Allow four days in Cairo to see the modern city, the historic mosques, the old Coptic quarter, the Egyptian Museum, and finally the important sites at Sakkara and the pyramids at Gîza. For trips to El Fayyum and Alexandria, add two more days. You cannot spend less than five days in Upper Egypt, two of them at Luxor visiting the site of ancient Thebes, two at Aswân, including a trip to Abu Simbel, and finally a one-day excursion to explore Abydos, the sacred city of Osiris, and Dendera.

▬ *ACCOMMODATION*

Egypt does not have adequate hotel facilities, despite the efforts being made to overcome this, and the contributions of the big American, French, Indian and other international hotel chains. Hotels that measure up to the expectations of western visitors can be found in the four main tourist and business centers: Cairo, Luxor, Aswân and Alexandria. At the beginning of 1981, a Sheraton hotel was opened at the new holiday resort of Hurghada, on the Red Sea, for people who enjoy sun-bathing and swimming in the sea. Nearly everywhere, hotels of international caliber are booked solidly six or seven months in advance, and individual travelers all too often find themselves stranded with nowhere to stay on their arrival. To ease the situation, the Egyptian tourist authorities have begun work on large new complexes that should increase hotel capacity by more than 3500 rooms of deluxe category in Cairo and over 750 in Luxor. An increase in the number of establishments providing first-class comfortable accommodation but with additional basic general facilities is being sought at the same time. New ones are being registered each year, either as first class superior (▲▲▲▲) or medium (▲▲▲), depending on their facilities. It is best to avoid hotels in lower categories, because these do not always come up to western standards.

Hotel charges vary, when adjusted according to the rate of exchange, and only travel agencies can keep up with the latest figures. Leave the calculations to them. Students can get accommodation at very low cost in youth hostels. There are 14 of these, divided among the various towns. For information, write to the Egyptian Youth Hostel Association, 7 Shari Abdel Hamed Said, Cairo (tel. 43-799).

FOOD AND DRINK

The standard international cuisine, varied by an occasional Middle Eastern dish, served at most hotels is quite acceptable. Cairo and Alexandria have many restaurants, the most luxurious of which are connected to nightclubs and are expensive. Do not be afraid to lunch in snack-bars or pastry-shops, where you can find delicious Middle Eastern specialties. Then there are countless small local restaurants where you can have a light meal at a reasonable price and try popular Egyptian dishes — but at your own risk.

Apart from kebabs, which are eaten all over the Middle East, and *mashwi* (whole roasted lamb), you may wish to try some popular local dishes. Among these are *fool*, a dish based on fava beans, which are first soaked in water to make them swell and then simmered in oil and spices; *mulukhia*, a mash of green vegetables used to give flavor to rice and chicken; *fattah*, a mixture of rice, bread, vinegar, garlic, curdled milk and lamb; or pigeon stuffed with *ferik* (wheat germ), which is delicious, and grilled fish, crab, lobster and other seafood.

With regard to drinks, you will most likely fall back on the local beer (Stella), which is light and pleasant; it is sold in half-litre bottles. Wine is more variable in quality. Among the red wines, try the Omar Khayyam, and among the rosé wines, the Rubis d'Égypte. Tap water is drinkable in major cities. Mineral water is quite expensive.

Fruit juices, especially lime juice, are excellent. You can also try mango, pomegranate and sugar-cane juice. *Karkadé*, a dark red infusion made from a Nubian plant, is drunk cold. Tea is served in small glasses that scald your fingers. Turkish coffee is one of the national drinks.

PRACTICAL INFORMATION

Local time

On arrival in Egypt, remember to move your watch forward (later) if traveling from Britain, the United States or any other country west of Egypt. Time differences are two hours ahead of Britain (Greenwich Mean Time), seven hours ahead of the United States east coast (Eastern Standard Time) and 10 hours ahead of the west coast (Pacific Time). Allowance should be made, however, for British Summer Time and American Daylight Saving Time in summer.

Visiting and business

Shops and monuments in the European quarters are open from 8.30 am to 1 or 2 pm and from 4 or 5 pm to 8 pm.

Museums are open every day, but close at the time of prayer — that is, from 11 am to 1 pm on Fridays. Each museum has its own hours of opening and it is wise to check beforehand. The Egyptian Museum in Cairo is normally open from 9 am to 4 pm, the Islamic Museum from 9 am to 2 pm, and the Coptic Museum from 9 am to 4 pm. The Luxor Museum opens its doors only between 4 and 9 pm.

Mosques are closed to visitors only at times of prayer and on Friday mornings.

The pharaonic sites are nearly all open the whole day. In summer they sometimes close at 2 pm but, if you can find him, you can always ask the attendant to let you in.

Newspapers

Egypt has one daily newspaper in English, the *Egyptian Gazette* published in Cairo. It is also possible to buy English-language dailies published in Britain and the United States, and the *International Herald Tribune*. The newsstands will also have *Arab News*, published in English in Saudi Arabia, and *Cairo Today*, an Egyptian monthly magazine, also in English. Daily newspapers in Arabic are numerous, the best-known including *El Ahram*, *El Gumhoria* and *El Akhbar*. In addition, there are several important weeklies.

Language

The official language is Arabic. English and French are also widely spoken by shopkeepers in the cities and larger towns. Expect some difficulty in making yourself understood in the country districts.

Holidays and festivals

Government offices are officially closed on Fridays. Most businesses, however, close on Sundays.

Public holidays are January 1; May 1; sometimes June 18, the anniversary of the founding of the Republic; always July 23, Revolution Day, and December 23, Victory Day. Finally, the Muslim New Year and all the important Islamic festivals are holidays. Their dates vary from year to year.

Shopping

The holiday souvenir industry, like tourism, is booming. It operates everywhere, and all sorts of articles specially made for visitors, (leather goods, copper items, jewelry, fabrics), lie in wait in the bazaars and souks. Amid all the junk, however, you may be lucky enough to come across attractive blown glassware, papyrus scrolls, various kinds of pots and simple but charming tapestries, mostly woven by children in the workshops of Garagos (Upper Egypt), Kerdassa or El-Haraniya (on the way to the pyramids). You can also have a *galabiyeh* (a long, loose robe) or even, at Luxor, western-style cotton dresses made to measure in a day.

At the archaeological sites you will be besieged by sellers of antiquities, who have all the gestures of conspirators and hand you poorly-made imitations of bas-reliefs, *ushabtis* (little tomb statuettes) or scarabs. You will find genuine articles only in a very small number of antique shops in Cairo and Alexandria. Bear in mind, however, that you will have great difficulty getting permission to take these out of the country.

Baksheesh

Always, wherever you are, remember to add the *baksheesh*, or a tip, on top of the price on the ticket or agreed through bargaining. Arm yourself with plenty of small change and save as much as you can, because as soon as you give a coin to a child or an attendant you will be surrounded by a cluster of outstretched hands. Remember that these people are poor compared to you, and that you are a foreigner with wealth that might seem provocative. When you refuse to give them anything, do it with a smile.

Useful addresses in Cairo

Australian Embassy (Map pp.66–67 D–2), 1097 Nile Corniche, Garden City (tel. 77–79–00).
British Embassy (Map pp.66–67 C–2), Shari Ahmed Ragheb, Garden City (tel. 23–077/29–850).
Canadian Embassy (Map pp.66–67 D–2), 6 Shari Muhamad Fahmi el Sayyid, Garden City (tel. 23–119/110).
United States Embassy (Map pp.66–67 C–2), 5 Shari Amrika Laliniyyah, Garden City (tel. 28–211/9).
British Council (Map pp.66–67 B–1), 192 Shari en-Nil, Aguza (tel. 34–60–206/577).
American Express (Map pp.66–67 C–3), 15 Shari Qasr en-Nil (tel. 75–31–42 and 75–08–92); desks in the Nile Hilton (tel. 81–03–83) and Meridien (tel. 84–40–17).
Misr Travel (Map pp.66–67 C–3), 1 Shari Talaat Harb (tel. 75–00–10/25–37).
Thomas Cook (Map pp.66–67 C–2), 4 Shari Champollion (tel. 74–39–55/67).

Tourist Information offices: main office: (Map pp.66–67 C–3), 5 Shari Adly (tel. 91–26–44/92–30–00); airport (tel. 96–64–75); pyramids (tel. 85–02–59).
Egypt Air: 6 Shari Adly (tel. 92–09–99/92–24–44).
Bank of America (Map pp.66–67 C–2), 106 Shari Qasr el-Ayni, Garden City (tel. 27–500).
Banque du Caire/Barclays International (Map pp.66–67 D–2), 12 Midan esh-Sheikh Ali Yusef, Garden City (tel. 35–49–422).
Emergencies: police (tel. 122); ambulance (tel. 123).

CAIRO

When traveling to the land of the pharaohs, the Nile Valley of Egypt, you land first at Cairo, the largest city in Africa and the Arab world. If the time of day and wind direction permit, you will get a panoramic view from the plane of the pyramids and the golden sands of the desert to the west. Then you will see the city, stretching away as far as the eye can see. Egypt may have the longest continuous history of any nation in the world but before you follow its course in the valley where it took place, your first experience of this country will be one of stark modernity.

THE SPRAWLING CITY OF CAIRO

On leaving the busy, crowded airport, you proceed along a modern expressway across the residential suburb of Heliopolis, built at the beginning of the century on the initiative of a celebrated Belgian businessman named Baron Empain. The beautiful villas and green space of Heliopolis are now giving way to luxury apartment buildings, while ever-increasing numbers of people bustle to and fro along the streets. You then enter Cairo itself along a long highway lined with squalid tenements straight out of the 19th century. Behind them, minarets rise above the working-class districts. By the time you end up in the ultra-modern city center and its jam of private cars, black and white taxis, and buses packed with men in local and European dress, you will have forgotten all about the Nile and the pharaohs! You will inevitably go though the Midan el-Tahrir, the immense Liberation Square (Map pp.66–67 C–2) , where the swirl of traffic, augmented by the coach station, is equaled only by the bustle of crowds who, to avoid it, go around the edge along a series of footbridges. You are sure to return here, because this is where the main streets containing the travel agencies, airline offices and finest shops converge. Indeed, you may be staying in one of the big hotels overlooking this square. You will, in any case, pass through it on the way to the Egyptian Museum (Map pp.66–67 C–2) nearby. The city of Cairo is currently involved in a widespread program of road repair and urban redevelopment. This is being done to create a city that matches the position of responsibility Egypt holds in the Arab world, its role at the forefront of the regional organization of the Nile nations and, on a wider basis, in African politics — in short, a city that matches up to Egypt's political and cultural importance.

Cairo, which celebrated its millennium in 1969, is a city undergoing considerable change and in which it is difficult to get around. Even the marvelous Nile Corniche is in the throes of a facelift amid the din of the traffic. Yet, on the slow and stately river early each morning and late in the evening, you can still see old *feluccas* sailing by, laden with cargoes of lumber while tourists take rides in the afternoon. Sometimes you may even see little ducks paddling around in the small cultivated plots at the water's edge where papyrus is grown at the foot of the concrete walls. It is now a long time since the city threw its many bridges across to the opposite bank via the two large islands of Gezira (Map pp.66–67 C–1–2) and Roda (Map pp.66–67 E–2), which are mainly residential areas. In doing so, it spread a continuous flow of cars and buses to the new districts to the north and to the built-up area of Giza (Map pp.66–67 E–F–1) by the pyramids to the south.

THE MUSLIM CAPITAL

Your hotel accommodation will probably be in one of the pleasanter districts of Cairo, and you will nearly always get to and from it by taxi or bus, because the city is so spread out and difficult to negotiate. Before setting out to explore, you should first go up to the top of the **Gezira Island tower** to get a general view. From the bar and restaurant 610 feet/186 metres above the ground, which you pay to reach by lift, you get a magnificent panoramic view over both sides of the Nile. In the distance, in the desperately dry landscape to the west, you will be able to pick out the pyramids of Giza, Sakkara and perhaps Abusir. Spread below you is a Muslim city bristling with minarets, and a modern urban metropolis criss-crossed by a maze of broad highways where between 11 and 12 million people live — twice as many as in 1967. Immediately below you, creating a few splashes of green, are the gardens. In the ring of popular suburbs to the east and northeast of the city, fringed on the outside by huge cemeteries, there are 156,000 people crowded into every square mile (60,000 per square kilometre), and as many as 280,000 in some spots. From up here, these figures will not suprise you. You will also begin to understand why the city is in such a hurry to do something about this alarming situation.

Meanwhile, you can trace the city's history in the immense panorama laid out before you. It began on the east bank of the river opposite Roda Island, where the Romans built a fortified village on the site known as 'Babylon in Egypt'. An important Christian community developed here between the 1st and 6th centuries A.D. In 639, after winning Egypt for Islam, Caliph Omar built a new city named Fustat (Map pp.66–67 F–2–3) opposite the walls that today enclose the old Coptic quarter of the city, and over the next hundred years it grew. But in 870 the governor Ibn Tulun succeeded in breaking away from the caliphs of Baghdad and built himself a private capital on a hill northeast of his predecessors' city. Nothing remains of the palaces, gardens and mosques with which he embellished it except the wonderful mosque (Map pp.66–67 D–3)

Cairo: typical street scene showing traditional lattice windows.

that bears his name, now lost in a teeming popular quarter of the modern city.

A century later, in 969, the Fatimids, a dynasty from Kairouan in Tunisia, which was then extending its rule across North Africa and into Syria and Palestine, established the capital of their empire at a spot northeast of the present citadel. They called it **El Kahira,** 'the victorious one'. The city enjoyed two centuries of glittering prosperity. Almost the only relics of the era in this incredibly crowded part of Cairo are the formidable Syrian-style walls and the two huge gates which can still be seen on the northern edge of the big suburban cemeteries.

In 1171, Fatimid rule gave way before the rising power of Saladin, the foe of the Crusaders. On one of the hills surrounding the city, he built a citadel (Map pp.66–67 D–4–5) that still dominates it and then undertook the task of uniting the two earlier cities within the same boundary. It was within this enlarged city that the Mamluk sultans, who reigned from 1250 to 1517, built the most outstanding monuments of Muslim Egypt. These extraordinary mercenary adventurers, who had come down from southern Europe and the Caucasus, were, in fact, the descendants of slaves and almost all of them were murdered by their successors. Through their passion for building and their love of ostentation, they managed to create a proud and grandiose style of architecture that was unequalled anywhere; the **mosque of Sultan Hasan,** at the foot of the citadel, is the most important example. It was during these years that Muslim Egypt reached the peak of its achievement. The seizure of power by the Ottoman Turks from the Mamluks at the beginning of the 16th century marked the start of what has been called the 'dark ages'.

The last of the great achievements of Islamic art in Cairo dates from the 19th century. This is the sumptuous mosque, inspired directly by the architectural masterpieces of Istanbul, with which Mehemet Ali (1805–1849) crowned the citadel of his predecessors. It still dominates the city and, in a way, marks the beginning of the modern era. Once he became master of Egypt, Ali, an Albanian officer in the Turkish army, tried to shake the country out of its lethargy by opening it up to western influence. Cairo then burst out from its medieval districts, through which broad highways were then cut, and work began on the construction of the great international metropolis that you can see growing and changing before your eyes today.

CITY INFORMATION

You arrive in Cairo at the Heliopolis International Airport, situated 10 miles/16 kilometres from the city. This is a huge complex used by both domestic and international airlines, and there is a constant bustle of people. If you are not traveling with a group, your first problem will be to get a taxi. When you arrive, get some small change from the 'bureau de change', because taxi drivers never have any. If you have any difficulties, go to the information desk of the Ministry of Tourism, which is in the airport. If you are coming by train from Alexandria, you will arrive directly in the city center. There are the same problems with taxis here as at the airport.

GETTING AROUND CAIRO AND THE SURROUNDING AREA

A large number of buses depart from Midan el-Tahrir (Map pp.66–67 C–2) for all destinations, including Alexandria, but, in practice, a visitor can only get about by taxi, especially if there is not much time. It is, however, difficult to find them. It is advisable to wait in front of one of the hotels. Not all taxis have meters, and you are advised to fix the fare before setting off. Reckon L.E. 5 per hour. A tip of around 10 percent should be added.

ACCOMMODATION

Since 1978, Cairo has made a remarkable effort to improve hotel accommodation to try to meet the various needs of visitors. Establishments coming up to modern luxury standards, or just first-class, now stretch from Heliopolis Airport, 10 miles/16 kilometres out on the east side of the Nile, as far as the pyramids, which dominate the river to the west. Hotels near the airport allow travelers to catch early-morning or late-night flights, which are now common in Egypt. Those near the pyramids cater for the holidays and archaeological visits for which most tourists travel to Egypt. Both of these hotel districts are linked to the city center by regular shuttle services. Most of the new hotel developments, however, are situated in the former residential districts of Zamalek and Doqqi. The hotels listed below are the ones generally used by foreign visitors because of their location and grade. The list, however, is constantly growing, and you may be offered a hotel that is not mentioned in this guide. If so, do not reject it immediately, because it may have opened after the guide was published. For convenience, hotel categories are included here under the following abbreviations: Deluxe: ▲▲▲▲; First-class ▲▲▲; Medium-class ▲▲; Tourist and economy class and 'pensions' ▲.

Near the airport
A number of hotels and establishments providing overnight accommodation have been built, among which two are particularly comfortable:

▲▲▲▲**Cairo Concorde** (tel. 66–42–42; telex 94066)

▲▲▲▲**Novotel** (tel. 66–13–30 and 69–47–72; telex 93711)

On the Heliopolis road
Two luxury hotels:

▲▲▲▲**Heliopolis Sheraton**, Shari el-Oruba (tel. 66–77–00 and 66–55–00; telex 93360), opened in 1979. The rooms, public areas and service are of international standard.

▲▲▲▲**Hyatt El Salam**, 61 Shari Abdul Hamid Badawy, (tel. 69–21–55; telex 92184 and 93009), open since 1979. 332 rooms, several restaurants, and conference rooms. Situated next to the El Shams Club, it has good access to holiday and sporting activities.

These two hotels have much to recommend them as places to spend a holiday; their drawbacks are their distance from the city center and the problem of traffic into Cairo.

At the city center
The number of top-grade hotels has increased. The following are worth mentioning:

▲▲▲▲**Cairo Marriott** (Map pp.66–67 B–2; tel. 65–08–40; telex 93464 and 93465), Shari Saray el-Gezira, opened in 1982 in a residential area on Gezira Island. It consists of two ultra-modern wings on each side of a French Napoleon III palace that still retains its charm.

▲▲▲▲**Cairo Sheraton** (Map pp.66–67 D–1; tel. 98–30–00 and 73–03–33; telex 92041 and 92322), in Midan Kubry el-Galaa, Giza, where it was built in 1978 in one of the new districts on the left bank of the Nile. You can see the pyramids from the room terraces overlooking the river. With its various restaurants, snack-bars, bars,

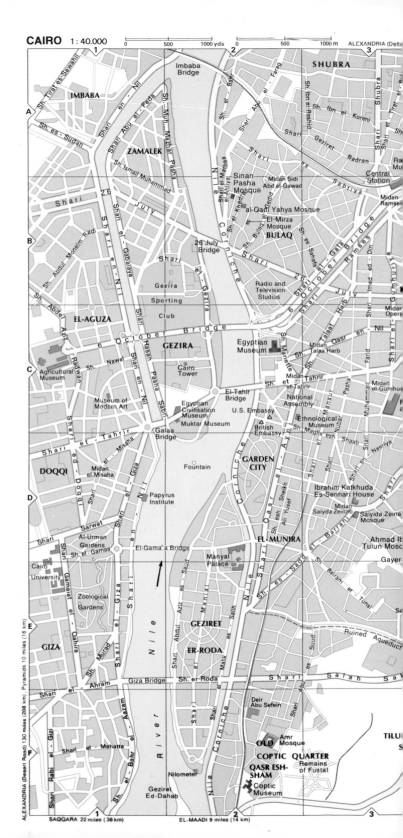

Cairo at a glance

★★★

Egyptian Museum
(C–2)

★★

Ahmad Ibn Tulun Mosque
(D–3)

Al-Azhar Mosque
(C–4)

Islamic Art Museum
(C–4)

Sultan Hasan Madrasa
(D–4)

★

Ben Ezra Synagogue
(F–2) (in old Coptic quarter)

Coptic Museum
(F–2)

Khan el-Khalili
(C–4–5)

Mausoleum of Kalaun
(C–4)

Mohammed Ali Mosque
(D–4)

Old Coptic quarter
(F–2)

Other sites of interest

Bab Zuweila
(C–4)

Blue Mosque
(D–4)

Church of St. Barbara
(F–2) in old Coptic quarter

Church of St. Sergius
(F–2) in old Coptic quarter

Citadel
(D–4–5)

City of the Dead
(C–D–5)

El-Barquq Mosque
(D–5)

El-Hakim Mosque
(B–5)

El-Maridani Mosque
(C–4)

Fatimid district
(C–4)

Gayer-Anderson Museum
(D–3)

Mouski district
(C–4)

Mausoleum of Qaytbay
(D–5)

Sultan el-Muayyad Mosque
(C–4)

lounges, shops, nightclub and casino, it attains the high standards of the finest international hotels.

▲▲▲▲**Meridien** (Map pp.66–67 D–2; tel. 84–54–44; telex 93918), at the tip of Roda Island beside the river. All 296 rooms, each with private terrace, have a superb view and are extremely comfortable. The hotel has three restaurants, a snack-bar, various bars and public lounges, a nightclub, two swimming-pools and a large number of shops catering both to tourists and the many business people who stay here.

▲▲▲▲**Nile Hilton** (Map pp.66–67 C–2; tel. 74–07–77 and 75–06–66; telex 92222), situated in Midan el-Tahrir, faces the square and the Egyptian Museum on one side, and the Nile on the other. It has 400 luxuriously appointed rooms. The four restaurants offer a choice of European and Middle Eastern cuisine. The Hilton's nightclub and casino cater to the varied interests of a clientèle that extends beyond hotel guests. This is one of Cairo's great meeting-places.

▲▲▲▲**Ramses Hilton** (Map pp.66–67 C–2; tel. 75–80–00; telex 92262), at 1115 Nile Corniche. An imposing building, it has twice as many rooms as the Nile Hilton and provides the same facilities.

▲▲▲**Manyal Palace** (Map pp.66–67 D–E–2; tel. 84–60–14; telex 93353) deserves special mention. Set in the beautiful tropical park of the former Manyal Palace on Roda Island, this is, by far, the most pleasant place to stay in Cairo. It accepts reservations from single travelers, such as archaeologists, teachers and businessmen, who come to spend a few days in Cairo but wish to get away from the noise and dust of the city. The accommodation is arranged in bungalows, each with double beds, laid out along alleys lined with imposing banyan trees. The main building contains a lounge, bar and restaurant. The swimming-pool is an irresistible attraction at lunch-time. This hotel is far removed from the international luxury palaces elsewhere, but it is right on the banks of the Nile and is very comfortable.

▲▲▲**Shepheard's** (Map pp.66–67 C–2; tel. 33–800 and 33–900; telex 9379), on the Nile Corniche. For a long time, this was the best hotel in Cairo. It has been renovated, but still retains the charm of a bygone era. Its restaurant, on a terrace, enjoys a panoramic view of the city. It unfortunately suffers from the traffic noise of the Nile Corniche.

Among the hotels that do not boast a special setting but which cater to the businessman's needs, the following may be listed:

▲▲**Pharaoh's** (Map pp.66–67 C–1; tel. 71–22–23; telex 93383), 12 Shari Lufti Hassuna, Doqqi, behind the Sheraton Hotel. A conveniently situated hotel in a quiet street.

▲▲**President** (Map pp.66–67 A–1; tel. 81–31–95; telex 93655), 22 Taha Hussein, Zamalek, in a leafy northern district of Gezira Island. Some of the rooms overlook the Nile. The restaurant is famous, as is the pub.

Other establishments offering acceptable accommodation include: ▲**Atlas Zamalek** 20 Shari Gamaat el-Dowal el Arabiya (Map pp.66–67 B–1 — falls just outside of map), tel. 80–41–75; telex 93281. ▲**El Borg** (Map pp.66–67 C–2), Gezira Island, tel. 65–18–27; telex 94148. ▲**El Nil** (Map pp.66–67 D–2), Nile Corniche, tel. 32–878; telex 9414. ▲**Garden City House** (tel. 28–126), 23 Shari Gamal el-Din Salah, situated in the Garden City, in the city center. ▲**Indiana** Ghana-el-Savaya, tel. 71–44–22; telex 94144.

For people looking for very simple accommodation, there are also two pensions at the same address, 21 Shari Ismail Mohammad (Map pp.66–67 B–1): **Horus** (tel. 61–86–82; telex 93655) and **Longchamps** (tel. 80–23–112).

Near the pyramids
Hotels on the edge of the desert that permit easy access to the pyramids and turn a stay in Cairo into a pleasant country holiday, are

increasing in number. Establishments of proven quality:
▲▲▲▲**Mena House Oberoi** (tel. 85–54–44 and 85–62–22; telex 92316 and 93096) is an historic hotel. It was originally a hunting lodge that the *khedive* Ismael had furnished to receive Empress Eugénie at the opening of the Suez Canal in 1869. Kings and poets have stayed here. Renovated by the Oberoi hotel chain, it now has a modern wing extending into the gardens. With facilities that include restaurants, bars, a nightclub, a swimming-pool and a golf course, this is a top-class hotel. It also offers facilities for horseback-riding over the dunes in the cool of the day.
▲▲▲**Jolie-ville** (tel. 85–55–10 or 85–56–12; telex 92567) is along the desert road to Alexandria. It is designed with separate bungalows, arranged in a garden around a swimming-pool. The cuisine is good. The hotel also offers opportunities for walks among the desert dunes.

Since 1984, three new hotels have been opened quite close to the pyramids. One is of top international grade: ▲▲▲▲**Siag** (tel. 85–60–22; telex 93522) Shari Sakara. The other two also provide comfortable accommodation: ▲▲▲**Green Pyramids** (tel. 85–26–00; telex 93701) which has 78 rooms in a single-story building beside a swimming-pool, and ▲▲▲**Radisson Oasis** (tel. 85–69–88).

▬ DINING OUT

In all the hotels you will find international and Middle Eastern cuisine, snack-bars or pizzerias.

The *Palme d'Or* and the *Qasr el-Raschid* in the *Meridien Hotel* (Map pp. 66–67 D–2) are specially recommended. The latter is the most select Middle Eastern restaurant in Cairo. It offers an enormous buffet of almost 50 different dishes every evening.

There are a large number of restaurants in the city itself. The following selection offer European cuisine and are expensive:
Caroll (Map pp.66–67 C–3; tel. 56–244), 12 Shari Qasr en-Nil.
Le Château (Map pp.66–67 E–1; tel. 98–14–87), Shari en-Nil, at Giza. Ties are compulsory.
Estoril (Map pp.66–67 C–3; tel. 74–31–02) 12 Shari Talaat Harb.

You may also wish to try restaurants specializing in Middle Eastern and Egyptian dishes, and there are several that are excellent:

In the city center:
Abu Shakra (Map pp.66–67 D–2; tel. 84–88–11), 69 Shari Qasr el-Ayni, serves some of the best kebabs in the city.
Arabesque (Map pp.66–67 C–3; tel.75–98–96), 6 Shari Qasr en-Nil, has authentic Eastern decor with a display of modern paintings; the menu offers unusual hors-d'oeuvres and a popular winter dessert called *Umm Ali.*
El Dahan, (Map pp.66–67 C–5), next to the Al-Azhar Mosque in the heart of Old Cairo, is famous for its specialty, casserole of young goat.
El Shimy (Map pp.66–67 B–3; tel. 55–345), Midan Orabi, is known for its chicken *mulukhia* and *fattet mulukhia* (a recipe with bread and rice).
Felfela (Map pp.66–67 C–3; tel. 74–05–21), Shari Sharawi at the corner of Talaat Harb, has a youthful atmosphere and offers a good *fool, taameyya* (fried chicken and vegetable rissole), *shashwa*, pigeon *ferik* and traditional *Umm Ali.*
Hag Mahmoud el Samak (Map pp.66–67 C–3), Shari Abdel Aziz, is one of the best fish and prawn restaurants in the city center.

Two of Cairo's most attractive restaurants are set in the open air along the road to Maadi, a long way from the city center on the right bank of the Nile:
Nile Garden is especially pleasant on hot evenings.
Seahorse (tel. 47–933) is renowned for its grilled fish and prawns and fish kebab. It overlooks the Nile at the spot where the boatmen hoist their mainsails on their way upriver after passing under the last of the

city bridges. In the distance, you can see the pyramids on the opposite bank.

Finally, the restaurants on the road to the pyramids should not be overlooked:

Andrea (tel. 85–11–33), on El Maruntia (on the right of the Pyramid Road, not the road to Sakkara). The specialty here is barbecued chicken.

The Farm (tel. 85–18–70), situated opposite the *Andrea* on the other side of the canal in a pleasant rural setting. This is one of Cairo's best restaurants.

Fel Fela Village (tel. 85–42–09), on El Maruntia next door to *The Farm* restaurant.

Casino des Pigeons (tel. 89–62–99), by the Abbas Bridge at Gîza, specializes in roast pigeon.

▬ PRACTICAL INFORMATION

Entertainment

Day or night you can hire a *felucca* in front of the *Meridien* and *El Borg* hotels, and go gliding down the Nile. This is a unique and very pleasant experience.

You should certainly go to see the *son et lumière* presentation at the pyramids, which is performed in several languages, including English. Check with your hotel for the days and times of the shows, because these vary. The hotel will probably make all the necessary arrangements for you to get there. You can also visit the casinos and nightclubs presenting traditional belly dancing. At the end of a long day, you will probably be too tired even to think about it but, if you feel up to it, you may try *After 8* (tel. 43–455), 6 Shari Qasr en-Nil, frequented by the younger set, good food.

There is also a string of countless nightspots along the road to the pyramids where the food is poor but where, from 10 pm till the early hours, you will find the best Middle Eastern singers and dancers in the world. Egyptians themselves, as well as visitors from neighboring countries go to these places.

Shopping: the Khan el-Khalili

Shopping in Cairo means, above all else, the Khan el-Khalili (Map pp. 66–67, C–4–5), the largest bazaar in the Middle East after the one in Istanbul. It was established in the Mamluk period and, at the center of the present market, you can still see a gate which dates from the 16th century. It was around this gate that bazaars selling carpets, silks and embroidered fabrics gradually gathered. Because of its fame, the Khan el-Khalili has lost much of its picturesque appeal. The big covered market selling local craft products is now filled with all sorts of merchants selling souvenirs of Egypt, specially designed and made for tourists. Here, you can find leather and copper goods, and necklaces made of amber and other semi-precious stones. You can also have a piece of silver jewelry or a *galabiyeh*, the traditional long robe, made for you, but it is perhaps preferable to have your *galabiyeh* made in the adjacent streets, where the merchants are pleasanter to deal with. You can also get perfume essences here, to which you can add alcohol or spices when you get home. Note also the blown glassware.

For old saddles, stirrups, or inlaid caskets, visit the covered alley near the Bab Zuweila, one of the old entrance-gates of Cairo.

Do not omit a visit to the **Papyrus Institute** (Map pp.66–67 D–1), 3 Shari en-Nil, Gîza where papyrus is still made as it was in ancient times. Very fine examples may be bought here, but at a high price if you do not bargain.

Popular restaurant in Cairo.

On the outskirts of the city, try shopping at the weaving and carpet workshops near Kerdassa, on the road to the pyramids, and at El-Haraniya, on the road to Alexandria. Make sure they are open for business before setting out. Check opening hours at the Tourist Office (see p.60).

VISITING CAIRO

THE OLD COPTIC QUARTER AND MUSEUM*
(Map pp.66–67 F–2)

Allow two hours for the round-trip by taxi from Midan el-Tahrir (Map pp.66–67 C–2). You can also reach the Coptic quarter by train from Bab el-Luk Station, alighting at Mari Girgis (Old Cairo) Station.

The name 'Copt' is used today to designate the ancient Christian community living along the Nile. Originally, it was simply the Arabic word for 'Egyptian', which the Arab invaders of the 7th century used for the inhabitants of the conquered country who, at that time, were Christian. After many ups and downs in their history, the Copts have become integrated into Egyptian society and today number between five and six million. They still practice their religion and observe their ancient traditions. They have, therefore, founded a museum that expresses their cultural identity on the site of the Qasr el-Shamah (Fortress of the Beacon), inside the Roman walls of ancient 'Babylon of Egypt'. Here, too, are the oldest Coptic churches. The site itself, enclosed within irregular high ramparts, is breathtaking. The entrance, opposite the little railway station, is between two immense towers, one of which is crowned by the two bell-towers of a Greek church built on top of it.

The Museum* (Map pp.66–67 F–2)

Visit: daily 9 am – 4 pm, from 10 am on Sundays. Admission charge.

Situated at the end of a garden, the museum was purposely built in a style in keeping with the collections kept there, and was embellished with woodwork, particularly latticework window-bays (*moucharabies*) from the ruins of houses or churches belonging to the Coptic community. The art on display here is neither naive nor sophisticated in style. It is the art of craftsmen who were not only skilled in the techniques of their day but who also stamped their faith on their work as it evolved in style over the centuries from Greco-Roman to Arabic.

On the **ground floor** are sculptures, reliefs, wall-niches, friezes, capitals and paintings, showing how Coptic art developed separately from the Greco-Roman art that was its original inspiration. Do not miss the huge fresco from El Fayyum in **room 9**; it depicts Adam and Eve after the Fall.

The upper floor, in **rooms 10, 11** and **12,** contains a beautiful collection of fabrics, some of which date from the 4th and 5th centuries. We know that Coptic fabrics were famous at this time for their fine quality, their astonishing range of colors and their varied subjects, in which Christian symbols and even Arabic interlaced scrollwork were later mingled with Hellenistic and Persian themes. **Room 13** contains a number of beautiful icons, rarely found outside churches. Do not miss the *St. George* and the *Virgin and Child*. In **room 14** there are three beautiful wooden crosses covered with geometric motifs. The next two rooms contain objects connected with the Coptic faith, and **room 17** has manuscripts decorated with miniatures and illuminated designs strongly influenced by the Arabic style. The last room contains examples of column capitals.

Do not miss, at the end of the garden, the wooden iconostasis, or icon screen, from the 10th-century church of St. Barbara. This beautiful composition, with its 45 exquisitely carved panels on various themes, is the best possible introduction to a tour of Coptic churches. One of the oddest of these is behind the museum and is known as the **Muallaka**, or 'Hanging Church'. It spans the two bastions flanking the southwest gate in the Roman walls. It may be reached by a flight of steps. Built probably in the

7th century, the Muallaka was last altered in the 18th century. Notice the 12th-century marble *ambo* (pulpit) and, especially, the cedar-wood door inlaid with ivory which is so fine that it is translucent.

The most typical Coptic churches are also to be found in Old Cairo. Go outside the walls from the Muallaka church and follow them along to the right. After about 218 yards/200 metres go through them again. This time you enter a maze of little alleys between high, bare, crumbling walls, in which the churches are not very conspicuous. The most famous of them is the **church of St. Sergius** (Abu Serga) (Map pp.66–67 F–2). A low gateway leads into a narrow passage at the end of which is the church. The church was probably founded in the 4th century, although the Holy Family is traditionally said to have found refuge in the crypt during the flight to Egypt. In any event, the church was rebuilt in the 11th century and altered in the 13th and 18th centuries. It is a typical Coptic church — that is, its design is that of an eastern basilica, with a porch, nave and two side-aisles demarcated by rows of columns supporting the vaults. Its distinguishing feature is the use of carved wooden screens to hide the altar from the faithful and separate the men from the women during services. These screens may also be seen in the **church of St. Barbara** (Map pp.66–67 F–2) not far away, where they show beautiful designs combining polygons and stars incorporating numerous crosses inlaid with carved ivory. About 110 feet/100 metres away is the **Ben Ezra Synagogue**★ (Map pp.66–67 F–2), which is shortly to be restored. The synagogue also possesses a number of very fine holy books and manuscripts.

▬ THE MOSQUE OF IBN TULUN★★
(Map pp.66–67 D 3)

Allow half an hour for a visit to this mosque, which may be combined with a walk either to Old Cairo or to the citadel.

The mosque of Ibn Tulun

Dating from the end of the 7th century, this is the oldest monument in Cairo. It is by no means easy to find among the many buildings and mosques packed into this area. Its most conspicuous feature is a spiral minaret visible from afar, which was inspired by the mosque at Samarra in Iraq. At close range, the mosque may be recognized by its high, fortified walls surmounted by a parapet with magnificent crenellations that recall the era of Islamic conquest. On entering the vast porticoed courtyard, you will immediately be struck by its dignified arrangement of low, pointed arcades on sturdy pillars, each with engaged columns at the corners. Ibn Tulun is a great classic mosque, identical in design to those built at the time of the caliphs of Baghdad.

The carved decoration follows beautiful, regular patterns. The spandrels between the arches have pointed windows cut into them below the continuous frieze. Interlaced decoration covers the inner surfaces of the arcades, and the pillars are also richly ornamented. Notice the wall at the back of the courtyard, which is pierced by latticed windows in a wide variety of different patterns. After walking through the arcades, visit the prayer hall in the principal *iwan* which fills the fourth side of the courtyard and broadens it with several more rows of arcades. The marble-clad *mihrab*, or wall-niche facing Mecca, is framed in foliated scrollwork executed in glass mosaic. The *minbar*, or pulpit, is a fine example of 13th-century Arabic woodwork. It has now lost the inlaid decoration that once embellished the pierced, polygonal-shaped panels on the sides. The little wooden dome above the *mihrab* has been restored. On the third pillar to the left is a plaque with an inscription in Kufic script commemorating the opening of the mosque. Your tour ends after crossing the courtyard. The splendid ablution fountain in the center dates from the 14th century. Take a look at the whole mosque complex from here, and then climb the minaret and look out over the district that was once the second capital of Muslim Egypt.

The Al-Azhar Mosque, Cairo.

The **Gayer-Anderson Museum** is at the exit, adjoining the mosque. (*Visit: daily except Friday mornings; 9 am – 1 pm in summer, 9 am – 4 pm in winter. Entrance ticket also valid for Museum of Islamic Art, p.76.*) Consisting of two former houses that were restored and refurnished by an Englishman before World War II, the museum is especially delightful with irregular levels, winding corridors, and galleries from which women, behind wooden latticework screens (*moucharabies*), could watch the men chatting and smoking the *nargileh*, or water-pipe. Its terraces, with their openwork screens, overlook the parapet on top of the mosque.

▬ THE MADRASA OF SULTAN HASAN★★ AND THE CITADEL

These two monuments are close to one other and both may be visited on the same tour. Allow a good two hours there and back from Midan el-Tahrir .

The madrasa-mosque of Sultan Hasan (Map pp.66–67 D–4)

This is perhaps the most remarkable mosque in Cairo and is, in any event, a magnificent example of Mamluk architecture. Built between 1356 and 1362, the structure is dominated by a minaret some 282 feet/86 metres

The madrasa of Sultan Hasan, Cairo.

high. The whole building stands just below the citadel, towards which a projection juts out, crowned with a Turkish-style dome 180 feet/55 metres high. From the street outside, the mosque looks quite different. Its plain, massive walls, slashed by long vertical recesses and narrow windows, give a dizzying sensation of height. The heavy cornice boldly projecting above the windows in several rows of honeycomb patterns, seems to hang menacingly above the head of anyone approaching. The building expresses both grandeur and austerity. A long flight of stairs leads to an enormous doorway, above which is a corbelled vault covered, like the finely carved side niches and beautiful cornice, with magnificent stalactite decoration.

The internal layout here is different from that of the classic mosque. You first enter a large vestibule and then, on the left, a narrow corridor. As you pass along it, you will be shown the remains of a hospital building. This corridor leads to the *sahn*, the great square courtyard onto which four oblong halls (the *iwans*) covered with immense, smoothly-curving barrel vaults open. In the center, there is the beautiful ablution fountain which is surmounted by a broad, spherical dome bearing inscriptions. Mamluk religious buildings always had *madrasas*, or theology schools, and often a hospital clustered around the body of the mosque itself. Each of the four *iwans* around you is linked to a college teaching one of the four orthodox rites of Islam. The buildings to which they are joined are simply the living-quarters of the students and teachers. The *iwan* on the southeast side, facing Mecca, houses the great prayer hall. Faced in marble and ringed by a frieze of texts from the Koran in Kufic script, it once possessed a special magnificence that is recalled today by the 70 lamp chains hanging from the high vaulted ceiling and by the splendor of the white marble* minbar. Here, you are at the very heart of a stronghold of the Muslim faith. A grille to the left of the minbar leads to the tomb of **Sultan Hasan,** who disappeared without trace. The simple catafalque was put there by his nephew. The chamber is covered by a huge dome dating from the Ottoman era. Windows set in the walls provide views of the citadel and the bustling streets outside. In this place you can readily appreciate the tranquillity and security the mosque must have given to worshippers during troubled times under the Mamluk sultans.

The citadel (Map pp.66–67 D–4–5)

After leaving the mosque of Sultan Hasan, a visit to the citadel is recommended. Before you embark on this, pause for a moment to look up from the square at the marvelous cluster of buildings on the top of the hill. The 'mosque with domes as bright as silver and minarets shaped like daggers' dominates ramparts directly inspired by Crusader architecture. The entire history of the citadel is included in this view. The citadel was begun, as we have already seen, by Saladin in 1176, enlarged by the Mamluk sultans and then, after them, by the Ottoman pashas. However, it was not finished until the beginning of the 19th century when Mehemet Ali demonstrated his power by building the monument that was directly inspired by St. Sophia in Constantinople and which still dominates the city today. This building is the object of your next visit. You reach it via the north side of the hill, preferably by car because the slope is steep. After passing through impressive fortified gates, you will find yourself in a huge square where rows of buses wait. The structure in front of you is faced all over with alabaster and looks like no other religious building in Cairo. However, the courtyard which you enter next is pleasantly proportioned, with slender columns and a pretty fountain in the center. Notice the little square tower housing a clock presented to Mehemet Ali by King Louis-Philippe of France. The interior of the mosque is immense and sumptuously decorated. It is surmounted by a large dome supported on four massive pillars and flanked by four half-domes, with octagonal domes at the corners. Inside stands the tomb of Mehemet Ali. Allow time to linger in the terrace garden behind the mosque and enjoy a marvelous panoramic view of the city stretching, when the air is clear, as far as the pyramids.

THE MUSEUM OF ISLAMIC ART★★

Allow up to an hour for a visit to this museum, which you can combine with a visit to the **Al-Azhar Mosque** (Map pp.66–67 C–4), a monument which is all too rarely included in organized tours.

Visit: daily, except Friday mornings; 9 am – 1 pm in summer, 9 am – 4 pm in winter. Entrance ticket also valid for Gayer-Anderson Museum, p. 74.

Tour

The Museum of Islamic Art is housed in the outbuildings of a mosque. Its collections rank among the most important in the world and they recall the elegance and splendor of the old palaces. Today, the museum's possessions fill 23 rooms. The first five rooms contain a wide range of objects from the great periods of Egyptian Islamic art. The arrangement is different in the subsequent rooms where objects are grouped according to the type of art, enabling the visitor to trace the development of a particular technique through time and through different styles. **Rooms 6** and **7,** and parts of **8** and **9,** are devoted to woodwork. Notice the simple methods used by local craftsmen, the detailed perfection of their creations, and the great flexibility in their arrangement of systematically interlocking squares, lozenges and stars. Do not miss the moucharabies, wooden latticework grilles that were placed over windows so that people could see without being seen, and the beautiful wood carvings from the caliphs' palaces, with their scenes of hunting, music, dancing and drinking.

Because the museum is constantly being reorganized, it is difficult to indicate the exact position of the objects in the rooms where they are exhibited. In one, you will admire a collection of 16th- and 17th-century weapons; in another, collections of Arab ceramics; some of these were found locally, while others came from a wide range of other sites. Their freedom of style and the versatility of their floral decoration are fascinating. Some of the rooms are hung with magnificent tapestries. Other items in the museum include lustre-painted faience, terracotta objects, delicate water-cooler filters as fine as lace, beautiful fabrics, rare glass, and a collection of mosque lamps, mostly from the mosque of Sultan Hasan, which is unique in the world. There is also a collection of very beautiful manuscripts. Do not leave the museum without seeing its Koran, one of the oldest in existence, nor the restored inner courtyard, which the keepers will light up on request.

▬ *THE AL-AZHAR MOSQUE*★★
(Map pp.66–67 C–4)

A tour of this mosque will take up a good half hour, and may be combined with a tour of the Museum of Islamic Art or a walk to the Khan el-Khalili.

The Al-Azhar Mosque, meaning 'the most radiant' or 'the most blossoming', was founded in 970 as the principal mosque of the new Fatimid city of Cairo.

The Mamluks endowed the mosque with a school of theology, which they took pleasure in loading with gifts. It is still one of the most famous universities of Islam. Most of the present leaders of the western Arab world attended it as students, attracted by its fundamental religious education, and the modern courses of study offered by its nine faculties. Al-Azhar now has about 20,000 students from Egypt and elsewhere. This is not only a monument of pure classic architecture, but also an immense living organism that has continuously grown and developed. It is an institution that has five minarets soaring over a complex covering more than 2½ acres/1 hectare and which is almost lost in the maze of buildings around it. The only part that may be visited is the mosque itself.

Tour

You enter the mosque from Midan Al-Azhar, first through the 18th-century double-arched gateway known as the Gate of the Barbers, then through a gate built in 1483 by Sultan Qaytbay. In between, you cross a small vestibule flanked by 14th-century buildings; those on the left are occupied by the present library with its collection of over 60,000 volumes, including 15,000 manuscripts. Passing through the gate of Qaytbay, which is surmounted by a minaret of the same period, you then enter the mosque itself, or rather its central courtyard where you can begin to see the importance and grandeur of the mosque. Designed as a standard porticoed mosque, Al-Azhar has more than 300 columns which, for the most part, come from ancient buildings and are extremely beautiful. In the courtyard itself, which owes its unusual elegance to the design of its Persian arches, the north and south colonnades have been doubled in size with additional pillars and, behind them, a second colonnade has been laid out which, unfortunately, is partly hidden from view. The impressive prayer hall has eight rows of columns arranged in twos and sometimes threes beneath the springing-line of the arches. There are, in addition, several *mihrabs*, empty niches toward which the eyes of the believers are directed as if toward some unapproachable god. The oldest of them was kept in its original position when the last additions were made to the building. It is now detached from the wall. You are expected to be as unobtrusive as possible when you enter this chamber, where many of the faithful will be prostrating themselves. In the silence you will realize how important Cairo's cultural role is in the Muslim world today. In a little street about 110 yards/100 metres on the left as you come out of the mosque, you will enter the Okel el-Ghuri, a beautiful restored *caravanserai*, or caravan hostelry, which today houses a school of handicrafts; here you may find a few things to buy.

THE FATIMID DISTRICT AND THE MAUSOLEUM OF KALAUN★
(Map pp.66–67 C–4)

This tour can be treated as a leisurely afternoon stroll, without taking your camera and without worrying about dirtying your shoes. Allow an hour and a half from the **Bab el-Futuh gate** (Map pp.66–67 B–5), where you will be set down, to Shari el-Azhar or Midan el-Ataba, where you can take a taxi.

Tour

You will begin your tour of Fatimid Cairo with the walls or, more precisely, the monumental gateways that still stand in the north of the city. The first impression is stunning. A market stretches to the foot of the thick, low walls which, over the years, have become buried over 12 feet/4 metres in the ground. With their sturdy arches, the two gateways of Bab el-Futuh (Gate of Conquest) and Bab en-Nasr (Gate of Victory), which are set between immense square towers and topped with projecting barbicans and machicolations, are reminiscent of Roman gates. They are said to have been built by the Syrians. You enter the district behind the walls by the Bab el-Futuh and you will find yourself in a huge square, on the left-hand side of which stands a Fatimid mosque, the impressive towers of which harmonize with the walls. This is the **El-Hakim Mosque** (Map pp.66–67 B–5), built between 990 and 1010 by a mad sultan, and its minarets were re-erected 300 years later. Used as a dungeon by the Crusaders, then as a stable and a magazine by Napoleon's army, the mosque was in total ruins when an Indian Shi-ite sect, the Bohra, began its restoration in 1980. Its paved marble courtyard is now sparkling white, but concrete has replaced brickwork in its columns, and the building as a whole comes as a surprise in these surroundings.

From the mosque, you will plunge into the milling crowds on Shari Muizz Lidin, which is the district's main arterial road. The street bustles with life and, bit by bit, you will get used to the thoroughly oriental mixture of pleasant and foul smells, delicate scents, dust, the placid gaze of the water-pipe smokers, the swarms of barefoot children, men in pajama-like robes, little donkeys, carts, cyclists, tourists, and women, both veiled and unveiled, but always wrapped in a black *melaya* and loaded with children and bundles.

Continue along the main street in the direction of the **mausoleum of Kalaun** (Map pp.66–67 C–4). There is nothing to tell you exactly where this mausoleum is, except a huge far-off minaret, which has three square sections of decreasing size superimposed one on the other. On top of these are an octagonal terrace and decorated cylindrical drum capped with an ovoid cupola of more recent date. As you approach it, you can identify the building by its facade, which is pierced by twin pointed arches and surmounted by parapets, all recalling the Norman architecture of Sicily.

Built by a Mamluk sultan between 1284 and 1293, the mausoleum of Kalaun belongs to the same period as the mosque of Hasan. The complex in which it stands is in a poor state of repair today, but it still contains the magnificent decoration with which these formidable sultans surrounded themselves. You will enter by a large recessed doorway which leads into a corridor decorated with false arches. Take the second small door on the right. This opens into a small inner courtyard. All the din of the street

Mamluk tomb, City of the Dead, Cairo.

outside suddenly evaporates into the silence and tranquillity of a holy place — and then you are struck by a dazzling sight. In the large square chamber, dominated by a huge dome resting on four columns, the catafalque of the sultan lies behind a turned and carved wooden screen of impressive ·design, bathed in a strange light flecked with color. As your eyes grow accustomed to the shadows, you will become aware of the remarkable harmony of the architecture, which combines a wide variety of techniques; · of the restrained decoration within the structural lines of the design; and of the overall mosaic veneer, which is enhanced by rows of arches formed of tiny marble pieces.

When you go back out into the street, turn to the right and continue past the stalls and craftsmen's shops. Eventually, you will emerge on a main thoroughfare, Shari Gohar el-Qaia. Further along, on the left, is the **Khan el-Khalili,** (Map pp.66–67 C–4–5), the big traditional bazaar.

An alternative route would be to cross Shari el-Azhar, (Map pp.66–67 C–4) and continue onward around the two districts via the monuments of Sultan el-Ghuri. You will come across more beautiful mosques on the way; first, the **mosque of Sultan el-Muayyad,** which has its minarets planted on top of the **Bab Zuweila,** (Map pp.66–67 C–4), the south gate of the Fatimid district which it adjoins; then the **mosque of El-Maridani,** set at an angle to the street. However, this is a long walk that will take you as far as the foot of the citadel, and you will not find any transport on the way.

You may prefer the shorter route back to the city center, walking down Shari Gohar el-Qaia, (Map pp.66–67 C–4), to the right. Along the way, you will cross Mouski district and its market, where you can do some shopping. You will be able to get a taxi when you get to Midan el-Ataba, (Map pp.66–67 C–3)

▬ THE CITY OF THE DEAD

If you are lucky enough to have a friend who knows the way, or there is a guide available, do not hesitate to spend an hour or two at the **City of the Dead,** (Map pp.66–67 C–D–5). This is one of the most fascinating places in Cairo. Here, the poorest people in the city camp around the mosque-mausoleums built by the Mamluk sultans. Whole families live there as squatters in the ruins of medieval schools or convents, while a shanty-town of brick and dried mud has grown up, with its own cafés, markets, donkeys and children, among the monuments. These monuments are much dilapidated, but their domes count among the most beautiful achievements of the 14th and 15th centuries.

Now crossed by an express highway, the City of the Dead stretches eastward across a broad, desolate sandy plain from the foot of the citadel. It occupies an immense area, because the tombs of caliphs and imams were put there in addition to those of the sultans. These were eventually followed by a growing number of private tombs, which are plainer in style but big enough to permit the relatives and friends of the deceased to stay there with him during important Muslim festivals.

About 220 yards/200 metres apart in the north cemetery, you can see both the beginning of Mamluk art, represented by the mosque of Sultan Barquq, and the peak of its achievement, in the form of the mosque of Qaytbay.

The **mosque of Barquq** was built between 1400 and 1411. It is recognizable by its twin domes decorated with zigzag patterns and flanked on both sides by smaller domes with a ribbed, melon-like design. These were the first stone domes to be built in Cairo. On the inside, you can admire their soaring lightness and their decoration; one of them covers the mausoleum of the sultan, the other that of his female relatives. Around the lovely courtyard, there is an arcaded gallery roofed with domes of smooth brick. The nearby dervishes' building is in ruins, but from the terrace, and particularly from the minaret, you will get a view of all the domes in the cemetery.

The **dome of the mosque of Qaytbay** is recognizable by the elaborate carved stonework decoration, which is repeated around the windows and doors. This mosque dates from the end of the 15th century. The building itself is laid out in the form of a cross, a plan that was later to become standard. Inside, note the play of colored light from the stained-glass windows set into the plaster walls.

▬ THE EGYPTIAN MUSEUM★★★
(Map pp.66–67 C–2)

Founded in 1857 by the French archaeologist Auguste Mariette, whose marble tomb and statue stand in the garden, the Egyptian Museum can today no longer keep pace with its continuously growing collections. The Egyptian government has, therefore, decided to undertake renovation work and, above all, to increase its area by at least a third. These works are sponsored by the International Council of Museums, based in Paris, and will provisionally be spread over five years.

Fortunately, this decision will not entail closing the museum, although some of the rooms that you are planning to see may be undergoing renovation at the time of your visit, and it is impossible to know which beforehand.

Tour

Visit: daily 9 am – 4 pm, except Friday, when it is closed at the time of prayer (11 am – 1 pm).

It is quite impossible to cover the whole museum in one visit. Even if you attempted to do so, your attention would flag after a while because Egyptian art belongs to a world that is completely alien to us today. Its creations were conceived for the other world and intended to accompany kings and men into eternal life; as such, they can be disturbing to the novice. Probably when you return from your visit to the great sites along the Nile Valley, you will be better able to grasp the supernatural significance, the beauty and the vital energy of the objects displayed here.

In any event, it will be less tiring to cover the museum in several visits of not more than two hours each. The collections are divided into two main sections. On the ground floor, sculptures are arranged in chronological order. On the upper floor, there are collections of furniture and various other objects found in the tombs, in particular the famous treasure of Tutankhamun.

To make your first visit easier, the most outstanding objects which should not be missed are indicated here. Some of these are occasionally sent abroad, and others may be put on display in temporary exhibitions in the museum itself. There are also countless other things that you will discover for yourself, simply because they attract you personally.

The ground floor

In the vestibule, you are greeted by two colossal statues of Ramesses II. In a window between them is the famous votive palette of Narmer, from the dawn of pharaonic history. This piece has been ascribed to the end of the fourth millennium B.C. It commemorates the conquest of the delta by Narmer (or Menes), a king from the Nile Valley who was the first to succeed in uniting the regions of the north and south, thus becoming the first pharaoh. The perfection of the relief carving is staggering when you realize it was executed more than 5000 years ago. Do not pass by without looking at the objects in a glass case on the left dating from the 5th dynasty,

As you enter the museum, you will see the collections of the **Old Kingdom** (2750–2180 B.C.) on your left.

The **sarcophagus gallery,** the first room you will encounter, contains two rows of sarcophagi. These monolithic coffins were placed in the farthest depths of the tomb before the pharaoh's death, ready to receive his mummified body. They were regarded as dwelling-places from which the soul — the pharaoh's double — could escape at will. On their sides you will notice the so-called 'palace facade' pattern. The most typical is the last one in the bay to the left. It has a leopard skin carved on the lid, which the priest had to leave there when the funeral ceremonies were completed.

The statues standing between the sarcophagi in the row on the left have the characteristic stiffness of this period. To the right, you will see three sculpture groups of Mycerinus, which were found in the ruins of his funerary temple. Carved in polished black slate, these portray the pharaoh with Hathor, the goddess of love, and a deity representing one of the 42 *nomes*, or provinces, of Egypt, who is bringing the pharaoh offerings from that province. It is thought that there were as many of these triad groups as there were *nomes*, although only a few have been found. Note the pharaoh striding out and the slight hint of movement on the part of the goddess.

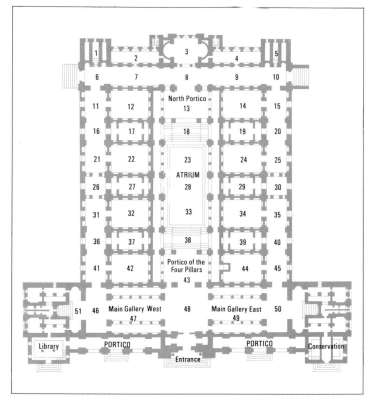

Egyptian Museum: ground floor.

Note, too, the similarity in the faces identifying the pharaoh with the god, and the pharaoh's false beard and pleated apron. During your visit you will come across these features over and over again in effigies of the god-kings; they are conventions. Do not miss, on the wall at the back, the false-door stelae, which were placed in the tombs between the permanently walled-up burial chamber and the chapel. It was through these 'doors' that the dead person was supposed to receive by magic the offerings of the living.

As a contrast to the powerful symbolism of these sacred sculptures, the glass cases in the center of the room provide a picture of the daily activities of ordinary people through a series of painted limestone statuettes. With their forthright realism and spontaneous expression, these bakers, potters, brewers, etc. are not unlike the simple folk portrayed on capitals in European romanesque architecture. However, their role is completely different. The Egyptian figures were meant to operate beyond the grave, continuing their occupations and providing their services in the other world. Alongside them, you will notice a number of 'reserve', or replacement, heads; these are strange sculpted heads found in the depths of the tombs, the purpose of which is still not known. As you leave the gallery, note the decoration of the burial chamber containing objects required by the dead person in the other world.

In front of you, in a glass case at the foot of the staircase, is the figure of Zoser, the oldest known statue of a pharaoh. He is seated on a throne in his full regalia of false beard, traditional *nemes* headdress, and a jubilee mantle that leaves the top of his shoulder bare. He gazes into the distance. Although his eyes have been torn out and his nose broken, his face wears an expression of intense tranquillity.

In **room 41** there is a particularly fine libation table, designed like a bed, with two lions forming the frame.

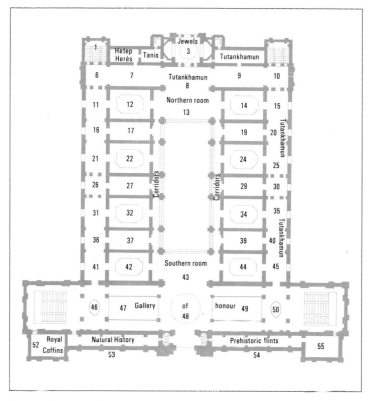

Egyptian Museum: first floor.

Room 42★★★ is one of the most important in the museum. The diorite statue of Chephren, in the center, is one of the great achievements of Egyptian art. The king is seated on a throne symbolizing the union of the lands of the North and South. The falcon Horus, the dynastic god, spreads his wings behind the king's head to protect him. Notice the harmony of the composition: the falcon does not extend beyond the pharaoh's headdress. Note, too, the carriage of the pharaoh's head, the majestic dignity of his gaze and bearing, and the different positions of his arms; in his upright, clenched right hand he holds the baton symbolizing the kingdom's heritage. The figure displays a remarkable youthful energy and royal power.

The marvelous wooden statue in the case on the left of the room is quite different. It is known by the name given to it by its 19th-century discoverers, who were struck by its close resemblance to a local dignitary, the Sheikh el-Beled, or 'village headman'. The figure, in fact, represents a contemporary of Cheops who occupied a high position in the priesthood. There is still a lively intensity in his eyes, which are made of white quartz, rock crystal and tiny pieces of polished ebony. His eyelids are outlined with strips of copper. Facing him is a magnificent wooden scribe of the 5th dynasty which still preserves traces of color; ancient Egyptian statues were customarily stuccoed and painted. Notice the faces of the two beautiful ebony statuettes at the opposite corners of the room, on the left as you go in and on the right at the other end.

Continue through **gallery 36** to **gallery 31.** Here, you should pause by the window in front of the wooden panels found in the *mastaba* (private tomb) of Hesi Re, a contemporary of Zoser. Admire the delicacy of the relief carving in the costumes and wigs of the main figure and the modeling of his face, created at the beginning of the third millennium B.C. Every hieroglyph is a work of art. Case B contains the oldest death mask known to mankind.

Room 32★★★ is full of masterpieces. First the famous statues of Rahotep and Nefret, consisting simply of a man and woman sitting side by side and gazing impassively into the distance. The woman's flimsy garment allows her hand to pass through and suggests the contours of her body. The strength of the man is expressed by his chest and arms. Created out of painted limestone, the twin figures have retained the freshness of their original colors and an extraordinary expressiveness.

To the left of this famous couple you will find the group statue of the dwarf Seneb and his family. The ancient Egyptians greatly respected dwarves and had no fear of their physical deformities; consequently, this is a man of some standing. The sculpture of him is equally impressive. Seneb is sitting cross-legged, and his two very young children, unclothed and with their fingers in their mouths, are standing in the place where his legs should be. As was the custom, Seneb's son is wearing a buckle on his side. His charming wife, seated next to him, is holding him tenderly in her arms.

On the right-hand wall you will see a bas-relief depicting a burial feast with musicians and dancers, and the famous *Geese of Medum*, the oldest painting yet discovered.

Before leaving this room, stop in front of the two statues of King Pepi I and his son (2350 B.C.), made in copper (bronze was not known in Egypt until later). These are disconcertingly modern. The pharaoh's expression is one of sadness. The boy has the plumpness of childhood; his inlaid, deep-set eyes seem puzzled.

Gallery 26. In the rooms devoted to the Middle Kingdom (2060–1785 B.C.) you enter a refined civilization stretching from Thebes to El Fayyum but whose great architectural achievements have unfortunately almost vanished. The sculptures found in their ruins call our attention to different new styles. Look to the right of the pillar at the crude painted sandstone statue of King Mentuhotep from Deir el-Bahari. With its heavy legs and red crown, this is an impressive figure. Nearby, there is a strange cube statue (also known as a block statue) of the noble prince Hotep, an important figure who lived around 2000 B.C. This new form, which appeared at that time at Sakkara, probably developed for technical reasons, in that it reduced the chances of the sculptor damaging the stone. Moreover, by placing the figure of the man in an attitude of passive contemplation, it reflected the growing spirituality of the period. Note, too, the delicacy of the face.

Gallery 21. Along the wall, there are a number of votive stelae from Abydos; these objects were left near the temple of Osiris, the god of resurrection, by people who came to ensure their own immortality.

Room 22. In the burial chamber of Horhotep, in the center, notice the friezes showing objects that the dead man carried into the after-world in the form of images, instead of real objects. The ten seated statues of Sesostris I, discovered in his temple at Lisht, near El Fayyum, have no special importance for ancient art history. On the other hand, they do give an idea of the mass-production of effigies adopted by kings for their tombs. As you leave this room, look at the bas-relief on the left-hand wall, which has preserved the likenesses and names of the dogs of Prince Antef. It confirms the marvelous ability of the ancient artists to portray animals.

Gallery 11. We now enter the New Kingdom (1580–1085 B.C.), the most magnificent period in pharaonic history, as shown by the splendid temples of the upper Nile Valley. On each side of the door into **room 12,** notice the fine slate statue of Tuthmosis III (1484–1450 B.C.) and the beautiful head of Queen Tiye (c. 1400 B.C.).

Room 12.★★ This is one of the outstanding rooms in the museum. The attention is at once drawn to the sandstone chapel facing the entrance, which is decorated with painted reliefs honoring the cow-goddess Hathor, seen protecting and feeding Amenophis II. Note the series of statues of the pharaoh on your left. On the other side, there is an interesting block statue of Senenmut, the favorite of Queen Hatshepsut (1505–1484 B.C.), which includes a little princess, the queen's daughter, whose face alone is visible. Next, there is a huge pink granite statue of Hatshepsut herself, dressed as a man. To appreciate this work, you must know the fantastic story of this royal princess who managed to seize power as pharaoh. The sculptors who carved her effigy had to invest her with all the attributes of majesty, but nonetheless, the Queen's charming little pointed face evidently left a lasting impression on them. On the wall to the left, a bas-relief recounts the return of the expedition mounted by Hatshepsut to the land of spices. Here, the enormous queen of Punt is seen following her skinny husband. Finally, on the way out, note the ebony statuette of Thay, the pharaoh's shield-bearer, to the right of the doorway.

From here, continue through **galleries 6, 7** and **8,** which notably contain a fine sphinx and various statues of Hatshepsut.

Room 3.★★★ Your attention will immediately be drawn to the sumptuous royal coffin inlaid with gold and carnelian, from which the gold mask has been torn, in the center of the room. Next, view the collection of objects testifying to the strange revolution that the schismatic pharaoh Akhenaton imposed on Egyptian art when he abandoned the cult of Amun and dedicated himself to Aton, the sun disk. It may be hard for us today to understand the connection between Akhenaton's aesthetic and religious ideas, but we can instantly grasp the novelty of the style that resulted. The colossal figures from Karnak in this room are the best examples of it. The body of the king, represented in the 'Osiris position', (the pose in which mummies were placed), is totally distorted. The shoulders and arms are thin; the chest is merely sketched in; the hips, short thighs and round belly are of indeterminate sex. One of the statues even seems to be asexual. It is easy to think the king was physically monstrous, yet he had six daughters. There can be no doubt that art has here exceeded reality, as if trying to convey some religious idea. But what? The question remains unanswered. The carved head of Akhenaton is equally astonishing. Each of the features seems to have been exaggerated, for no obvious reason. The bridge of the nose is very thin; the narrow almond eyes slant up toward the ears; the face is elongated by the extremely long false beard. On the other hand, the full lips and flaring nostrils betray an intense inner vitality, and the shadows, everywhere softened by the artist, endow the face with a spiritual quality that is almost supernatural.

You will find this style repeated, though less pronounced, in the glass cases containing royal portraits. The pharaoh's plaster mask nevertheless confirms his physical peculiarities. His hair emphasizes his receding forehead. The heads of the little princesses are also ill-proportioned. Do not miss the sculpture studies; the king facing himself, chiseled in outline on a slab of limestone and then carved. Out of this collection of family portraits only Queen Nefertiti retains an unalterable beauty. Look at her unfinished head from all angles, on which the colored working lines can still be seen.

The king and his family are usually represented worshipping the solar disk — especially on the beautiful limestone altar, where Akhenaton is seen offering libations above some lotus flowers. Behind, Nefertiti is imitating him, and a little princess is doing the same. The sun's rays which taper into hands, are striking them; the hands hold crosses (*ankhs*) representing the sun's life-giving force before their faces. There is a spiritual element in the expressions on the royal features that is found nowhere else in Egyptian art. Lastly, do not leave this room without a look at the exquisite floral pavement in the curve of the wall, and at the vivid scenes showing ducks taking flight above marsh-grass or papyrus thickets. Although it lasted for only 20 years, the Akhenaton interlude still continues to intrigue and amaze the world.

Before leaving the room, if you are interested in history, stop for a moment at the glass case on the right containing terra-cotta tablets incised with cuneiform script. These tablets reveal the diplomatic relations the pharaoh maintained with the rulers of Asia.

At this point you have a choice; you can either end your visit to the ground floor of the museum and proceed to the central atrium through **room 13,** (where there are large stelae celebrating various royal victories), or carry on along the gallery, where there are several beautiful rooms that make the detour worthwhile.

Room 4 contains an interesting collection of medals.

Gallery 15. Three masterpieces are displayed in the first case: first, the bust of one of the daughters of Ramesses, who is wearing a heavy crown on top of a high, blue-colored wig; then the two figures, unfortunately badly damaged, of Nakhtmin the *flabellum*-bearer, (the *flabellum* was a kind of ostrich-feather fan, identified with royalty), who is holding the insignia of his office, and his wife. The modeling of the faces and of the woman's body, which is visible through the folds of her clothing, is of extraordinary perfection. On each side of the door to the next room are two colossal heads of Ramesses.

Room 14. Here there is a solar sanctuary, found at Abu Simbel, in which a solar scarab beetle and a baboon, enclosed in a *naos*, or shrine, are worshipped by four dog-faced baboons.

Room 24 is devoted to Saite, Ethiopian and Persian women and contains a striking statue of Thoeris, the hippopotamus-goddess, from Karnak.

Galleries 30 and **35** contain objects from the Ethiopian and Persian periods. **Room 34** has Greco-Roman marbles and heads. **Galleries 40** and **45** and **room 44** are devoted to Nubia.

In **galleries 50** and **49** (late period), do not miss the coffin of Petosiris at the exit, which has highly detailed hieroglyphs fashioned from glass paste.

The tour ends in the **atrium,** where you will find yourself surrounded with wonderful things: first, two Middle Kingdom boats which remind us that ancient Egypt was a land in which all trade, commerce and travel was waterborne. Also, three fine sarcophagi, decorated with huge eyes that were meant to allow the dead to see the earth from the other world. The most interesting is the one belonging to an obscure delta king named Psusennes (1050 B.C.), who would have remained unknown had his tomb not been found intact at Tanis. The heavy lid of his granite sarcophagus is raised, and you can see the figure of the pharaoh, in the mummy position, carved on the bottom of the container.

The most important object here, however, is the colossal figure group of Amenophis III and Queen Tiye, which was discovered in the temple of Medinet Habu. Young women or princesses shelter between the king's legs. There is remarkable femininity in the look in the queen's eye. These giant figures, which nevertheless belong to the world of human beings, leave an indelible impression of grandeur.

The upper floor

Allow an hour and a half, or more, to visit the exhibits here. Begin with the famous treasure of Tutankhamun, but do not omit the other collections.

The treasure of Tutankhamun★★★ (1354–1345 B.C.) is a collection of 177 items distinguished by their use of gold and inlaid precious stones and comprising the king's tomb furniture, jewelry, chests, statuettes, amulets, weapons, games — all of staggering beauty. Discovered in 1922 by the British archaeologist Howard Carter, it astonished the world's Egyptologists who, until then, had been acquainted only with tombs that had been broken into and plundered of their treasures in the Valley of the Kings. The objects that were heaped up in the two small chambers of Tutankhamun's narrow tomb and which represented the 'celestial house-removal' of the young king who had died at the age of 18, allow us to imagine the sumptuous wealth with which the greatest pharaohs must have surrounded themselves in order to live with the gods in eternity.

It is preferable to approach the collection from the landing in **room 50,** after coming up the staircase to the right at the museum entrance. Standing here are two life-size statues of the pharaoh in black wood and gold-leaf that once guarded the walled-up doorway to the burial chamber. Tutankhamun is portrayed advancing, with a club in one hand and a long baton in the other. Beyond the entrance you find shields displayed next to a pretty little ostrich-feather fan, caskets for games and amulets. So numerous are the wonderful objects here that, even if you came back a hundred times, you would still discover some new item or detail that you had not seen before.

It is possible only to point out a few of the main highlights, which the museum has fortunately numbered.

Near the door to **room 44,** do not miss a pretty wood and ivory casket, inlaid with ebony, faience and colored glass. On its lid, the queen is offering flowers to her husband. With the passage of time, the whole piece has taken on paler colors.

Below the central scene, young girls are gathering mandrake roots, symbolizing love. In **gallery 40,** note a gilded wood chest surmounted with a figure of the god Anubis, and some beautiful model boats. In **gallery 35,** see the cases displaying large numbers of *shawabtis*, small figurines intended to accompany the dead king in the other world, where they would act as his slaves. Then take a close look at the 32 gold statuettes, 23½ inches/60 centimetres high, showing the king in triumphant postures, which might be concluded to be ceremonial. In one, he is standing on a panther, leaning on a cane and wearing the tall white crown; in another, he is in a flimsy papyrus boat, brandishing a spear and wearing the red crown of the delta.

In front of the door to **room 24,** look out for the casket depicting the desert hunt, which bears scenes of unusual vitality. In **gallery 25,** there are numerous seats, carved and sculptured stools inlaid with ivory, and foot-rests with figures of Asians or Africans, some of them on the ground, representing the new lands that the king held under his power. The outstanding item in this collection is a small throne, with arms in the form of winged serpents wearing the double crown that protects the name of the king. On the back-rest, which is gold-plated and inlaid with carnelian, turquoise and lapis-lazuli, there is a charming scene in which, beneath the rays of the solar disk, the queen is tenderly leaning forward to anoint her husband, who is sitting casually on a chair. The king's pleated loin-cloth is covered by an apron studded with precious stones. Note the delightful papyrus plant on the back.

In **gallery 20,** you will find wooden chests, canes or batons with knobs representing Egypt's traditional enemies, both Asian and African, fan handles, jars, etc.

Gallery 15 contains a series of five beds, one of which is covered with gold-leaf. Do not miss the case displaying head-rests, nor the finely carved ivory casket near the wall at the back, which is striking in its simplicity. The baby's head emerging from a lotus flower facing it is that of Tutankhamun as a child.

Before turning into the long North Gallery, note the bunches of persea flowers, the queen's final expression of love for her too-soon-departed husband.

At this point, you encounter the mass of gold forming the royal tomb treasure. First are three funeral beds in gilded wood, with frames that look like the stretched bodies of three sacred animals, a cow, a lion and a hippopotamus. Their heads, inlaid with glass paste and crystal, form the posts.

Room 4, on the right, contains the most precious objects in this impressive collection. Among these is the famous gold mask that covered the royal mummy, with eyes of lapis-lazuli. The collar and *nemes* headdress are made of glass paste and precious stones, as is the double diadem combining cobra and vulture heads. Two of the three mummiform coffins, which were placed one inside the other to protect the mummy, are also displayed here. The largest has been left with the mummy itself in the tomb in the Valley of the Kings. The second one is made of gilded, inlaid wood, and the third is of pure gold almost one inch/two centimetres thick. The king is portrayed on it with his arms across his breast in the Osiris position and holding his royal insignia.

In the surrounding cases are quantities of beautiful jewelry and precious amulets picked up in the tomb or taken from the mummy.

Along the **North Gallery** you will come to an amazing *naos*, or box-like shrine, of gilded wood and nearly seven feet/two metres high, lying on a sledge like a large reliquary. Above this is a canopy supported at the corners by four pillars bearing the king's names and titles. Four delightful small figures on the sides seem to watch over it, with their heads slightly inclined and their arms gracefully extended. These are the funerary goddesses Isis and her sister Nephthys, Neith and Selkis. The shrine they are guarding is the one that enclosed the canopic chest which, in turn, held miniature coffins containing the canopic jars, a kind of alabaster urn in which the king's internal organs, wrapped in fine linen, were placed. The canopic chest itself is displayed next to the shrine. It is itself an object of considerable beauty, with its immense sloping lid and its hieroglyphs. These are outlined in black on the white alabaster and record the ritual words spoken in the after-world by the four goddesses who appear again at the corners.

Four shrines in gilded wood follow, the last one inlaid with amulets in blue enamel. They were fitted inside one another. Were these chapels? No one knows. The first of these is nearly 19½ feet/6 metres long. A canopy frame of gilded wood separated it from the second one and supported a veil decorated all over with little flowers and gold rosettes. You will see the remains of this awning. Pause by the third shrine to admire the wonderful gold image of the goddess Isis, with her wing-like arms, that decorates the inside of the door. She is promising the king eternal life.

Do not leave the treasure of Tutankhamun without seeing the three great war chariots facing the atrium and the victory scenes portrayed on their sides.

The **Jewel Room (room 3)** opens off the gallery devoted to Tutankhamun and is strictly guarded. Begin at the back of the room on the left, where the oldest items are. The cases are in chronological order, demonstrating the development of the goldsmith's art and techniques over thousands of years. Do not miss: case 1, pendant necklaces of the 1st dynasty (3000 B.C.); case 3, the gold falcon's head of the 6th dynasty (2350 B.C.); cases 5 and 9, jewelry of princesses of the Middle Kingdom (2060–1785 B.C.); large case 10, ceremonial jewelry and weapons of a 17th-dynasty queen (c. 1600 B.C.); case 14, jewelry of queens of the New Kingdom (c. 1400 B.C.); cases 11 and 12, the treasure of Tanis (9th century B.C.); case 20, a gold mask found at Sakkara. Also note, in case 27, the Asiatic treasure discovered in a Middle Kingdom temple.

Room 2, on your right at the exit, contains objects from a tomb dating from the beginning of the third millennium B.C. and belonging to Queen Hetepheres. In the small adjoining room, you will see the jewelry found at Tanis in tombs dating from the end of the second millennium, together with two large coffins, one of which is of silver.

The next collections on your tour are arranged around the gallery overlooking the atrium. The most interesting are to your right (along the west wing).

The collections of the New Kingdom (1580–1085 B.C.)

Room 13 contains magnificent chariots and the intact furnishings from the private New Kingdom tomb of Yuya and Tuyu, which skillfully copy royal luxury. **Room 12** contains a collection of objects from royal tombs of the 17th dynasty; **Room 17** contains funerary objects and the work implements of Sennedjem, a supervisor of construction works in the Valley of the Kings. **Room 22** offers a fine collection of multicolored stelae, along with funerary objects and statuettes.

Statuettes of the Middle Kingdom (2060–1785 B.C.)★

Room 27 contains the first objects of a wonderful collection including statuettes, found in different private tombs of the Middle Kingdom; these were originally grouped together in the tombs to form various model tableaux representing the daily lives of the dead. They are generally made of wood covered with painted stucco or plaster, with additional fabric accessories, such as loin-cloths, robes, or the sails of a ship, and they possess remarkable vitality. Note, first of all, the woman bearing offerings, who is wearing a dress and pearl-studded hairnet and balancing a basket filled with wine glasses on her head. If you lean over the cases you will discover a model taken from the tomb of a certain Meket-Re, which includes a garden, a house, a weaving workshop and a carpenter's booth; this is a captivating piece of work. The display continues in **room 32** with boats and boatmen, woodworkers, kitchens, butchers' shops, and so on, from different tombs. As you proceed along the corridor by **room 32,** do not miss the statue of a naked god-king in its wooden shrine. This outstanding piece was once partly covered in gold. In **room 37,** a whole army, from light to heavy infantry, is set out. It was taken to the grave by a general named Mesah, so that he could deploy it in the other world.

The protohistoric collections (3000–2700 B.C.)

Room 42 takes us back to the dawn of Egyptian history. Note the section of turquoise faience on the outside wall of the gallery to the right of the exit. This came from the tomb complex of King Zoser at Sakkara (2780 B.C.).

Room 43 is devoted entirely to a collection of objects of the Thinite period (the end of the fourth millennium B.C.), which were found in the tomb of the chancellor Hemaka at Sakkara. This consists of flints, weapons, vessels and vases of great interest to experts.

There are now only the collections in the six rooms along the east side of the atrium to see. Begin with the room at the far end.

Portraits from El Fayyum (1st century A.D.)*

Room 14. Among a number of interesting funerary masks of the Greco-Roman period, you will find the famous portraits from El Fayyum. During the first centuries A.D. these figures were positioned over the upper parts of mummies. Made in wax, according to a process originated by the Greeks, they are highly unusual.

Room 24 is devoted to artists' trial pieces and rough sketches; **room 29,** to drawings and writings ranging from tablets to papyri. In **corridors 34** and **39** you will find linen articles; in **room 34,** all sorts of documents relating to toiletry, music and even agriculture; in **room 39,** bronzes, glassware and terra-cotta items of the Greco-Roman period; and in **corridor 44,** faience articles of various periods (all of great beauty), and glass mosaics.

Room 48, above the museum entrance, is well worth close examination. It contains two sarcophagi of the Middle Kingdom belonging to princesses Aashait and Kawit; both are decorated with friezes colorfully illustrating daily life. Among the illustrations are a bull's carcass being cut up, a cow with a calf tied to its leg being milked, wheat being poured into the grain-stores, etc. The display case between these sarcophagi has many beautiful items on display: a small figure of Cheops; a blue faience hippopotamus, which seems to be emerging from a marsh, from which it is still carrying leaves and flowers on its back; a little soapstone head of Queen Tiye and a *shawabti*, or tomb statuette, of Ptah.

Continue through **rooms 47** and **46** toward the staircase, passing a collection of coffins of kings, queens and priests of the New Kingdom.

(Note: The **mummy room** has been closed since 1981.)

THE BIRTHPLACES OF
PHARAONIC EGYPT

Situated only about 19 miles/30 kilometres north of ancient Memphis (the first capital in Egyptian history), Cairo provides the visitor with his first contact with the world of the pharaohs, through its oldest ruins. All the burial-grounds stretching along the cliff overlooking the west bank of the Nile between this ancient site and today's city date, in fact, from the Old Kingdom (2750–2180 B.C.). From their evidence, archaeologists are trying to piece together an idea of the civilization that developed along the valley.

THE SPHINX AND THE THREE PYRAMIDS OF GÎZA★★★

These 'star attractions' of Egyptian tourism will probably form the centerpiece of your visit. In order to understand, right from the start, the strange mystery of this unique site, your best course is to view it first from the foot of the Sphinx, and then, move across to the pyramids rising in the background, on the rim of the plateau. Unfortunately, organized tours rarely go this way. You may also have to resort to your own initiative to reach the *Sahara City* restaurant up on the plateau; from this vantage point, you will see the three pyramids standing out alone against the desert sky.

▬ *GETTING THERE*

It is 7½ miles/12 kilometres from the center of Cairo (Midan el-Tahrir) to the pyramids. There are buses, but it is best to go by taxi, which will cost L.E. 5 for the round trip.

The Pyramids Road was inaugurated by Empress Eugénie of France in 1869, at the time of the opening of the Suez Canal. Around 20 years ago, it still crossed the open desert. Over the years, however, it has gradually been overtaken by new buildings in the suburbs of Gîza, which has spawned a rapid growth of shops and the most famous nightclubs in Cairo. Today, the buildings along the road are spreading to the plateau where the pyramids were built 5000 years ago.

From time to time along the route, on your left, you will get a glimpse of a pyramid, yellow against the blue sky and disappearing again behind walls or palm trees. The turn-off for the sphinx is on the left before the final bend. However, under normal circumstances you will go straight on to the pyramid of Cheops, which suddenly looms above you on top of the ridge. Then you will find yourself surrounded by donkey- and camel-drivers and souvenir sellers, from whom you will have to defend yourself. Once clear of this hazard, you can contemplate the strange spectacle presented by the three immense geometric shapes standing in a row across the plateau.

The pyramids at Gîza.

TOUR OF THE PYRAMIDS

There is an admission charge to the three pyramids themselves and to the valley temple of Chephren below the sphinx. The monuments are open from 8 am to 5 pm. Tickets can be bought near the pyramid of Cheops.

Admission to the general site is free. You will probably want to come back again, either to see the sun awakening the sphinx at daybreak or to watch the pyramids growing enormously as their shadows lengthen at sunset.

You will certainly return for the *son et lumière* spectacle, which detaches this majestic group of buildings from its present commercial trappings and restores its mystery.

The **pyramid of Cheops,** known as the Great Pyramid, highest and the oldest of the group, is the nearest. Take a few steps around the Great Pyramid of Cheops. It measures 754 feet/230 metres along each side and 449 feet/137 metres high (479 feet or 146 metres in ancient times). Experts have uncovered evidence of three stages of building that testify to the pharaoh's growing taste for splendor. Herodotus recounts that 100,000 men condemned to forced labor worked in shifts for 10 years to excavate the stone quarries at Tura and to transport the blocks of stone to the site, and another 20 years to build the pyramid. This has lost its outer casing and now reveals a series of irregular tiers that tempt you to climb them but, because of the poor footholds that make it dangerous, climbing the pyramid is more or less forbidden. If you are fit and energetic, however, you can nevertheless risk going up the east face, and you will be rewarded with a stunning view from the top.

Most visitors are invited to explore the interior of the pyramid instead, but the walk to the burial chamber is strenuous, and not everyone can manage it. It necessitates a long, stooping walk in a confined atmosphere along passages scarcely more than three feet/one metre high. These lead to an amazing gallery the height of which suddenly soars to 28 feet/8½ metres, while its width, reduced to three feet/0.9 metre at ground level by side ramps, shrinks into an extremely narrow roof. Beyond this constricted passage, the polished stones of which make the slope treacherous, you pass through two low chambers and come out in the burial chamber. The sarcophagus is still in place. You will be impressed by the structural perfection of the walls, the evenness of the stone courses and the fineness of the joints. The roof, formed by nine granite slabs altogether weighing 440 tons/400 tonnes, was cracked as a result of an earthquake. We know that five 'relieving chambers' were built above it to support the weight of the pyramid above the tomb. Along the walls on your way to the burial chamber you will notice slots designed to take granite portcullises that have now disappeared. You will be glad to take deep breaths of fresh air when you come out!

As you walk around the pyramid of Cheops, you will see large pits dug into the rock on the south side to house the sacred boats that were to permit the pharaoh to wander over the celestial ocean. One of these was discovered during excavations in the 1950s. Made of Lebanese cedar, it is quite magnificent, and a museum has been set up on the site to exhibit it. There is an entrance charge.

East of the Great Pyramid, there is a row of three subsidiary pyramids, probably intended for the pharaoh's sisters, wives, or daughters.

Proceed to the **pyramid of Chephren.** This, of the three, is in the best state of preservation, and the upper part is almost intact. The main burial chamber, cut into the bedrock and reached by a steep, narrow passage, still contains the granite sarcophagus which, strangely, bears no inscriptions or decoration. On the way, notice a series of cells partly buried in the sand, which were probably used to house the workmen on the site.

You can cover the short distance from here to the **pyramid of Mycerinus** on foot. From the rocky plateau, which was leveled to meet the kings' wish to build their tombs there, you will be able to see the little villages in the valley 130 feet/40 metres below and think of the poor *fellahin* of centuries ago. The approach to the pyramid is through the low walls of its ruined temple. You have to climb over these blocks to appreciate the impressive size of this building, just as you do over the skillfully shaped pink granite blocks from Aswân used to dress the lower part of the pyramid. The pyramid of Mycerinus is the smallest of the three: 354 feet/108 metres along each side, and 217 feet/66 metres high. It is said that the pharaoh, a kindly man, wished to spare his people from hardship! You can enter the pyramid along a low, sloping corridor, divided by portcullises, which takes you 20 feet/6 metres below ground to a first burial chamber and then down a slope to the side to the real tomb which is now empty. The basalt sarcophagus was removed and went down, with the ship transporting it, off the coast of Spain. As you leave the pyramid of Mycerinus, you will notice its three subsidiary pyramids, the smallest of which belonged to his wife.

You will then come back the same way. The hillside you cross is a vast necropolis, where all the important people at court or members of the royal family were buried. It is, unfortunately, not yet cleared, so you will not be able to visit any of the *mastabas*, the entrances of which you can see here and there. Descend the gentle slope to the sphinx along the remains of the great paved causeway that led from the pyramid of Chephren to the valley temple, where his body was mummified. This is known as the Granite Temple, its great hall now open to the sky. It was here that marvelous statues of the king were found, one of which is now in the Egyptian Museum in Cairo.

Now you can finally look at the **Sphinx** from the front. It was created out of a natural outcrop of rock that blocked the way, and was sculpted in the shape of a lion with a human head wearing the *nemes* headdress with the *uraeus* on the front. Is this the image of Chephren guarding his burial-place, or that of the god Horus keeping watch over the horizon? No one knows. Between its paws, a stele relates that the pharaoh Tuthmosis IV was ordered in a dream to free the Sphinx from the sand that, so often in its history, engulfed it. The king undertook the task without delay and so attained eternal glory.

THE SITE OF MEMPHIS
AND THE NECROPOLIS OF SAKKARA★★★

This is a wonderful trip which will take a whole day if you really want to make the most of it. Hire a taxi or arrange to share a minibus, and take a light picnic meal with you; you can get drinks at the rest-house at Sakkara. The first part of the journey follows the road to the pyramids, but about a mile/1500 metres before the *Mena House Hotel*, there is a good small local road to the left, which runs beside the canal and goes on to the site of Memphis. On the way, you will go through small villages and pass little carts and people riding bicycles.

The road runs close to the edge of the desert plateau to the right and eventually arrives at a palm-grove where a few scattered ruins recall the existence of the city that, from the third millennium to the Greco-Roman period, was one of the most important religious, cultural and commercial centers of the ancient world. When you have bought your ticket to enter the site, you will be greeted by an alabaster sphinx more than 13 feet/4 metres high, which probably stood beside a temple dedicated to Ptah, the patron god of the city, during the New Kingdom (1580–1085 B.C.). Among the jumbled mass of ruins 200 yards/180 metres further on, you will see an alabaster embalming table more than 16 feet/5 metres long and about 9 feet/3 metres wide. It was dedicated to the sacred bull Apis, the most sacred of all animals which, like mankind, was destined for eternal life.

As you wander through the palm-grove at Memphis, you will come across many interesting stone fragments. Do not spend too much time over these, because there are many masterpieces ahead of you. Do, however, go into the building housing a colossal figure of Ramesses II which is lying on its back because it has lost its legs. Sculpted out of fine-grained limestone, this sculpture has the pharaoh's name carved on the right shoulder, pectoral and belt buckle. To get the best view of it, go up to the gallery surrounding it. Even without legs, it is still 33 feet/10 metres long. Curiously enough, its two profiles do not have quite the same expression.

As you leave Memphis for Sakkara, returning the way you came, you will see the two pyramids of Dahshur (attributed to Sneferu, the father of Cheops) on your left. One of them, the red pyramid, is somewhat flattened. The other has two angles of slope, like a mansard roof, which probably correspond to two different periods of construction; this has become famous as the 'rhomboidal' or 'bent' pyramid. You will then pass by the necropolis of South Sakkara, which is badly ruined and of minor interest. Beyond this is one of the most important sites in Egypt.

Sakkara is an immense necropolis about a mile/1.6 kilometres wide and 5 miles/8 kilometres in length. It was used from prehistoric times until the Greco-Roman period. You will visit mostly remains of the Old Kingdom, and they will fill you with wonder. The archaeologists are a long way from having exhausted their mysteries and treasures.

▬ *THE TOMB OF KING ZOSER*★★

This enormous complex which dominates the site of North Sakkara, is one of the most staggering and puzzling monuments left by the ancient

Egyptians. It is the work of the first architect whose name history has preserved — Imhotep — and, in the form of the first known pyramid, it provides us with the world's first manifestation of architecture in stone. It is an amazing piece of ingenuity which surrounds the royal tomb with a mock palace, as if the architect had to fix in stone an image of the timber and reed dwelling in which the pharaoh lived on the banks of the Nile. This, so that he or, more accurately, his non-earthly double, or *ka*, could pursue his destiny in the other world. No one knows why this innovation was not taken up. These great mock facades form part of a decorative scheme designed to last forever, yet behind them, only pebble filling has been found. Excavation and reconstruction work that has gone on for the last 50 years has not yet enabled all the pieces to be put back in place.

The complex begins with an enclosure formed by a magnificent wall buttressed with projecting bastions like that of a fortress, around which are spaced 14 simulated closed double gates, but no real gate. The entrance is through another mock gate, this one permanently open at the southeast corner. A small vestibule leads on to a marvelous narrow stone passage lined with 40 'bundle' columns engaged in short wing-walls and arranged in two rows. These originally supported a heavy roof of limestone slabs imitating the leaf-stems of palm trees. They still bear traces of red paint and recall the wooden columns which, in turn, imitated the bundles of reeds that were frequently used as roof supports. Divided into two sections of unequal length, the passage is unique in Egyptian architecture. It opens into a small hypostyle hall with eight columns in the same style — but not so high — which have been restored to their original proportions by making use of the many intact drum sections found in the sand.

Eventually, passing through another door, you will reach the vast court where the famous 'step pyramid' stands. It forms a gigantic staircase with six broad steps ascending to the sky, clearly suggesting the shape of the *mastaba* from which it originated. We know that this structural form, which was revolutionary at the time, was a response to theological considerations and was the result of a long series of experiments. Unfortunately, you will not be able to view the interior layout of the tomb because entry is forbidden. Its complex plan involves numerous galleries 82 feet/25 metres below ground, some of which were reserved for queens and royal children. In its storerooms, an amazing hoard of royal tableware has been found, consisting of 30,000 to 40,000 stone vases in addition to many other items. (Of special interest is the blue faience tile panel from the royal burial chamber on view in the Egyptian Museum in Cairo, where it has been restored). You will then proceed along the right-hand side of the great court. In the middle of a buttressed wall, three elegant fluted columns stand amid the ruins of a small temple. Here you will notice another simulated half-open door and, between the slabs on the ground nearby, numerous pieces of ceiling rounded at the bottom and painted red to resemble logs.

A narrow passage to the right leads to the end of another court, known as the Jubilee, or *Heb Sed*, Court. This was intended, it seems, to permit the king's *ka* to observe in the eternal world the extremely impressive ceremony that, on earth, had the effect of revitalizing the pharaoh's power. Here you will see chapels and simulated wooden screens carved on beautiful stone walls. Note the double staircase at one end and the feet of four vanished statues at the other. You will then emerge from the east side of the pyramid. This still has a few courses of the original casing, and in the sloping side you will notice the opening to the burial shaft belonging to one of the members of the royal family, with original lintels over the top.

The small sanctuary on your right is known as the House of the South because one of its columns is decorated with two bindweed tendrils, symbolizing Upper Egypt. The façade, partly rebuilt, is embellished with four fluted columns without a base, the tallest of which was originally 40 feet/12 metres high but now measures only 10 feet/3 metres. An arched cornice ran along the top of the building. The capitals have been discovered almost intact. The inside of the sanctuary contains little of interest but a short distance further on, you will arrive at the House of the North,

Entrance to the tomb and pyramid of Zoser, Sakkara.

announced by three small engaged columns on its right-hand wall, on which the papyrus, the emblem of the delta, appears. It is thought that these two practically identical buildings symbolize the king's power over the two lands. Turn, now, towards the north side of the pyramid, where the *serdab* occupies a corner. This is a doorless chamber in which the statue of Zoser — his 'replacement body' — could breathe fresh air and receive emanations of life. The statue is now in the Egyptian Museum in Cairo, but a cast stands in its place. On the front wall of the *serdab*, two halves of a door are carved into the stonework to the left and right. Opposite the one at the western end you will see a section of wall with beautiful capitals. This is all that remains of the mortuary temple that abutted on to the pyramid. In front of you, there is a huge altar, on the left of which there was once a series of store-rooms for provisions.

After walking right around the pyramid via the west face, you will again cross the great court, the western edge of which is demarcated by the corner of the pyramid. In the thickness of the south wall, the opening to a large shaft leads to the granite burial chamber which contained, it is thought, Zoser's canopic jars. A storeroom has been constructed next to it to hold the most important blocks of stone dug out during excavations in this part of the site. Note the wooden bars used to shift these great stones, still perfectly preserved, which were discovered in the large shaft and date from the third millennium B.C. Note, too, the partly restored frieze of cobras on the wall dedicated to the goddess Buto. From the terrace formed by the enclosure wall at this point, the view extends as far as Dahshur. On the way to the exit you will again go through the marvelous colonnade you passed on the way in.

▬ THE PYRAMID OF UNAS

Your visit will continue with the pyramid of Unas. Although the smallest of the Sakkara pyramids, this is not the least known, because it was in the beautiful burial chamber here that the first texts of funerary hieroglyphs, known as the 'Pyramid Texts', were discovered. The chamber is reached by a sloping passage which penetrates the rock as far as a vestibule lined with granite. A long horizontal shaft leads to an antechamber in which the fine limestone walls are inscribed with long vertical rows of hieroglyphs painted in green. The roof is decorated with stars and the rest of the walls with carefully and deeply cut rows of hieroglyphs in blue.

▬ THE NECROPOLIS

After leaving the pyramid of Unas, pay a visit to some of the great private tombs, or *mastabas*, the decoration of which perpetuates burial ceremonies and daily customs which are 5000 years old. It is not possible to see everything, and because you will not be able to wander alone around the dunes, you will also have to rely on your guide. However, the most attractive tombs are included here so that you may make your own choice if the occasion arises.

The mastaba of Princess Idut, near the pyramid of Unas, is worth visiting for the exquisite water scenes in the first two chambers. The next two are devoted to scenes of offerings.

The mastaba of Mehu★★, immediately below, contains well-preserved painted decorations executed with incredible freshness. The image of the dead man, portrayed on each side of the entrance, greets you at the threshhold, as in all the tombs. Do not forget that you are now entering a home. Mehu is old and fat, a sign of his importance. The first small chamber is devoted to paintings of water sport. The long gallery has scenes on several themes: work in the fields, harvesting, fishing and so on. The gathering of 39 women and one man represents Mehu's property. In the offerings chamber, the colors are virtually as new. On the right of the entrance, note the dwarf sitting beneath his master's chair during a concert. The chapel is in a perfect state of preservation and, if a number of the scenes are repeated, they are nearly always enhanced with additional new details.

The mastaba of Nefer-her-ptah, the 'tomb of the birds', is below the causeway quite close to the complex of Unas and contains decoration in the form of sketches of great delicacy and quality.

Two other important *mastabas* have been dug out of the sand about half a mile/700 metres northwest of the Zoser complex.

The mastaba of Mereruka is a huge family sepulchre 132 feet/40 metres long and 79 feet/24 metres wide; it comprises no fewer than 32 rooms, half of which served as storerooms. The decorated chambers do not possess great delicacy of style, but they do depict a large number of new or unusual themes. Do not miss the following: entrance vestibule, marsh and cultivation scenes; chamber 4, fishing in the marshes; chamber 7, harem scenes; chamber 8, the false door, complete with bolt and hangings. Chamber 13, with six pillars supporting the roof, is the largest and contains a perfectly preserved statue of Mereruka in a niche behind a libation table. On the right-hand wall, there is a series of mourning scenes which were rarely seen in houses at this time. The small chamber (no. 18) in the corner by the tomb of Meri-Teti includes many delightful details. Do not leave without seeing the curious scenes of women dancing and taking part in sporting activities (chamber 23), next to the tomb of Princess Seshseshet (Har-Watet-Khet) at the opposite end of the *mastaba*.

The mastaba of Kagemni, on your left as you leave the *mastaba* of Mereruka, should be noted. It contains only five rooms, but the decoration is of exceptional quality.

By this time, you will probably be ready for some refreshment at the rest-house. This was built near the site of the house occupied by the French archaeologist Mariette when he decided, after discovering the Serapeum in 1851, to devote himself to the site and, in doing so, laid the foundations of scientific Egyptology.

The Serapeum★, which is the next objective of your tour, was a quite extraordinary complex of catacombs where the Apis bulls were buried from the time of the New Kingdom to the Greco-Roman era. Unfortunately, you will find practically nothing left of this enormous cemetery and its temples and numerous outbuildings, priests' quarters and pilgrims' lodgings. However, there remain rock-cut chambers staggered along both sides of a dark passage so as not to face each other, each containing an enormous sarcophagus hewn from a single block of granite, basalt or limestone. As you walk down into this labyrinth, imagine the tremendous shock received by the excavators when, after months of patient digging in the desert, they one day came across 24 mummies of Apis bulls lying intact in their coffins. This at once raises the controversial subject of the Ancient Egyptian cult of sacred animals, the significance of which we still do not fully understand. All along the Nile Valley, excavations have yielded numerous animal cemeteries. At Sakkara itself, vast catacombs of ibises were discovered in 1965, followed by the tombs of the Apis mothers in 1970.

The mastaba of Ti, which was excavated by Mariette in 1865, is today below ground level because of the accumulation of sand. The figure of Ti, carved with all his titles in hieroglyphs on the two rectangular pillars of the facade, shows that he was a man of some importance. On the splayed surfaces of the doorway, he receives visitors into a large pillared courtyard. In this part of the tomb, the low reliefs are sadly damaged. In the narrow corridor that follows, however, the decoration is well preserved. The figure of Ti appears several times, sometimes accompanied by his wife and various servants. The first small chamber on the right was devoted to offerings, as the decorations indicate. Continuing along the corridor, you will notice the musicians and dancers above the entrance to the large chapel, in which you will find some of the finest bas-relief carvings of the Old Kingdom.

On the left-hand wall as you go in, life-size figures of Ti and his wife preside over farming activities. Workers are stacking wheat, winnowing, putting the grain into sacks and transporting sheaves on donkeys. The building of a boat is also depicted. Note the simplicity of the tools. The next wall round the chamber is that of the *serdab*, which has openings beneath the feet of Ti and his wife. On either side, two servants are burning incense. The rest of the wall is covered with scenes of extraordinary realism, showing craftsmen at work. After passing quickly along the third wall which has two stelae and offering tables, you will pause for a long look at the beautiful north wall, every detail of which is a feast for the eyes. Note, especially, the hunting and fishing scenes in which the action, though placed in a conventional setting of reeds and papyrus bushes, is treated with unusual movement, expressiveness and vitality.

The mastaba of Ptah-hotep and Akhet-hotep, situated 218 yards/200 metres from the rest-house on the way to the site exit, should not be missed. The decoration here, which employs the usual themes, is remarkable for its delicacy of execution. It is unfinished in the entrance passage, where the methods used by the carvers can be followed. In Ptah-hotep's chapel, the decoration forms one continuous tapestry, while that of Akhet-hotep's chapel is one of the wonders of the art of relief carving. Note, especially, the scenes in which the standing figure of the dead man is present at a series of mock battles and contests on the water. The small seated figure to whom a child is giving a drink is probably the chief artist.

If there is enough time before leaving Sakkara, take a walk around the ruins on your own.

On your return journey go through Abusir. Of the many pyramids which have been identified here, only four have kept some semblance of their original shape. The rest are no more than mounds, but the view from here over Sakkara is worth the short detour.

THE OASIS OF EL FAYYUM AND THE PYRAMID OF MEDUM★: A TRIP FOR RELAXATION

Length of the excursion: one day with long stops. Distance: about 156 miles/250 kilometres. Transport: taxi or minibus. A hostel by the lake offers good fish dishes.

■■■ *EL FAYYUM*★

This is an amazing oasis inhabited by almost a million *fellahin* and fishing people clustered in large villages, who still live at the slow and tranquil pace of the time of the pharaohs. Beneath the green fields and orchards of the oasis are the vestiges of thousands of years of civilization. Collections of jewelry, libraries of papyrus documents, and statues now preserved in the museums all bear witness to the existence of such a civilization — above all, the famous portraits from El Fayyum (now in the Egyptian Museum in Cairo, upper floor, room 14), which, some 2000 years ago, replaced masks over the faces of mummies and have since toured the world. Today, practically nothing remains of the impressive temples built during the Middle Kingdom (2060–1785 B.C.) or the many buildings constructed by Greek colonists in the first centuries A.D., except ruins for archaeologists. What awaits you in El Fayyum, therefore, is the spontaneous and exciting traditional way of life of the Egyptian people. After leaving Cairo, skirting the pyramids and crossing 50 miles/80 kilometres of harsh desert plateau, you suddenly arrive in a land shimmering with water and cultivated fields lying beside the broad bowl of a lake. You will then descend 145 feet/44 metres below sea level into an ocean of greenery stretching as far as the shores of **Lake Karun,** which shrank in size over the ages, leaving behind the rich terraces of silt that created the land's fertility. Today, a pale-tinted sandy desert enclosed by rocky hills borders it to the west. You may have the opportunity of finding a boat to take you there, and a guide to show you the way to the Greco-Roman ruins in the little village of **Dime** (Dimiet es-Sebaa), which once lay on the caravan route across the Libyan desert.

Otherwise, take a drive along the lush green shoreline of the lake. You will see the inhabitants of the little port of **Shakshuk** fishing in the slightly salty water for enormous fish like the ones served at the small hotels along the shore. When the sun becomes less fierce, continue your drive to the heart of the oasis. Traveling along roads lined with palm trees, you will pass groves of lemon, orange, mango and guava trees and then numerous little canals running with water from the Nile, which has been channeled off 125 miles/200 kilometres upstream by the Bahr Yusuf (the Canal of Joseph), to turn the countless water-wheels in the fields and orchards. When you have had your fill of the *joie de vivre* of the likeable, hard-working local people, set off for **Roda** and from there take the road to Cairo. On the way you will pass the site of **Medum** with its curious pyramid, the 'False Pyramid', which now only looks like a sort of bare castle keep rising above a sturdy base and surrounded by the splendid stone blocks that once encased it. This construction is attributed to Sneferu, the father of Cheops. It certainly dates back to the beginning of the third millennium. You can go inside it if you are prepared for acrobatics. The internal structure is novel, and cedarwood beams still exist in the burial chamber. Otherwise, take a look at one or two of the *mastabas* around it. The **mastaba of Atef,** for example, contains enameled bas-reliefs, which are unique in their kind. It was among these ruins that many of the masterpieces in the museum in Cairo were found, for example, the painting of the geese of Medum and the famous sculpture group of Rahotep and his wife, Nefret.

Some 13 miles/20 kilometres from here on your way back to Cairo, you will
see two low hills on your left that are barely distinguishable from
undulations in the ground. These are the remains of the two **pyramids of
Lisht,** where the 10 seated statues of Sesostris I, now in the museum in
Cairo, were discovered.

LUXOR AND KARNAK

Until recent years, a journey up the Nile Valley involved taking a plane to Luxor or Aswân or perhaps the overnight sleeper train connecting Cairo with Upper Egypt. The main archaeological sites in Middle Egypt are now being opened to the public and, although the glorious remains now coming to light are often incomprehensible for the non-specialist, travel organizations almost invariably include a journey up the Nile in their holiday programs.

Problems with basic food and accommodation still remain, but air-conditioned buses now enable tourists to travel in comfort, among landscapes and people that have remained much the same since the days of the pharaohs.

THE ROUTE UP THE VALLEY

The journey up the Nile Valley is usually taken with two stops, one at **Minya,** 150 miles/250 kilometres from Cairo, on the first night, and the second at **Nag Hammadi,** 90 miles/150 kilometres from Luxor.

The coach leaves Cairo by the road to Memphis and at once enters rich farming country watered by countless canals. In some places, the plain broadens to fill wide amphitheaters of land, while, in others, it squeezes between barren cliffs. It fills the land between the desert and the banks of the river, from which it never strays all the way to Aswân.

Soon after your departure, you pass the silhouettes of the pyramids of Sakkara, Dahshur, Lisht and Medum, outlined on the horizon against the Libyan hills. Sometimes the itinerary includes an excursion to the rich oasis of El Fayyum.

▬▬ A TOUR OF THE SITES

At **Minya,** your archaeological 'Grand Tour' begins. The first site you will come to is **Beni Hasan,** with its necropolis cut into the limestone cliffs on the right bank of the Nile. Make the ascent by donkey and, after passing an impressive series of mysterious holes, follow a track passing along the vertical facades of some 40 *hypogea*, or rock-cut tombs. It was here that the great feudal rulers of the *nome*, or province, of the Antelope were buried at the beginning of the second millennium B.C. Inscriptions and paintings surviving in the last two tombs provide a picture of their lives. Scenes of work in the fields, everyday chores, battles and desert hunts alternate with the usual supernatural subjects in long columns. In the next-to-last tomb, note the Asian caravan bringing perfumed eye make-up to the prince, a scene often reproduced elsewhere.

You will then recross the river to reach the little village of **Ashmunein,** about 6 miles/10 kilometres to the south where, according to pharaonic tradition, the sun rose for the first time above the earth — where, as it were, the world was born. We know that the Greeks built the settlement of Hermopolis at this spot, where Thoth, the moon-god whom they identified with Hermes, was worshipped. Mummies of baboons and ibises, animals sacred to Thoth, were found in huge numbers in three underground galleries here; they have done more to give the site its air of mystery than the ruins themselves.

Eventually you will arrive at the necropolis of **Tune el-Gebel★**, where local notables were buried between the 4th century B.C. and the 3rd century A.D. The tombs are largely intact. The tomb of Petosiris is probably one of the oldest, and was discovered in 1920. It dates from about 300 B.C. and Petosiris was clearly an important person. The decoration inside shows the attraction educated people of the time felt for foreign culture, the existence of which was brought to their attention by Greek settlers at Naucratis, in the delta. Seven centuries separate this tomb from the ones closer to the edge of the desert; during those centuries, Egypt fell under the political control of Greece and Rome. When it yields up its secrets, the necropolis of Tuna el-Gebel will perhaps show how this happened. When you leave, make for the site of **Tel el-Amarna★**, which Akhenaton, the husband of Nefertiti, chose for his new capital in the 4th century B.C. On the way, do not miss seeing the stelae which Akhenaton had carved high on the cliff-face on both sides of the Nile to mark the boundary of the city where he was to dedicate himself to the worship of the solar disk, Aton. It is all the more moving because, on his death, all traces of the revolutionary pharaoh were systematically obliterated and his capital, Akhetaton or 'Aton's horizon', was destroyed. Despite the efforts of the archaeologists, there is hardly anything left.

After leaving Tel el-Amarna, continue south for 150 miles/250 kilometres without stopping, except perhaps at two famous Coptic monasteries near Suhag. At **Nag Hammadi**, a small sugar-refining town which you will probably pass through during the night, you will enter the tourist area around Luxor. The sites you visit from here on are included in the travel itineraries or cruises available in the capital of Upper Egypt, and are described below.

The first site is **Abydos★★** (see p. 135), the sacred city of Osiris, the remains of which extend beneath the sand for many miles along the edge of the Libyan hills. The wonderful decorations in the temple of Seti I have, fortunately, been largely uncovered.

You will then go back in the direction of the Nile along a short track through the fields of sugar cane that supply the mills of Nag Hammadi. A short distance from the town, you will rejoin the road to the south. On your right, a few miles further on, is the town of **Egplum,** where the government has built a large aluminum factory with Russian aid. You will then cross the desert for 18 miles/30 kilometres before coming to the **temple of Dendera** (see p. 137), the dwelling-place of Hathor, goddess of love and happiness, which stands in isolation in the surrounding country. You will probably wish to stop here for a while. It is the last stop before Luxor, which is only about 40 miles/65 kilometres further on. The road crosses to the right bank of the Nile at **Qena,** the principal market for large jars and water-bottles, and then plunges on into the countryside. At **Kus** and then at **Kift,** it crosses the routes to the Red Sea used by ancient caravans seeking the perfumes and spices of the mysterious land of Punt. On the right, 15 miles/25 kilometres further on, is the turn-off for Luxor. The three or four days usually allowed for a stay in the old capital of Thebes will not be enough for you to see all its treasures, and you will be left with a strong desire to return. However, other wonders await you further south.

The first temple you come to is that of **Isna★** (see p. 137), which is dedicated to Khnum, the god of the floods. To reach it you have to cross the river over a dam which provides the region with irrigation water. The temple's superb columns are now in the center of a large market town,

where, since Roman times, they have been gradually sinking into a depression in the ancient river sediments.

From here, continue your journey along the right bank of the Nile. The valley broadens out at first, then contracts, as if teasing the desert, and the road passes on through. It skirts the walls of **El-Kab** and threads its way along the river as far as the small town of **Idfu★★**. Here, on the left bank of the river, is the most grandiose and best-preserved temple left by the Ptolemies, the house of the falcon-god, Horus (*see p.137*).

After Idfu, the road turns away from the right bank into the countryside. It rejoins the Nile at the defile between the sandstone hills of the Gebel Sikila (the 'Mountain of the Chain'); then veers away again through the sugarcane fields of New Nubia, reclaimed from the desert. Here, a number of villages have been built to resettle people from the communities inundated by the Aswân Dam. The road eventually rejoins the Nile at **Kom Ombo** (*see p.140*), where the romantic remains of a temple overlook the town from the top of a hill. The road does not leave the river again, and the landscape becomes increasingly rugged as the valley narrows. Belts of palm trees extend towards the golden sand dunes on the right and the brooding cliffs on the left, as the sandstone rocks give way to granite. Suddenly, the broad plain of Aswân opens out with the Nile flowing in from the distant interior of Africa. The water boils among the polished boulders of the first cataract and embraces verdant islands basking in the permanent sunshine. This is journey's end.

LUXOR★★★

Luxor is the heart of Upper Egypt and, even if the amount of time at your disposal limits your stay in this quiet, small provincial city, you will find it well worth the trip. The setting is quite exceptional. This is the site of Thebes, the 'hundred-gated city' sung by Homer. Under the protection of the god Amun, Thebes remained the spiritual capital of Egypt for more than 15 centuries until the middle of the first millennium. The river is almost a mile wide at this point, and edged with a green and brown tapestry of fields, river silt, reeds and canals. Nearby, at the foot of the Arabian mountains to the east, is the spot where, over the centuries, **Karnak** grew. To the west, in the immense bare rock amphitheater of cliffs formed by the Libyan hills, the great pharaohs of the New Kingdom built their funerary temples and concealed their fantastic tombs while, on the edge of the cultivated fields, the most important people of the time dug their own separate burial grounds.

The modern city of Luxor is now growing on both sides of the famous temple to which the Place de la Concorde in Paris owes its obelisk. A string of hotels, from modest to luxurious, lines the Corniche along the right bank of the Nile. Coaches and taxis come and go at the landing-stages, where cruise-boats are lined up along the jetties. Luxor spares no effort to make it easy for visitors to reach not only the sites in the immediate vicinity, but also those up to 80 miles/150 kilometres away — Abydos, Dendera, Isna, Idfu and Kom Ombo, the ruins of which are being restored by archaeologists. It is also from Luxor that visitors embark for Aswân, Abu Simbel and Philae.

Today, Luxor is the world's leading center for archaeological tours.

Temple of Luxor, obelisk of Tuthmosis II.

▬ *PRACTICAL INFORMATION FOR LUXOR*

Getting there

By air
There are three daily flights between Luxor and Cairo, two of which leave from Aswân. There are also charter flights catering to the flood of tourists at peak periods. The airport is 6½ miles/11 kilometres northeast of the city in the desert. If you are traveling independently, make sure on your departure that a coach or taxi will be waiting for you on your arrival.

By train
The station is situated in the center of the city. Sleeper trains from Cairo arrive in the morning (a 12-hour journey) and go on to Aswân (a 4-hour journey). The return journey is also overnight. Several colorful stopping trains operating during the daytime serve Aswân and the sites around Luxor. They are not air-conditioned.

By road
As described previously, the main road along the Nile passes within a few miles of Luxor. The branch road leading off is clearly signposted.

By boat
The journey can only be made by cruise-boat. The landing-stage is along the Corniche.

Getting around Luxor

The traditional mode of transport in the city, and between Luxor and Karnak, is the horse-drawn carriage.

The use of bicycles is increasing. They are a good way to travel to sites when it is not too hot. They can be rented in many different places, in particular beside the *Horus* and *Isis* hotels. Bicycles can be taken across to the left bank on the ferry.

Buses and minibuses are specially operated by the travel organizations.

Taxis can be ordered by the hotels or travel agencies for people traveling independently.

For crossing to the left bank (the west bank), there are two choices: the tourist ferry, which serves the big hotels and arrives at a landing-stage where the bus, minibus or taxi ordered for you will be waiting; or the ferry used by local people, which provides a non-stop shuttle service and is infinitely more colorful and lively. The crossing is itself quite a spectacle; however, you will not find any taxis at the landing-stage. The best arrangement might be to take the tourist ferry in the morning and the local ferry back in the evening.

A tour of the west bank can be made by car, but this involves going downriver for 36 miles/60 kilometres to cross the **bridge at Qena,** which is a lot of time wasted.

Accommodation

Luxor is gradually building adequate facilities to cope with the growing number of tourists. For the moment, however, the number of rooms available is still insufficient. Many visitors stay on board the cruise-boats, which sometimes remain tied up along the quayside for two or three days.

Three top-class holiday hotels have opened since 1983 by the river to the south of the city:
▲▲▲▲**Akhenaton** (Map pp.106–107 D–2; tel. 77–75–75; telex 93159), the hotel village of the *Club Méditerranée*, which owes its high reputation to the facilities and excellent food provided, the comfort of its bungalow-style accommodation amid the greenery, and the fine swimming-pool, from which you can watch the activity on the river and the passage of the sun over the opposite bank.
▲▲▲▲**Isis** (Map pp.106–107 D–2; tel. 82–750; telex 90276), Shari Khaled Ibn el-Walid is more impersonal. A hotel of international

caliber, with all the extra services you could wish for, its 250 rooms occupy a multistory building and look out over the countryside where the Valley of the Kings lies hidden. The swimming-pool is surrounded by the lush vegetation of a little garden.

▲▲▲▲**Mövenpick-Jolieville** (tel. 84–400; telex 93825) has proved a great success. Situated on Crocodile Island, 4½ miles/7 kilometres from Luxor, and connected to the bank by a bridge, it has 16-room bungalows in a terraced garden setting, a swimming-pool, tennis courts and jogging track. All sporting activities are catered to.

In the midst of the bustle at the center of Luxor itself, there are two other first-class hotels:

▲▲▲▲**Etap** (Map pp.106–107 C–3; tel. 83–800; telex 92080), situated on the Nile Corniche near the temple. Its rooms overlook the river and provide the highest standards of comfort. The restaurants are good. With its lounge, shops, swimming-pool and bars, the *Etap* is a popular and lively meeting spot and place to stay.

▲▲▲▲**Winter Palace** and **New Winter Palace** (Map pp.106–107 D–3; tel. 82–000; telex 92160) are next to each other on the Nile Corniche. The first-named of these two related hotels is now some 20 years old. The other, now renovated, dates back to colonial days. They share the same garden and swimming-pool. At the back, there is a restaurant, a nightclub and several shops. Note that half-board is compulsory here.

To this list two other pleasant hotels can be added: the ▲▲**Savoy** (Map pp.106–107 C–3; tel. 82–200; telex 92160), overlooking the river, and the ▲▲**Luxor,** (Map pp.106–107 C–3; tel. 82–400; telex 24–126), near the temple. The rooms in these hotels are not air-conditioned.

The modestly priced hotels include: the ▲**Windsor** (Map pp.106–107 C–3; tel. 82–847), ▲**Philippe** (Map pp.106–107 C–3; tel. 82–284), ▲**Dina** (Map pp.106–107 C–3; tel. 82–620) and ▲**Horus** (Map pp.106–107 C–3; tel. 82–165).

An accurate and up-to-date list of hotels in Luxor is impossible to compile because the situation is constantly changing.

Dining

The only restaurants are those provided by the hotels. In rest-houses, which you will come across on your various trips, you will get only cool drinks, excellent fresh lemon juice in particular.

Be careful about picnic meals, which can quickly spoil. Lunchtime is a hot time of the day, and it is best to go back to your hotel or, if you are spending the whole day visiting the tombs on the west bank, to get a meal (ordered in advance) at the local *Mersam* or *Abu* hotels, both on the left bank.

There are small ordinary restaurants along the Corniche in Luxor itself, and one on a terrace, called the *Merhaba*, where it is pleasant to linger, if only for the view.

Entertainment

An absorbing spectacle that lasts throughout the day is provided by the changing light of this marvelous setting. It begins about 5 o'clock in the morning, when the first golden rays of the sun strike the Western Peak, which stands like a natural pyramid above the amphitheater formed by the cliffs of the Libyan plateau. Bit by bit, the light creeps across the green fields and brown farmland, while the river swarms with overladen *feluccas*, the local ferry and boats of every shape and size.

Bathed in glaring white light at midday and tinged with blue in the afternoon, the landscape takes on violet tints as evening approaches. If you take a *felucca* trip on the river at this time, look up at the three sharp peaks known as the 'Three Brothers' outlined behind the town; their shapes have contributed distinctive signs for 'mountain' and 'desert' to hieroglyphic writing.

In the evening, you can see the *son et lumière* spectacle at Karnak, given in

LUXOR AND KARNAK   1 : 25.000

QENA 38 miles (61 km)

WESTERN THEBES

QURNA EL-GEDIDA

River Nile

Ticket Office

Vehicles

Department of Antiquit

Coptic Ch

Evangelical Church

Fran Chur

Temple of Luxor

Midan el-Hurriya

Souk

Post Office

Winter Palace

Stati

ISNA 42 miles (67 km)

EL-BAIRAT

Shari Salah ed Din

ASWAN 149 miles (240 km)

English on Saturdays, Mondays and Wednesdays, and in other languages on the other days. This is very evocative and should on no account be missed.

Shopping

(Map above C–3)

Market stalls are set out in the alleyways of the town center and in the tourist bazaar. Traditional souvenirs and mock antique-leather bags can be found here. You can have a *galabiyeh* or cotton kaftan made for you in a day.

Useful addresses

Egypt Air and the travel agencies have offices under the arcades of the *Winter Palace*.

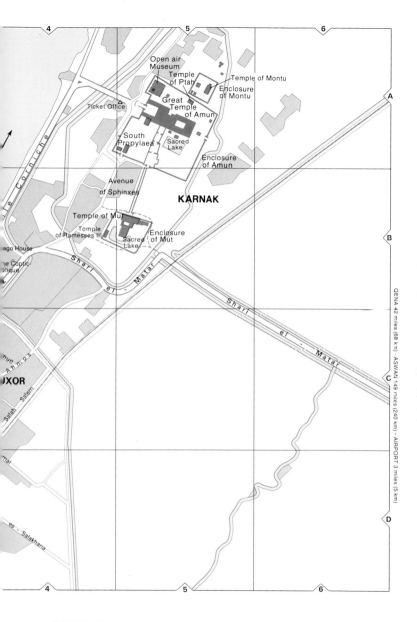

4   5   6

Open air
Museum
Temple
of Ptah

Temple of Montu

Enclosure
of Montu

Ticket Office

Great
Temple
of Amun

South
Propylaea

Sacred
Lake

Enclosure
of Amun

A

Avenue
of Sphinxes

KARNAK

Temple of Mut

Temple
of Ramesses III

Sacred
Lake

Enclosure
of Mut

B

ago House

e Coptic-
tique

S h a r i

e l - M a t a r

S h a r i

e l - M a t a r

nue
A h m o s

Salah Salem

JXOR

C

QENA 42 miles (68 km) - ASWAN 149 miles (240 km) - AIRPORT 3 miles (5 km)

D

mat

es - Salakhana

4   5   6

▬ VISITING THE SITES

Remember that Luxor is a sunny place and that, in order to enjoy
the beauty of its buildings and ruins to the fullest, you must take
account of the light. Certain temples should be seen early in the
morning, others late in the evening. The burial grounds and
hypogea, or rock-cut tombs, are best visited during the daytime.

The temple of Luxor★★★ (Map above C–3)

This should be included in the itinerary on your first visit. Go at dawn to see
the subtle changes of color in the sandstone and granite in the growing
light. Come back in the evening, if you can — up to 9 o'clock in winter and

10 o'clock in summer — because at that time the temple is perfectly lit. From the Corniche, you will see the handsome series of the colonnades; as you continue on into the courtyards, you will discover the scenes carved into its walls, indicating its special purpose.

The Egyptians called this building the 'harem of Amun'. It was used only at New Year, when the god's procession left Karnak to take part, amid great pomp, in the festival of Opet, which lasted nearly a month here. This perhaps explains the temple's comparatively modest size — 758 by 224 feet/260 by 59 metres and the long *dromos*, or walled avenue, flanked by human-headed sphinxes, which connected it with the temple at Karnak. The remains of long stretches of this have been discovered beneath the present road.

We know that the temple of Luxor was mainly the work of two of the great pharaohs, Amenophis III, the Memnon of the Greeks (1408–1372 B.C.) and Ramesses II (1298–1235 B.C.). The former had a temple of classic design built on the site of a Middle Kingdom temple, placing it on a raised platform to escape the Nile floods. Ramesses, a century later, added a double-colonnaded courtyard of impressive size, which he had to place askew, east of the central axis, to respect an ancient boat sanctuary which was found to be in the direct line of the central aisle. He then enclosed it by a monumental pylon, with two obelisks and six colossal statues in front. The enclosure wall, built in the 9th century B.C. by the Ethiopian pharaohs, and the chapel converted by Alexander the Great, did not detract from the splendid orderly arrangement of the building. The clearing of this temple nevertheless required immense effort on the part of archaeologists. This was begun by Gaston Maspéro in 1883 and is continuing today, because large sections were added to the structure over the centuries. Remains of Roman columns and Coptic churches have been found west of the sanctuary, and traces of a forum and military encampments on the east side. Even today, it is still not possible to dislodge the mosque from the solid masonry in the court of Ramesses II.

A suitable place to begin your visit is the pylon that Ramesses II added and had decorated, like all his temples, with scenes of the famous battle he fought against the Hittites at Kadesh. You will probably take only a brief look at this curious scuffle, in which the enemy is knocked head over heels and put to flight, while the Egyptian chariots, which fill most of the picture, remain in perfect order. Indeed, the pylon is nearly always in the shade except at sunrise. However, the original grandeur of this place is embodied in the perfectly-proportioned single obelisk. This bears hieroglyphs high-lighted in red and carved into each of its sides in three vertical rows; it stands on a plinth bearing four baboons worshipping the sun. In former times, the obelisk's pyramidion, tipped with gilded bronze, must have sparkled in the sun. In 1831, its twin was donated to France by Mehemet Ali. Flanking the gateway, there are two colossal seated figures of the king, with the figure of Queen Nefertari represented up to the height of the seat. Four other colossal standing figures in pink granite once accompanied them, but only one (badly damaged) survives. **The great court of Ramesses,** which you will enter next, is cluttered on the left with a mosque and on the right with the sanctuary of sacred boats built two centuries earlier. A peristyle of columns encloses it around the wall, and a wonderful row of colossal pink granite statues is slotted between the sandstone shafts now worn smooth. Take a look at this pharaoh, whose image is repeated 11 times, with his pleated loincloth and his left leg forward. On the connection fixing his leg to the column behind, you will also see the shaped or incised figure of one of his queens. The effect is stunning. You will then pass between two colossal seated statues of Ramesses in black granite. Note the figures of peoples conquered by the king on the base. You will then enter what remains of the **temple of Amenophis III,** a succession of porticoes and colonnades which time has endowed with extraordinary power and mystery while, at the same time, destroying the walls and ceilings that stood between them. There is first a grand colonnade consisting of two rows of seven columns; the immense shafts blossom into papyrus umbels and support massive architraves beneath the open sky. The arrangement then broadens out into a vast court in which the capitals on the bundle columns represent papyrus buds. Beyond this court, which is framed on three sides by a double colonnade, is the small hypostyle hall, with 32 columns in the same style. These gigantic arrangements of columns, which preserve, on a royal and divine plane, the petrified forms of the fragile plants of the Nile, lead into the secret part of the temple, which was altered in the Greco-Roman period. The shrine of the sacred boat, preceding the main temple sanctuary, was converted by Alexander the Great to contain an inner sandstone chapel open at both ends and decorated with scenes in which he appears. In one of the little rooms off to the left, you can see, with the help of a flashlight, the damaged reliefs illustrating the divine origins of Amenophis III, from his 'conception' by Amun to his birth, and his being suckled by goddesses.

From here, retrace your steps and try to imagine what the procession of Amun was like as it passed along these immense stone alleyways. Scenes carved on the sections of the walls and blocks of stone that have been spared by time will help you. In what was once the hypostyle hall you will see the procession of the *nomes*, the provinces of ancient Egypt; in the grand colonnade, its walls decorated by Tutankhamun, the ceremonies of the Opet festival; and finally, in the court of Ramesses you will be able to examine the well-preserved scene depicting the inauguration of the first pylon.

The Luxor Museum★★ (Map pp.106–107 B–3)

Situated on the Nile Corniche, this should not be missed. *Visit: daily 4 – 10 pm in summer, 4 – 9 pm in winter*

The objects on display relate to the art and history of Thebes. They are few in number, but are aptly chosen and displayed to best advantage. Beyond the entrance you will find two major items: a colossal head of Amenophis III in red basalt and, in a case, a painted wooden head of the cow-goddess, Hathor, found in the tomb of Tutankhamun.

All the objects on the ground floor are worth a mention, among them the head of Amenophis II, on the left; the basalt statue of Tuthmosis III, in the center; the limestone block with the profile of the same king outlined in deep colors; and the alabaster group representing the crocodile-god and Amenophis III.

In the loggia, there is a long display case containing a number of fascinating objects but the museum's most impressive items are exhibited inside. There is, first of all, the superb head of the revolutionary pharaoh Akhenaton, whose excessively elongated features convey his intense spirituality, while the mouth, with its full lips, reveals his zest for life. Next you come to the wall of *talatats*, or stone blocks, a patiently reconstructed wall from one of the temples to Aton, the sun disk, which the pharaoh built at Thebes and which were all destroyed by his successors. The 283 blocks were taken from the ninth pylon at Karnak. Measuring 60 feet long by 10 feet high (18 metres by 3 metres), the wall shows the king and queen paying homage to Aton on one side, and the store-rooms and warehouses attached to the temple of Aton on the other. The scenes are treated in a lively manner and reveal a number of previously unknown details about the methods used by the Egyptians to store their produce and to feed their livestock. They also throw new light on certain craft techniques. Above all, they present us with one of those very rare artistic achievements condemned to oblivion by contemporaries but seen by today's archaeologists as a major revelation of Egypt's genius.

As you go back down the stairs to the ground floor, note the niche taken from a Coptic church in the area.

Do not leave the museum without visiting the two rooms open downstairs. You will see photographs of the site of Karnak which will help you to know more about it, and a number of items showing amazing freedom of style created at the time of Akhenaton.

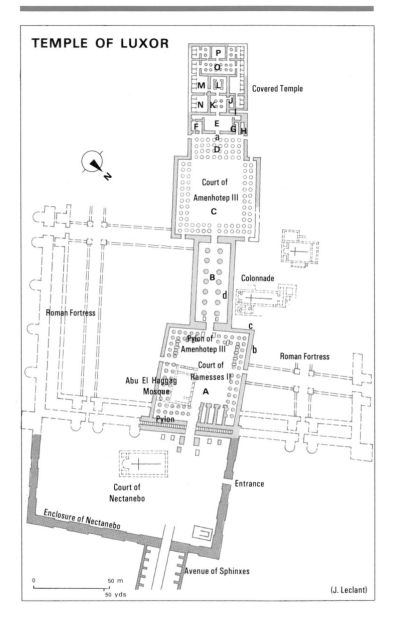

TEMPLE OF LUXOR

Covered Temple

Court of
Amenhotep III
C

N

Colonnade

Roman Fortress

B
d

c

Pylon of
Amenhotep III
b

Court of
Ramesses II

Roman Fortress

Abu El Haggag
Mosque
A

Pylon

Court of
Nectanebo

Entrance

Enclosure of Nectanebo

0   50 m

50 yds

Avenue of Sphinxes

(J. Leclant)

KARNAK★★

The **temple of Karnak,** (Map pp.106–107 A–5) dominates the entire site of ancient Thebes. It was built at the beginning of the second millennium B.C. by the city's founder-pharaohs in honor of Amun, its patron god, who had brought them victory. No one knows what the building was like at that time, because it has virtually disappeared. The temple you see now was built by the New Kingdom (1580–1085 B.C.) pharaohs: Amenophis, Tuthmosis,

Temple of Luxor, colonnade of Amenophis III.

Ramesses II and their successors. When they returned from their
glorious campaigns in Africa and Asia, from places as far afield as
Nubia and the Mitanni Empire (Armenia), they offered the bulk of
their booty to the god who had led them and, with it, made him the
richest property-owner in the country. Karnak is not the only
temple in Thebes to be dedicated to Amun. The pharaohs, who
were all considered sons of the 'king of gods', linked their own cults
to his in the funerary temples they built on the left (west) bank of
the Nile near their tombs. We know that, every year, on the

occasion of ritual festivals, Amun (or rather his effigy) left Karnak in procession to go by sacred boat on a visit to one or other of his 'secondary dwellings'. Thebes, in time, became a kind of metropolis of gods, among whom Amun reigned supreme; avenues lined with sphinxes led from one sanctuary to another. It is difficult for us to imagine life in that world, in which royal prestige and divine power were completely indivisible.

The history of Karnak throws some light on this concept. Karnak is based on a succession of gigantic buildings and campaigns of blind destruction. We know that the pharaohs, anxious to link their own glory to that of Amun, set their hearts on raising new pylons, statues and obelisks; many of them did not hesitate to usurp the achievements of their predecessors and to place their own cartouches upon them. What is more difficult to understand is why this destruction went far beyond its original purpose of clearing space and became acts of revenge. In ancient Egypt, people believed they could have the gates to eternal life closed to a dead man by breaking statues of him or works marked with his seal. Thus, all signs of the reign of Akhenaton, the revolutionary pharaoh, who had attempted to substitute the cult of Amun with that of Aton, were obliterated by his successors. Fortunately for us, the rulers of ancient Egypt, although destroying in this way some of the works of their predecessors, systematically reused the debris in the filling material, foundations and walls of their new buildings. Over the ages, Karnak became a gigantic, chaotic storehouse of stones, a puzzle on a scale measuring thousands of years which archaeologists are still trying to unravel. The best course for the visitor is merely to observe the splendor of these buildings, and leave the puzzle to the experts.

▬ *PRACTICAL INFORMATION FOR KARNAK*

Getting there

Karnak is about 2 miles/3 kilometres north of the temple of Luxor. You can get there by horse-drawn carriage by two different routes. The first follows the pleasant, shady Nile Corniche. About 1½ miles/two kilometres from the temple of Luxor, a road turns off to the right at right angles to the river. It ends at the entrance to the great temple. The other route goes right through Luxor from south to north along Shari Markaz. After passing a bridge over the canal and leaving the main road to Cairo on the right, it follows the visible part of the sacred avenue linking the two temples to the southwest gate in the Karnak enclosure, which it then follows round to the left. Either way, you will arrive at the jetty that once stood on the canal leading from the Nile and from which the sacred boat departed during important processions. You will have to use your imagination to recreate it as it was in its heyday because all you will see is a platform raised above the mud; all the gardens that once surrounded it have vanished.

However, the **avenue of sphinxes** is still in place and, as you walk along between the two rows of strange creatures with ram's heads towards the towering mass of the first pylon, you will understand the emotion of the explorer Champollion when, on discovering Karnak, he wrote: 'No people ancient or modern has ever conceived architecture on a scale so sublime, so vast, so grandiose.'

Tour

The **first pylon,** which forms the monumental gateway, is one of the most recent parts of the temple. It dates from the time of the Ptolemies, that is, from the 3rd century B.C., but it was never completed. By its sheer size and that of the prospect visible between its two towers, it makes you aware of the unique nature of the site before you even enter it. It comprises, in fact, a broad area of ruins surrounded by a quadrangular mud-brick enclosure 7920 feet/2400 metres in circumference and 26 feet/8 metres thick.

The **great temple** itself occupies not more than a tenth of this area, but its remains dominate all the other buildings that appeared over the ages to add to the splendor of the site: a succession of courtyards, stretches of wall and columns extends straight ahead of you. The various structures, which follow one after the other, are separated by five pylons that get smaller and smaller. To them are attached the names of the pharaohs who undertook the most extensive alterations to the building. They lie, for the most part, in ruins, and you will be able to identify them only with difficulty. What you will be able to pick out, on the other hand, is the line of five major features that make up the temple today: first, the great court, which extends before you and, measuring 328 feet wide and 263 feet deep (100 by 80 metres), is the largest of all known Egyptian courts; then the famous hypostyle hall of Ramesses II, followed by a curious maze of ruins above which obelisks rise; after this comes a strange open area where a Middle Kingdom temple once stood; and finally, the festival hall of Tuthmosis III, known as the 'Akh Menu'. This layout is quite unusual for Egyptian temples, due more to everyday practicalities than to architectural rules, and it reminds you of the way western cathedrals grew. A sort of processional avenue, or sacred way, also unique in the history of Egyptian architecture, completes it. This is preceded, on the same level as the hypostyle hall, by a furniture store-room to which the priests sent statues for which there was no longer any use. More than 17,000 of them have been discovered. Beyond it, to the south, there is a transverse complex consisting of a series of courts separated by four largely ruined pylons. The gateways to the south are difficult to pick out in the ruins if you do not know that they are aligned in the direction of the temple of Mut, to which they are linked beyond the enclosure wall by an avenue of sphinxes.

The sacred lake, on their left (east side), has been restored. The temple of Khonsu, on their right (west side), still has its pylon. Buried in the sand on the other side of the great temple, the small temple of Ptah contains two fine statues amid its ruins. The temple of Montu, which faces it beyond the enclosure wall, is closed to the public.

The wonderful story of archaeological discovery at Karnak is far from complete, as you will learn when you enter the great temple.

The first courtyard you will cross is the **Ethiopian Court,** where an immense sacred kiosk covered by a wooden roof was built in the center by King Taharka in the 9th century B.C. Of this, only one magnificent column remains, bearing its open papyrus capital high above the scattered fragments of identical columns lying round about. Rows of columns and ram-headed statues line the court on both sides. Two older structures complete the layout. On the left, in the northwest corner, the **temple of Seti II** retains its air of mystery. It comprises three sandstone chapels with doorways of pink quartzite, like the platform on which it stands. The **temple of Ramesses III,** the facade of which is embodied in the enclosure wall on the right of the courtyard, is a more imposing structure. This is a temple of the purest classic design. Its entrance is through a massive pylon decorated with traditional victory scenes, in front of which are two colossal statues of the pharaoh. Its courtyard is surrounded on three sides by Osiride pillars — that is, pillars with highly realistic mummiform figures of the king. Opening off on the right at the far end of the courtyard is the **Bubastite gateway,** which dates from the 10th century B.C.

A single damaged colossus of Ramesses II in pink granite stands before the **second pylon,** having lost its twin. The pylon itself and the vestibule preceding it are considerably damaged, but beautiful offering scenes still decorate the side walls of the vestibule. The gateway through the pylon is 97 feet/29.5 metres high and, although it has lost its upper part, it gives an indication of the size of what is to follow — the hypostyle hall.

The **hypostyle hall**★★★ is one of the finest spectacles on earth, a forest of

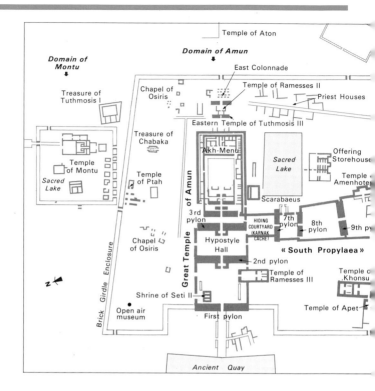

proud, simple columns that lead the eye up to the sky. It is said that the 12 columns of the central nave could accommodate 50 people on top of the open corolla of their papyrus capitals. Rising to a height of 76 feet/23 metres, they support the enormous architraves of a ceiling that is now partly missing.

Arranged on both sides of this royal avenue are 122 monostyle columns with papyrus bud capitals, forming a dense checkerboard pattern in each of the two wings. They rest on thin stone foundations at ground-level and are only 43 feet/13 metres high. The difference in height between the central nave and the side aisles or wings permitted an arrangement of clerestory windows in the form of stone grilles. You can imagine the unreal, mysterious atmosphere created by this dense screen of columns in the half light when the roofs were in place. Everything leads to the conclusion that this magnificent achievement was the fruit of a long period of gestation. It would have begun about 1375 B.C. as a simple colonnade leading to the shrine of Amun. Then, half a century later, Horemheb undertook the task of turning it into a huge station chapel along the route taken by the procession conducting the sacred boat to the temples on the west bank of the river. Ramesses II and his successors would then have completed his work. Indeed, ceremonial scenes, both large and small, that decorate the walls and columns are filled with their cartouches. Some still preserve traces of fairly crude color, which was intended to act as a background for the carvings and to make them stand out in the half light. You will probably remain in the hypostyle hall a long time but, before leaving, do not forget to have a look at the facades of the outside walls. On the north side, on your left, they recount the military exploits of Seti I, the father of Ramesses II; on the south side, on your right, they illustrate yet again the celebrated battle of Kadesh and the victorious campaign of Ramesses in Palestine.

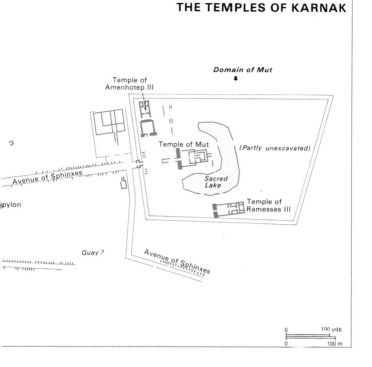

THE TEMPLES OF KARNAK

Domain of Mut

Temple of
Amenhotep III

Temple of Mut

(Partly unexcavated)

Avenue of Sphinxes

*Sacred
Lake*

pylon

Temple of
Ramesses III

Quay ?

Avenue of Sphinxes

Temple of Karnak, avenue of sphinxes.

In the debris from the **third, fourth and fifth pylons,** a jumbled mass of ruins, you can follow the continuous alterations indulged in by the ancient architects. Here, you will recognize one of the pink granite obelisks erected by Queen Hatshepsut rising out of the mass of masonry in which Tuthmosis III encased it after demolishing the other one. The **sixth pylon,** the last and the smallest, can be recognized by the two fine granite pillars standing detached from it on the far side. The one to the south is decorated with the plant emblem of Upper Egypt. The other, to the north, is decorated with the plant symbol of Lower Egypt. These were intended to support the roof of the chamber of historical records depicting the important events of the reign of Tuthmosis III.

Do not miss the **sanctuary of the sacred boats,** known as the 'Granite Chamber', the decoration on the outside of which was heightened with color. It illustrates the procession of the divine boats. You then come out into open ground where the original Middle Kingdom temple was built, a building that historical research will never be able to reconstruct.

The great temple continues with the Festival Hall of Tuthmosis III, the **Akh Menu.** This is another hypostyle hall, flanked by small chambers connected with the cult, and is entered by a narrow vestibule on one side. On your left you will, at once, notice a double row of columns, 10 columns in each row, and, around them, there are two rows of square pillars forming a peristyle. The columns in the center are unusual, a stone version of the wooden poles used to keep the canvas of large tents in place. No doubt their use by the architects conveys some meaning that is lost to us today. The decoration in the small adjoining rooms is of a rare perfection. Note the walls completely covered at the bottom with a jungle of intermingled exotic plants and animals, in what is known as the 'Botanic Garden', or 'Botanic Room'.

You can now enter the surrounding precinct through an opening in the wall enclosing the temple proper. You will be drawn at once towards the **sacred lake,** where the priests came at dawn to complete their ablutions; this has been restored. On the opposite bank, you will notice the remains of storehouses for offering and of the **aviary** where aquatic birds were kept. In front of you stretch the ruins of the priests' houses, one of which has been rebuilt.

Walk on along the lake to the northwest corner, noticing on the way, a large **granite scarab** dedicated to the sun-god and, at its feet, the debris of the upper part of Hatshepsut's south obelisk, which Tuthmosis III had embedded in masonry. Continuing in this direction, you will come to the remains of the pylons on the south side. Do not miss the limestone and quartzite colossi, nor the pink granite gateway with sunken relief decoration, which is all that remains of the **tenth pylon.** This opens onto the avenue of sphinxes leading to the temple precinct of Mut. Continuing to the right, however, you will come to the small **temple of Khonsu** standing among scattered blocks. This is a temple of classic design which must date from the end of the 20th dynasty, although the gateway belonging to it in the main enclosure wall is of the Ptolemaic period. It is not always open to the public.

If you enjoy exploring, go back through the hypostyle hall of the main temple and on to the little **temple of Ptah,** hidden in a grove of palm trees against the enclosure wall. The seated statue of the god in the central chapel is damaged but, when the door is closed, it is illuminated as if by magic by light coming in through the roof. The powerful black granite statue of Sekhmet, standing in the chapel to its right, also breathes an air of mystery.

End your visit to Karnak with a look round the open-air **museum,** for which you will need special permission. Situated in an enclosure a few yards to the left of the main entrance court, it has a classified and indexed collection of all the blocks found during the course of excavations. This highly specialized work would scarcely draw your attention had it not permitted a Middle Kingdom **station chapel,** known as the 'White Chapel of Sesostris', to be reconstructed in its original form. It is a kiosk or pavilion standing on a base measuring 21 feet/6.5 metres along each side and with a staircase on opposite sides providing access. Its roof is supported on 16 pillars arranged in four rows and decorated on the inside, like the low walls between them, with shallow relief carving of outstanding quality showing offerings being made to Amun. Carved on the outside is the only known geographical gazetteer of the Middle Kingdom. The building is a masterpiece. It is also an extremely rare example of Middle Kingdom architecture, which has almost completely disappeared.

As you leave Karnak, you will pass once more through the hypostyle hall with its forest of magic columns erected by god-kings and you might ponder the countless revelations this unique site still holds in store for mankind in the future.

Son et Lumière

The *son et lumière* spectacle will lead you through the labyrinth of this timeless temple and take you on an easy but complete tour through its various courts and from one evocative scene to the next, as far as the sacred lake.

WESTERN THEBES

At the time of the pharaohs, the west, or left, bank of the Nile at Thebes was a strange world inhabited only by the dead of high rank and by the living who were there to serve them — that is, the priests, workmen and staff of the necropolis who ensured that the daily funerary rites took place. What you will encounter when you cross the river, therefore, is the elevation of New Kingdom society to an eternal plane. In the rugged, steep-sided valleys hidden in the Libyan plateau, you will discover the tombs where the mummies of the pharaohs once lay, and, on the edge of the cultivated lands, the remains of temples where they received the offerings needed for their survival in the after-world and the homage of the people. Amid the bare hills below the cliffs, lie the tombs of notable people, viziers and courtiers of the second millennium B.C. Their decoration, even down to the details, depicts the vicissitudes in their contented lifestyle, which they hoped would continue into immortality. Finally, at the separate site of Deir el-Medina, where the laborers, masons, painters and sculptors who worked on the necropolis were gathered into a community, you will find rare evidence of the tombs and villages of ordinary folk in ancient Egypt.

It is, of course, impossible to fully explore all these vast sites with their countless secrets. Of the tombs and remains which it has been possible to identify, a large number are reduced to ruins while a good many others are undergoing repair and restoration work and are therefore closed to the public. It is, thus, difficult to plan a precise itinerary for your tour in advance. Only general guidelines can be given here.

THE TOUR OF THE SITES

Getting there

When you get off the ferry bringing you across the river from Luxor you will have a choice, if you are not with an organized group, of taking either a taxi, which may be expensive, or a bicycle, which is tiring in the midday sun but gives you a lot of freedom to get around. A donkey can only be used within the ruins and for short trips.

Valley of the Kings, tomb decoration.

Visiting the sites

Admission tickets for the various sites are obtainable only at the tourist landing-stage. Students and holders of discount cards can go to the Antiquities Service office near Qurnat Murai on the edge of the ruins. Take a small flashlight with you. Visits to the various monuments present no problems because there are always attendants on duty at the sites who will open them up in return for a few piastres.

Planning your visit to the sites depends on the time you have available. A circular tour is suggested here: traveling northward from the landing-stage and returning from the south. Every one of the sites described here is worth several return visits. Remember that the temple of Medinet Habu, its relief carvings among the finest in Egypt, should be seen when the sunlight is striking it at a low angle — that is, as late as possible in the afternoon.

▬ ON THE WAY TO THE VALLEY OF THE KINGS

After following the Dendera road a little more than a mile (2 kilometres), with the canal on your right, you will come to a country lane on the left that immediately passes close to the temple of Seti I at Qurna.

The temple of Seti I (Map pp. 122–123 C–6)

The temple built by Seti I, the father of Ramesses II, once headed an avenue of sphinxes used by processions coming from Karnak. Today it lies in ruins and, though not lacking in grandeur, it can be saved for a second or third trip to the west bank. Some 550 yards/500 metres further on, the road makes a broad sweep along the foot of the hills and enters the desert. After about 2 miles/3 kilometres, the road forks into two valleys hidden amid the surrounding rock debris. The tombs of the greatest pharaohs of the New

Kingdom are concealed here. We now know that all trace of them was supposed to disappear. Yet they were rediscovered in ancient times, and they aroused such public curiosity then that tourists came, it is said, from all directions to see them. Nevertheless, they were then forgotten for nearly 15 centuries, and when Napoleon's expedition happened by chance to open the tomb of Amenophis III, it brought about a worldwide revolution in archaeology. Discoveries followed, one after another, often the result of individual endeavor. The latest was the discovery of the tomb of Tutankhamun in 1922 which, for the first time, revealed those 'celestial households' destined for the pharaohs as they moved into immortality, and from which tomb-robbers nearly always managed to reap the benefit. The treasure of Tutankhamun has toured the world, and is, today, preserved in the Egyptian Museum in Cairo.

▬ THE VALLEY OF THE KINGS★★★
(Map p.122–123 B–2)

Of the 62 *hypogea*, or rock-cut tombs, which it has been possible to identify in the **Valley of the Kings,** some are no more than holes; others are in ruins. Only 10 can be visited. Their general layout is nearly always the same. An opening cut into the rock gives access to a long corridor reaching deep into the hillside. This is divided up along its length by constrictions, has a pit dug into it and is flanked by niches and side chapels. It opens out into one, or sometimes several, spacious chambers with ceilings supported by pillars. Next comes the tomb chamber, where the mummy, which has nearly always vanished, rested in a massive sarcophagus. It is, in a word, a sort of descent into Hades. Decoration unequaled in quantity and richness covers the walls, its themes taken from the great royal funerary texts: the Litany of the Sun, the Ritual of the Opening of the Mouth (which describes the rites required to reanimate the mummy to receive offerings), the Book of the Underworld (or *Amduat*) and the Book of the Gates (which identifies the king with the sun and traces the adventures of the sun as it journeys through the world of darkness). You will follow the pharaoh, in the guise of Osiris, as he navigates the underworld river the banks of which are peopled by demons, his solar boat piloted by the jackal-god accompanied by Hathor and Horus. You will witness the ceremony of the weighing of the soul. And as you do so, you will be penetrating a secret royal world that should have been closed for all eternity and which the heavy and somber atmosphere of the tomb invests with supernatural power.

Each of the tombs follows its own interpretation of certain general themes. Each speaks of the personal qualities of the king, the importance of his reign, and the length of time he was given in life to bring about the completion of his tomb. This was begun as soon as he ascended the throne and was sealed up, with nothing more being added to it, by his successors on the day of the funeral ceremony. Four of these tombs are especially noteworthy. You will approach them from the rest-house, where you will probably stop for a moment to gather your strength and escape from the implacable sunshine.

The tomb of Seti I★★★ (**no. 17** restoration in progress)

This is the most famous of all the tombs, and is on the left as you leave the rest-house. Beyond the entrance, you descend into 'Hades' by a flight of 27 steps leading to a corridor, from which a second flight of steps descends to another corridor ending at a deep pit designed to confuse robbers. A beautiful chamber with four pillars follows, concealed behind a wall by the builders. From it, another staircase leads through a further series of corridors to a chamber with six pillars flanked by small chapels. Finally comes the vaulted chamber, broader than it is long, where the sarcophagus was found. It is now in the Sir John Soane Museum in London. The royal mummy was discovered later, hidden at Deir el-Bahari. Another corridor, once hidden by a slab and now partly filled with fallen rock, leads off behind the sarcophagus. It seems that only the death of its owner prevented this immense tomb from being dug even deeper into the earth. In any event, it was left unfinished: in places, the decoration covering the walls is only sketched in with red lines. Its subjects are taken, one after the other, from the royal funerary books. On the second flight of steps, however, note the 75 transformations of the sun from the Litany and then the scene showing the god Horus and the peoples of the earth, symbolized by four Egyptians, four Asians, four Africans and four Libyans, which appears on the far wall of the first chamber. Do not miss the celestial cow dominating the starry vault in the little chapel to the right of the six-pillared chamber, and the sky of Egypt in the sarcophagus chamber.

The tomb of Ramesses III★★ (no. 11)

Situated along the road in front of the rest-house, the tomb of Ramesses III is famous for the decorations in the first corridor down. The scenes in the small chambers on each side are also of interest. Here you will see bakers and butchers preparing food; boats sailing up and down the Nile; the river making offerings of its produce to the gods of the fields and crops, and so on. The allegorical tilling of the fields of Yaru is also pictured, along with two harpists singing the praises of the king before the gods. It is to them that the tomb owes its popular name of the 'Harpers' Tomb'. After seeing the 12 figures of Osiris, you can end your visit at the end wall blocking the corridor. At this point, the tomb is displaced to the right and continues on into the rock for another 137 yards/125 metres, but the decoration is badly damaged and becomes conventional. When you emerge from the tomb, turn to the left and take the path that forks up to the right.

The tomb of Amenophis II★★ (no. 35)

The entrance to this tomb is at the foot of a sheer rockface at the end of the path. When it was discovered, the mummy of the pharaoh was found intact in the coffin. Around his neck was a garland of flowers and on his breast, a small bunch of mimosa blossoms. Placed nearby were offerings, provisions of food, vases and mummified birds. The tomb had, however, been robbed, as you will see during your visit. You enter by a steeply sloping corridor broken by several flights of steps and barred as usual by a pit many feet deep. In the chamber following it, there are the remains of the wall knocked down by the robbers. The walls and ceiling are completely bare and roughly finished, and still bear the marks left by the workmen. A flight of steps, followed by another corridor, leads into a chamber with six pillars. The yellow-gray walls are made to resemble an immense unrolled papyrus scroll on which the text and figures from the Book of the Underworld are outlined in black. The restraint of the decoration is powerfully moving. On the pillars, the pharaoh stands before the gods of the underworld. The dark-blue ceiling is adorned with yellow stars. Beyond the pillars, it lowers to form a sort of alcove containing the sarcophagus, which is still in place.

The tomb of Tuthmosis III★★ (no. 34)

This tomb is one of the most unusual in the whole necropolis. The entrance is 33 feet/10 metres above the level of the valley. Retracing your steps from the tomb of Amenophis II, take the first path on your right, and then turn off onto a track on the left 165 feet/50 metres further on. This track winds up a rocky cleft in the mountains that soon narrows to no more than 3 feet/1 metre wide. The setting is forbidding. You will find a staircase fixed to the rockface which provides access to a passage running into the cliff. You then descend a 45-degree slope to the usual pit, which completely bars the way. The large antechamber that comes next turns to the left. Its two square pillars are decorated with paintings in which the figures of 740 divinities can be recognized. In a corner, a flight of steps leads to an even larger chamber, its rounded corners giving it the shape of a huge royal cartouche. The walls are embellished with figures drawn in outline and with black and red cursive hieroglyphs that are not far from being graffiti and which stand out from a grayish background imitating the color of papyrus. All of this has something strangely modern about it and is quite different from everything else you see round about. Can this originality be attributed to ceremonial requirements or linked to the development of tomb art? No one knows.

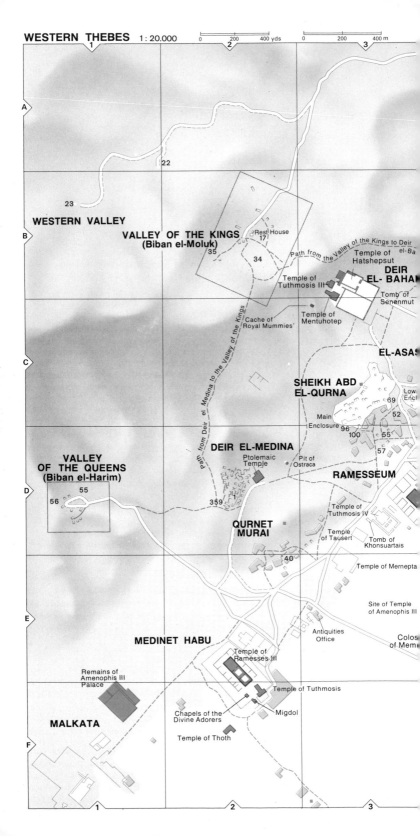

WESTERN THEBES   1:20.000

0   200   400 yds
0   200   400 m

1   2   3

A

B

22

23

WESTERN VALLEY

VALLEY OF THE KINGS
(Biban el-Moluk)

Rest House
17
35
34

Path from the Valley of the Kings to Deir el-Ba

Temple of
Hatshepsut

**DEIR
EL- BAHA**

Temple of
Tuthmosis III

Tomb of
Senenmut

C

Cache of
'Royal Mummies'

Temple of
Mentuhotep

EL-ASAS

**SHEIKH ABD
EL-QURNA**

Low
Encl

69

52

Main
Enclosure 96
100

55

57

Path from Deir el Medina to the Valley of the Kings

**VALLEY
OF THE QUEENS**
(Biban el-Harim)

56   55

DEIR EL-MEDINA

Ptolemaic
Temple

Pit of
Ostraca

D

359

RAMESSEUM

Temple of
Tuthmosis IV

**QURNET
MURAI**

Temple
of Tausert

Tomb of
Khonsuartais

40

Temple of Mernepta

Site of Temple
of Amenophis III

E

MEDINET HABU

Antiquities
Office

Colos
of Mem

Temple of
Ramesses III

Remains of
Amenophis III
Palace

Temple of Tuthmosis

Chapels of the
Divine Adorers

Migdol

MALKATA

Temple of Thoth

F

1   2   3

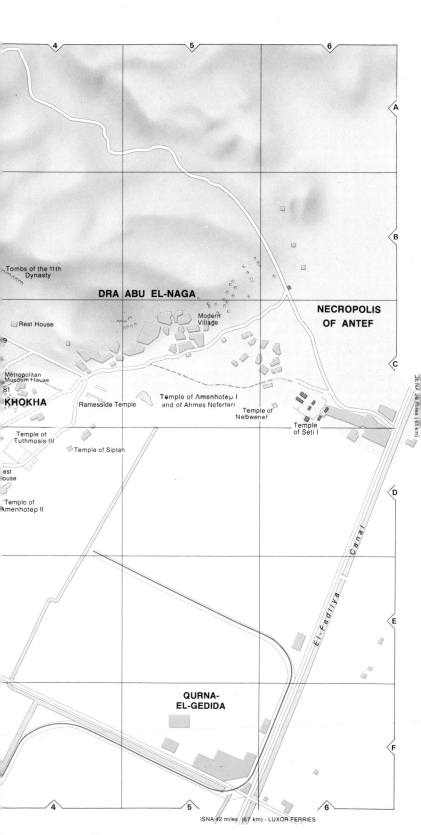

Other tombs you may wish to visit are:

The tomb of Ramesses IX (no. 6)

This is damaged but has a stunning long corridor. The sarcophagus chamber has preserved its decoration. The ceiling is covered with astronomical scenes across which is stretched the body of the goddess Nut who, according to myth, swallowed the sun each evening before restoring it the next morning. She has a lovely face.

The tomb of Merneptah (no. 8)

This tomb has an extremely steep and impressive corridor leading to the tomb chamber, which still contains the royal sarcophagus.

The tomb of Ramesses VI (no. 9)

The scholars accompanying Napoleon's expedition called this tomb 'the triumph of the transmigration of souls'. Its decoration gives the complete text of the books that helped the dead man to find his way in the afterworld.

The tomb of Tutankhamun (no. 62)

The entrance is opposite the rest-house. This is the only tomb to have come down to us intact. Soil and rubble from the tomb of Ramesses VI above it hid the entrance. It is scarcely believable that all the objects exhibited today in the Egyptian Museum in Cairo, even if taken to pieces, could have been packed into these four tiny rooms. The sarcophagus is still in position, and the mummy lies in it, protected by four goddesses. The paintings on the wall showing the pharaoh's funeral are fairly poor in style and bear no relationship to the richness and refinement of the treasure now stored in Cairo. The dissimilarity admirably illustrates the dramatic story of the prince who died too young to have prepared his tomb or to have mapped out his path to immortality.

▬ *THE TEMPLE OF DEIR EL-BAHARI*★★

(Map pp. 122–123 B–3)

The amphitheater of cliffs, where the **mortuary temple of Deir el-Bahari** was built for the queen-pharaoh Hatshepsut by her favorite, the great architect Senenmut, is quite close to the Valley of the Kings.

You can reach it from there by a track that climbs up the cliff-face. From the 980-foot/300-metre summit you will look down over the surrounding country and the marvelous terraces of the temple before clattering down the rocky slopes toward them. Although tiring, this walk, which takes about three-quarters of an hour, gets you away from the tourist atmosphere for a while. Find a guide to go with you but refrain from buying his antiquities. You can also go straight to Deir el-Bahari by taxi or coach. In this case, you follow the same route you took to get to the Valley of the Kings but you turn off to the right less than a mile (1 kilometre) before Qurna. You will go through the huge necropolis of Dra Abu el-Naga, where the tombs are too ruined to be worth stopping for on your first visit. You will eventually arrive at a complex of buildings that is unique in world architecture — or, at any rate, in Egyptian architecture.

Once preceded by an avenue of sphinxes, the temple complex has three magnificent colonnaded terraces anchored to the cliff behind. Ramps cutting through the center link them together and lead to a sanctuary cut into the rockface and out of sight. The site on which this sanctuary is laid out is of special significance. From the earliest times, it was dedicated to Hathor, the beautiful goddess with cow's ears who was the goddess of love and happiness. It is rich in sacred ruins. However, only the temple of Hatshepsut has been rebuilt and it is this which gives the landscape its superhuman aspect today. The Polish expedition responsible for its reconstruction is concentrating on the task of restoring its features and proportions down to the last detail. Of course, they cannot resurrect the bustling activity of the time of Senenmut and, in its restored state today, it seems somewhat cold. Nevertheless, the work being done here will one day give us a faithful reproduction and that, in itself, is quite a feat.

Tour of the site

Your visit will be restricted to the first two terraces and the adjacent remains. The **lower terrace** is bounded by broad, low walls and has a row of 15 columns arranged behind square pillars on each side of the first ramp. The retaining wall behind them is completely covered with bas-relief decoration illustrating, on one side, the erection of the obelisks at the temple of Amun at Karnak and, on the other, ritual fishing and hunting scenes. Little T-shaped fountain basins, arranged symmetrically in front of the colonnades, were once adorned with decorative plants. As you go up the ramp you will see the large lion which protects the royal name of Hatshepsut.

The **second terrace** is, by far, the most beautiful. It is bounded on the right by 15 proto-Doric columns noted for their purity of style; behind these are four niches. The deep colonnade along the back of the terrace forms a unified structure of wonderful classic style. On each side of the second ramp, there is a double row of square pillars which, at the right-hand end, leads to a small chapel cut into the rockface and dedicated to Anubis. Behind the colonnade, there is a beautiful limestone wall decorated with flat reliefs that are among the most interesting in Egyptian sculpture. On the right, you will see the divine conception and birth of the queen and her accession to the throne. On the left, note the wonderfully illustrated chronicle of the trading expedition the queen sent to the land of Punt (Somalia), which was one of the principal events of her reign. The carvings depict boats at anchor in a river and inquisitive native people. Next comes the exchange of Egyptian manufactured goods for local treasures, and the loading of the ships with precious objects, rare animals, gold, ivory, ebony, panther skins; also represented is the enormous queen of Punt following her thin husband. These last scenes are only casts, because the originals were removed and are now on display in the museum in Cairo. The story of this expedition ends on the upper register of the wall with a triumphal procession to the temple of Amun. Here the proceeds are recorded by the god Thoth and the incense measured by Hatshepsut herself, who finally appears before the god who gave her life. The carvings tell a delightful story that is unique in Egyptian art and provide an insight into the political and religious activities of a pharaoh.

From here, go around to the left-hand edge of the terrace to reach the **chapel of Hathor,** which was also built by the architect Senenmut. This is a small rock-cut temple, at the front of which are two hypostyle chambers containing very beautiful Hathoric capitals. The bas-reliefs in the second chamber have preserved the decorative scheme celebrating the festivities held in honor of the goddess. Note, especially, the bird and boat races on the rear wall. The chambers cut into the mountainside are decorated with scenes of worship and offering ceremonies. The architect of this complex took care to sign his work by having a picture of himself carved behind the doors of several small niches, presumably so that he could take part in the cult ceremonies without being seen!

The **third terrace** is in a badly dilapidated state and you will probably not be allowed access to it. There is not much to see in any case, except the great serpent twisting up the low parapet wall of the ramp and the pink granite doorway opening into the sanctuary court. The court itself is in ruins, as are the hidden underground chambers beyond.

Before leaving Deir el-Bahari, take another long look at the temple's setting amid the surrounding country. Then try to persuade the attendant to open the tomb of the man to whom the world owes this unequaled masterpiece, the architect Senenmut, which lies about 33 feet/10 metres to the right of the lower terrace. A long corridor broken by flights of steps leads down to a small chamber. Opposite the entrance, Senenmut has left his own portrait. In the next room there is an astronomical ceiling indicating the houses, or regions, of the sky and the constellations.

THE PRIVATE CEMETERIES

After leaving Deir el-Bahari, you will begin your visit to the private cemeteries, which are immense. Not many of their surface structures are left; the courtyards or terraces laid out in front of the tombs are often in ruins, and the small pyramids that rose above a number of them have all disappeared. You will see, however — and you are unlikely to tire of it — the decoration of their wide vestibules, which is brimming with extraordinary vitality and reflects Theban society through its activities, work, pastimes and sports. The wall paintings here repeat, after an interval of a thousand years, the scenes you have already marveled at in the *mastabas* at Sakkara, but they are now the product of a more flexible and homely attitude to art. They are full of flashes of humor but also include sensitive touches. They reveal, too, a change in fashion, with large, enveloping, heavily pleated white robes replacing the earlier short tunic. Musical instruments are slightly different. New animals such as the pig and the horse have appeared, but there are still the same *fellahin* bent over the same labors, the same marshes, the same landscape of reeds and river mud such as you find today along the banks of the Nile — the eternal landscape of Egypt.

Tour

The first cemetery you will pass through after leaving Deir el-Bahari is the one at **Asasif** (Map pp. 122–123 C–3). Its tombs are in ruins. Those on the hill at Khokha, nearby, are more interesting. You may wish to break your journey to see the courtyards of the **tombs of Kheruef** (no. 192) and **Puymre** (no. 39), and the **double tomb of Nebamon and Ipunky** (no. 181), sculptors to the king.

The huge necropolis at **Sheikh Abd el-Qurna** (Map pp. 122–123 C–3) has a collection of masterpieces on a totally different scale. This is the cemetery of officials of the 18th dynasty, the period of the conqueror-kings. It is vast and extends in a series of clearly-marked sections over a hill crowned by a village. The tombs have entrances that stand out as dark brown blobs against the light-colored background of the rocks. They all have the same general plan. In front, there is a terrace, or court, in which biographical stelae are arranged. The facade is broken up by close-set bays. It opens into a broad vestibule decorated with scenes showing the owner in the exercise of his earthly duties and occupations. A corridor follows in a straight axis from the entrance and leads to a recess where statues of the dead man and his near relatives stand above the tomb. The walls of the corridor are generally given over to scenes depicting the funeral rites. In following this simple plan, some of the tombs attain a rare beauty. Begin with the tombs in the smaller precinct, which is demarcated by a low boundary wall surrounded by bare rocks.

The tomb of Nakht★ (no. 52), the scribe and astronomer of Amun in about 1400 B.C., is one of the best preserved. Its decoration is unfinished, but it wonderfully evokes scenes of country life in great detail. You will particularly admire those showing the cultivation of cereal crops on a plain watered by a little meandering canal. In it, the people are laboring, breaking up the soil hardened by the river mud, sowing seed and digging. The scenes of fishing and harvesting in the delta, where the owner probably had estates like everyone of his station, are equally charming. You will also notice the beautiful offertory tables. Equally noteworthy is the scene depicting the funeral feast with its musicians, dancers and blind harpist and the cat devouring a fish beneath the chair in which Nakht's wife is sitting.

On the hillside behind the village, look for **the tomb of Menna** (no. 69) which is very well preserved; the colors of its decorations are fresh and attractive. The scenes are arranged in their usual positions, the most interesting on your left as you enter. In these, the scribes, palette in hand, are checking the measuring of the harvest. On the wall to the right, there is a long procession of Menna's sons and daughters. In the corridor beyond, note also the funeral scenes taking place in the presence of Osiris, and the pilgrimage to Abydos.

Three tombs close to the road to Medinet Habu are also worth a visit:

The tomb of Kenamon (no. 93), chief steward to the king (1450 B.C.), is in a dilapidated state but has preserved its vestibule of eight pillars and its funerary chapel, also of eight pillars, both of which are extremely impressive.

The tomb of Sennefer (no. 96) is often referred to as the 'Tomb of the Vines'. It is cut into the rock at the bottom of a flight of 43 steps and the decoration on the ceilings forms a veritable bower of bunches of black grapes. The walls are covered with scenes of offerings. On the left, as you enter, note the dead man and his wife, first sitting in the stillness of the tomb, then standing and emerging from the ground to see the sun in the courtyard.

The tomb of Rekhmire★★ (no. 100), the vizier of Tuthmosis III, though damaged in many places, is one of the most intact tombs of the period. On the walls opposite the entrance there is, in addition to the usual agricultural scenes, an illustration of the ceremony in which foreign peoples brought their tributes each year. Filing past, one after the other, are envoys from the land of Punt, wearing short clothes and bringing ebony, ivory, monkeys and leopards; people from Kefti (Cretans), with their long tresses and sandals, bearing vases and gold objects; black people from Kush (Nubia), dressed in panther-skin loincloths, leading jaguars, monkeys, giraffes and sturdy oxen with long horns; Syrians laden with various offerings and, finally, black women leading their children by the hand or carrying them on their shoulders or in baskets. Up and down the procession, scribes are recording the 'revenues'. Note the chapel, which has a curiously sloping ceiling that rises into the mountain.

Your visit will end with two of the most beautiful tombs, which are hidden among the buildings of the village itself.

The tomb of Khaemhat, also known as **Mahu** (no. 57), royal scribe and inspector of the granaries of Upper and Lower Egypt, is at the back of a courtyard which has several other tombs of the same period opening onto it. It contains relief decorations. The funerary recess is here hollowed out to make a chamber containing six finely modeled statues. The decoration combines the usual scenes with scenes of deeper meaning.

The tomb of Ramose★★★ (no. 55), who was the grand vizier of the schismatic pharaoh Akhenaton, remains the finest of all the tombs. Its vestibule is nothing less than a hypostyle hall. Its decoration, though unfinished, is magnificent. You will note the fine quality of the carving as well as the variations in style. In some scenes, the decoration keeps to the accepted rules and proportions, as in the banquet scene covering the walls on each side of the entrance. In others, it is marked by the characteristic 'Amarna' style — that is, by the freedom of expression injected into the art of the time by the pharaoh in accordance with his new religious ideology. The scenes filling the walls opposite the entrance, which are unfinished, follow the same trend. Here, Ramose is seen before the king and queen, receiving his honorary collars. He is also being acclaimed by his servants and congratulated by his peers and foreign representatives. The scene of the funeral banquet, filling the whole left-hand wall of the chamber, is a mixture of both styles. It is a remarkably arresting picture, and you will not tire of gazing at even its smallest details.

▬ THE RAMESSEUM★★
(Map pp. 122–123 D–3)

The remains of the **Ramesseum,** the mortuary temple of Ramesses II standing on the edge of cultivation about 1600 feet/500 metres from the necropolis of Sheikh Abd el-Qurna, marks a return to classic art in all its grandeur. Today, the Ramesseum consists of nothing more than great stretches of walls and a magnificent cluster of columns standing out against the desert sky. It was once one of the most beautiful temples of antiquity. A colossus of Ramesses lies in fragments on one side of the court, its huge tranquil face buried in the grass. It gives the site a dramatic, unearthly atmosphere. The temple's first pylon, to the left, is still partly standing. On it are carved military scenes that can only be picked out in an oblique light. They record the campaigns of Ramesses against the Hittites and Syrians, and the battle of Kadesh. Beyond the immense ruined court, which is now open to the surrounding countryside, you will find a pictorial account of the pharaoh's legendary battles, carved on what remains of the second pylon — that is, the right-hand tower. It is a terrifying spectacle. Standing in his chariot, the pharaoh charges over piles of corpses, while the river encircling Kadesh carries along countless bodies of drowned men. Note the soldiers holding their commander up by his feet to expel the water he has swallowed. The carnage is all the more striking because, in the upper register of the wall, a peaceful agricultural festival is taking place in honor of the god, Min.

The second court may be identified by a number of Osiride pillars and papyrus columns that demarcate the original layout. Before passing on, look at the double procession of Ramesses' sons and daughters on the wall containing the entrance to the next chamber; this may be reached by a short flight of steps.

You will then enter the **hypostyle hall,** where 29 of its 48 columns are still standing. They are of considerable beauty, even though damaged. In the center, they are arranged in two rows of columns with bell-shaped capitals while, on each side, there are rows of shorter columns with papyrus capitals. The ceilings are still partly in place and painted dark blue with yellow stars.

The small hypostyle chamber following the main hall still has its eight columns and astronomical ceiling. The next chamber is partly demolished while the sanctuary has completely gone. All around, as you walk through, you will find traces of countless other features of the temple, among which storehouses, a school for scribes, and priests' quarters have been identified. This tremendous complex once filled the ancient Greeks with wonder, and it is sometimes compared to the Parthenon.

▬ DEIR EL-MEDINA★
(Map pp. 122–123 D–2)

After leaving the Ramesseum, continue on to the most interesting part of the Theban west bank, comprising the remains of the village that once housed the quarrymen, masons, sculptors — all the workmen, in fact, from the royal necropolis. A path leads straight to it but you will need a guide. It is better to go by the road used by taxis and coaches. You will first pass through the necropolis of Qurnet Murai, but do not stop here. Its tombs, which are decorated with paintings on plain rough surfaces, are only of real interest to experts, since they are badly damaged. Beyond a gentle curve in the road, you will enter the little valley of **Deir el-Medina.** The houses in the village, of which a few walls survive, were piled up one against the other. They are very simple structures made of sun-dried brick. Occasionally you may be able to pick out a few traces of paintings. The bottom steps of a number of staircases indicate the presence of cellars or terraces. Walk as far as possible around the tombs, which are scattered over the hillside. Two of them are open to visitors. They are small but their decoration is remarkable for its freedom of style and brilliant colors. The more interesting of the two is the **tomb of Sennedjem,** whose grave furnishings were recovered intact and removed to the museum in Cairo. The effects achieved by the use of white, blue and brown in the scenes on the ceiling are delightful. The **tomb of Ipuy** is of cruder construction but it has lively representations of animal deities set among hieroglyphic texts. At the edge of the village, you will see a small **Ptolemaic temple** which has preserved its main features. About 250 yards/200 metres away is the excavation site from which nearly 5000 flakes of limestone known as *ostraca* were removed. Overseers of work did their calculations on them, and they have allowed us to get an idea of the activities of the workmen whose lives were dedicated to the dead.

THE VALLEY OF THE QUEENS
(Map pp. 122–123 D–1)

On your right after leaving Deir el-Medina is the Valley of the Queens. Its tombs are currently being restored. You will, however, be able to visit one built for a young son of Ramesses III, unequaled in the freshness of its colors and draftsmanship. Beside it is the tomb of a baby prince whose mummified remains have defied the passage of time.

MEDINET HABU★★★
(Map pp. 122–123 E–1–2)

The temple of Medinet Habu, which you will now discover set back against a nearby hillside, is one of the most splendid in Upper Egypt.

You will probably be glad to take some refreshment at the little *Habu* hotel by the entrance to the ruins, while waiting for the light of the setting sun to splash the various structures, pylons and large expanses of relief carvings with its changing colors. The temple emerges in all its beauty at this time.

Medinet Habu is an immense complex of buildings dominated by the presence of Ramesses III (1198–1166 B.C.), who had a palace built in it next to his mortuary temple; traces of this may be found on the ground. Grouped around the temple proper, the complex contains various chapels and additional structures of the Ethiopian and Greco-Roman periods, as well as the remains of a temple of Tuthmosis — that is, a temple dating from the beginning of the New Kingdom (1580–1450 B.C.). After sheltering a Christian community among its ruins in the first centuries A.D., the site was to become a source of stone for the local *fellahin*, who were only too happy to plunder its ready-cut blocks. As a result, restoration work here is particularly difficult. It has, nevertheless, managed to bring back the original impressive grandeur of the site.

Medinet Habu is entered by the triumphal gateway Ramesses built into the thick walls of his enclosure, the military nature of which is quite clear. This is the Migdol, a sort of fortress modeled on the ones the pharaoh had laid siege to in Asia and which you will see in battle scenes in the relief decoration of the temple. Two groups of captives, from the North and the South, are carved in relief at the top of the sloping walls; they symbolize the pharaoh's victories. We know there was a similar gateway built on the west side of the precinct. On the inside, the gate tower is like the central portion of a royal pavilion that has now vanished. Its upper floors are inaccessible but their decorations and pretty harem scenes have been preserved.

The first remains, on the left, are those of the **temple of the Divine Adorers** which consisted of the two adjoining funerary chapels of princesses of the 25th and 26th dynasties (750–650 B.C.) who were adorers of Amun. The earlier contains the oldest example of stone vaulting in history. Turn to the right, where pungent-smelling plants are everywhere overrunning the stones, and wander through the remains of the **temple of Tuthmosis.** It is said to have once possessed a rare elegance and, although numerous later additions have altered its appearance, you will recognize the beauty of its proportions. Finally, you will come to the great **temple of Ramesses III.**

The massive first pylon has a facade 207 feet/63 metres wide that is decorated with the customary fighting scenes. Here they are devoted to the pharaoh's victories over the Sea Peoples of the Mediterranean. Ramesses is seen sacrificing captives to Amun, who holds out a sword to

The Colossi of Memnon.

him. Note the deep ruts worn in the paving by chariots passing through the gateway. The next courtyard provided the setting for great ritual festivals. It is bordered on the right by seven Osiride pillars with engaged figures of the king and, on the other side, by a portico of eight columns with bell capitals. This curious arrangement came about because the portico formed the facade of the royal palace, the ruins of which you will see during your visit. The wall behind the columns is pierced by three doorways and a balcony, from which the king watched the ceremonial processions. The wall is decorated with martial scenes and fighting sequences in which there seem to be movements like those in judo. It is worth walking around the courtyard to admire its decoration, which is carved surprisingly deeply and which combines military and religious themes. Then pass on through the second pylon by the pink and black granite doorway.

The second court is very impressive. It is framed by colonnades, two of which — those on the right and left sides — have columns with bud capitals, while the others have damaged Osiride pillars. The different treatment of the fourth colonnade, leading up to a gently sloping ramp, and the additional depth provided by the row of columns set behind the pillars, lend the whole court considerable splendor. Significant traces of color can be detected on the columns, reliefs and ceilings. The decoration on the walls reads from left to right. You will be particularly interested in following the procession of the god Min, which continues from the doorway at the rear of the court along the wall to the right-hand tower of the pylon.

Beyond the hypostyle hall, of which only the shafts of a few columns remain, the temple lies in ruins. This part was exploited as a quarry for stone. Nevertheless, take a moment to go up the aisle leading to the innermost recesses of the sanctuary. Climb on to the terraces and look out over the ruins and the plain beyond. Then turn left and return along the outside of the temple. You will soon come to the remains of the **royal palace,** which consists of just a few brick walls. The vestiges of extremely well-appointed apartments can be identified here.

At this point, you will be facing the outside walls of the temple's first court and, if the light is right, you will be able to enjoy one of the most wonderful relief scenes in the whole of Egyptian art. It fills the return wall of the pylon and depicts a royal hunt with exceptional freedom and vitality. The detailed observation is astounding, especially in the sequence where wild bulls, to escape the danger, are plunging into the marshes and disturbing its customary tranquillity. The scenes adorning the other walls catalogue the pharaoh's campaigns. Medinet Habu's masterpiece, a splendid naval battle which ran along the outside of the north wall of the great court, has unfortunately been removed to the museum in Cairo. It depicts the ships and weapons used in the dramatic encounter and perfectly captures the physical characteristics of the pharaoh's adversaries. It is the first appearance of the Sea Peoples in art. Before continuing on your way, climb to the top of the main pylon as the sun is setting and, in the distance, watch the last rays striking Karnak and Luxor, the ancient city of Thebes.

▬ THE COLOSSI OF MEMNON
(Map pp. 122–123 E–3)

To return to the Nile from Medinet Habu, take the road to the right at every fork. After passing the Antiquities Service building you will come to the famous **Colossi of Memnon.** These stand imposingly below the road amid the cultivated land where the children play. These two impassive giants, whose gaze is directed above their earthly surroundings, once flanked the entrance to the funerary temple of Amenophis III, one of the most remarkable at Thebes. They are figures of the pharaoh. The one on the right collapsed during a terrible earthquake that destroyed the temple in 27 B.C. It then became famous because it was said to emit a musical sound at sunrise, and people came from far and wide to marvel at it. The Greeks, in particular, were much struck by this, so much so that they identified it with Memnon, the son of Aurora. Two centuries later, however, the Roman Emperor Septimius Severus had it repaired and from then on it stopped singing.

NILE CRUISES

When you return to the Nile at dusk, you will see people with their square faces and narrow eyes expressing friendly cheerfulness and occasionally, malice — so very much like the people you have briefly mingled with in the ancient cemeteries. You can continue your journey through this vibrant country along the river which gave it life.

TRAVELING INTO EGYPT'S PAST

You have a choice of several methods of traveling. The first, the details of which have been described on previous pages, involves going by road, either by bus or private car, to any one of the major sites around Luxor: north to **Abydos** 93 miles/150 kilometres, the sacred city of Osiris, and **Dendera** 37 miles/60 kilometres, where a temple dedicated to Hathor was built during the Roman period; south to the three temple complexes of **Isna** 31 miles/50 kilometres, **Idfu** 62 miles/100 kilometres and **Kom Ombo** 106 miles/170 kilometres, dating from the centuries around the birth of Christ. These trips are exciting but tiring, and you will not find much at the rest-houses except drinks that are fairly cool.

You can also travel along the valley by train, using the slow train that everybody takes and which stops everywhere you could possibly want it to stop. The scenery might lose some of its lively impact this way but, on the other hand, you will gain by spending a few hours in close company with delightful people who are otherwise difficult to get to know. Be prepared, however, to be trapped in the crush of people piled up to the luggage racks and bustling to get on and off at every station, with sellers passing incessantly offering cool drinks, kebabs, toys and footwear.

There is, finally, the boat, which is the most restful way to travel and the one most used by tourists. You may miss many of the ordinary, everyday sights but you will be retracing the route used in ancient times by the gods to travel from temple to temple, by the pharaohs to launch their expeditions into deepest Africa or the famous land of Kush, and by the Nubian slaves who came to work on the estates of the kings and priests. This was also the route taken by the architects, quarrymen and sculptors seeking the granite of Aswân or the sandstone of Silsila, these artisans to whom Egypt owes its wonderful heritage of monuments.

▄▄ *BOAT TRAVEL ON THE NILE*

Nile cruises are available only as part of an organized tour. For a long time, they were the special preserve of only the most privileged travelers. But, today, they are available to everyone as a result of the increase in the number of boats in service, a list of which is, unfortunately, impossible to forecast six months in advance. The biggest hotel chains have their own fleets, as do many of the travel organizations, and the boats available, like the hotels they link up with in the itineraries, range in grade from 'deluxe' to simply 'tourist'.

The **Nile Emperor,** put into service in 1982, is the leading ship in the Nile fleet at present. As well as 60 double cabins, it also has 20 single cabins, which is unusual. It provides the same services as any hotel of international caliber.

The **Hatsheput,** brought into service in 1984, is a cruise-boat of the ultimate in luxury, with 33 double cabins and suites with panoramic lounges.

The **Aton, Any, Tut** and **H Top,** which belong to the Sheraton hotel chain, are of the highest standard of comfort and service, as are the **Isis** and **Osiris,** which are owned by the Hilton chain. Restaurants, panoramic lounges, bars, boutiques, a sun-deck, swimming-pools and promenade deck all contribute to the enjoyment of a voyage on these boats.

The **Club Méditerranée** has two boats: the **Nile Queen,** with 40 cabins, and the **Nile Prince,** with 30. The sun-deck, swimming-pool and wide windows in the cabins and restaurant allow you to take full advantage of the scenery. The particularly relaxed atmosphere and the excellent cooking contribute to the success of a cruise on these boats.

Other top-grade boats include the **Nile Concorde, Nile President, Nile Sphinx** and **Nile Dream,** as well as the **Imam, Horus** and **Triton.**

Boats with accommodation ranging from 16 to 30 cabins seem to be in favor with travel organizers. They allow smaller groups to be accommodated conveniently and facilitate shorter trips, although the services provided are not always up to standard. These include the **Hoda, Rev'Vacances, Pyramids, Ramsis, Nefertari** and **Cleopatra.**

Other boats, such as the **Memphis, El Salam** and **Nile Explorer** are used at peak tourist periods.

The most important new development in 1984 was the setting up of *felucca* trips for tourists. It is now possible to go down the river, just carried along by the breeze that barely makes the huge sails move and stopping on the way at the sites you wish to visit. It is a fascinating adventure, because it allows you to live for a week or two in the company of Saidis and Nubians, with their traditional customs, and to discover the real country. However, it can be very tiring because you have to share the same boat and meals prepared by the *felucca*-man with eight or ten other people and to sleep in the open wrapped in a sleeping-bag.

As a final choice, the first motorized inflatable rubber boats appeared on the Nile in 1984, and you can take a trip up the river in groups of two or four, camping along the banks as you go.

Whatever means of travel you choose, the itinerary planned for you will be the same. The boat will leave from Luxor for Aswân, or vice-versa, and you will stop off at the temples of Kom Ombo, Idfu, Isna and sometimes Dendera and Abydos.

Some agencies are willing to arrange cruises for eight people on private boats but the itinerary remains the same.

STOPPING-OFF POINTS

A tour of the more northerly sites is only rarely included in Nile cruises but this is a wonderful trip and it takes in Abydos and Dendera. You leave ancient Thebes (that is, modern Luxor) via the royal route that follows the broad meanders of the river between its busy shores. Overloaded *feluccas* with their tall sails glide by upon the calm waters, passing barges heavily laden with stones and ore and rafts stacked high with porous jars, some of which hang in nets. After 37 miles/60 kilometres you will reach the Qena bridge, and then, 43½ miles/70 kilometres further on, the Nag Hammadi barrage. At the point where the barren Arabian mountains close in on the right, you will disembark at **Baliana.** From here a track will take you to the edge of the cultivated land and the site of Abydos, one of the most mysterious centers of pharaonic Egypt.

Abydos★★

Abydos was once the holy city of Osiris, the god of resurrection, and the world's first place of pilgrimage for people in search of hope. Today, it is just an expanse covered by sand which looks as if some ancient cyclone had blown over it but a strange atmosphere still haunts the site. It is thought that some of the cemeteries lying along the foot of the Libyan escarpment date back to the end of the fourth millennium B.C. What is known for certain is that, for a thousand years, from the beginning of the Middle Kingdom to the end of the New Kingdom, people of all ranks thronged there to take part in a yearly celebration. This celebration commemorated the quest of Isis, who restored life to Osiris by finding the various pieces of his dismembered body. According to legend, the head of the martyred god was buried there. It was here that the pharaohs erected cenotaphs, or memorial tombs, in order to be near the god who presided over the judgement of souls in the underworld. Leading figures of Egyptian society also raised family stelae here. These have been found in the thousands and can now be seen in museums around the world. Nothing remains at Abydos except the wonderful ruins of the temple built by Seti I, (father of Ramesses II), the cenotaph known as the Osireion which he added to it, and the remains of the temple of Ramesses II.

The temple of Seti I does not resemble any of the ones you may have visited at Thebes. It is a tremendous votive offering made to seven gods all at once: first to Amun-Ra; then to Osiris, Isis and their son Horus; next to Ptah, the god of death and of the world's creation; then to Ra-Harmakhis (Ra-Harakhte), the sun-god associated with the gates of the afterlife; and finally to the deified Seti himself. As for the decorations, there is nothing particularly awesome about them: they celebrate the immortality rites of Osiris. The first two courtyards of the complex have been completely leveled, and the entrance to the temple itself is through a portico completed under Ramesses II, the decoration of which records the cult dedicated by the pharaoh to his father after death. Go straight into the first hypostyle hall, which has two rows of papyrus columns aligned with seven doors opening into the second hypostyle hall, which is deeper. There is then a third row of columns standing on a low platform, beyond which seven more doors open into seven chapels. These are arranged in a line side by side and are dedicated to the gods whose images appear all over the columns and walls of the two previous chambers. The complete design, modulated around the number seven, has a mysterious simplicity about it. What will undoubtedly impress you most, however, is the decoration of the second hypostyle hall and the seven chapels. The composition, which is both self-assured and charming, the relief carving, the profile figures with their purity of line, all painted in pastel tones on the finest and whitest stone, are among the most beautiful left to us by

Nile felucca.

pharaonic Egypt. Here you will wait for the sun to illuminate the innermost chambers, which are divided into two parts by columns and darkened by the restoration of the curved stone ceilings. As a precaution, it is a good idea to take a flashlight with you.

The back of the temple is of less interest but in the long passage known as the Gallery of Kings or Hall of Ancestors, which opens from the second hypostyle hall at right angles to the temple's main axis, you will find the famous **Abydos list of kings.** Here Seti I is seen burning incense and reciting prayers of offering before the cartouches which represent the names of the 76 pharaohs who had reigned over Egypt before him from the time of the legendary Menes (Narmer). This is one of the clues used by historians to decipher the succession of ancient dynasties. The rooms off this corridor are in a very bad state of ruin. You will scarcely be able to distinguish the abattoir of the sacred animals. A flight of steps midway along the corridor leads up to the flat terrace roof of the temple, and you will go up it to get to the Osireion.

The **Osireion** is a fantastic hole in the ground which is flooded for much of the year and in which enormous pink granite pillars supporting architraves are still standing. On these, a roof may have rested, and on top of this it is assumed there was a little wooded hillock. Entered by a passage that makes a right-angled turn and passes through antechambers or vestibules lined with texts from the funerary books, the Osireion is closely related to the *hypogea* of Thebes but this is a *hypogeum* that time has opened to the sky. This deep and empty tomb is reflected in the stagnant water of the pool from which a little island rises as a symbol of the creation of the world. It is likely to leave a deep impression on you.

If you have a moment left to wander through the ruins of the **temple of Ramesses II,** you will not regret it. Here, notice the subtle effects created by the use of different kinds of stone: alabaster with black granite, and sandstone with pink granite and white limestone. The reliefs on the remaining sections of wall and the lower parts of the structure, filled with fascinating details, are also worth a mention. Be sure to see the great procession in what was once the second court, with its bulls and gazelles, soldiers rallying in response to a trumpet and lines of Libyan, Nubian and Asian prisoners, and then the scene of the sacrifice of the bulls. You will then sail back up the Nile through the same shifting but unaltered scenery as far as the track that leads off to Dendera on the right, less than a mile/1 kilometre before the Qena bridge.

Dendera★★

Wonderful ruins standing amid peace and silence beyond a screen of palm trees on the edge of cultivation — such is your first glimpse of the temple at Dendera dedicated to Hathor. Hathor was the goddess with the cow's ears and the symbol of happiness and love whom the Greeks renamed Aphrodite. Built during the Greco-Roman period — that is, 15 centuries after Karnak — the temple was undoubtedly preceded by other sanctuaries the remains of which have long since disappeared. A partly ruined gateway and two fountains stand at its entrance. The gate forms an opening in the thick mud-brick wall that encloses the sacred precinct. Here you enter a huge forecourt, where you will be immediately confronted by the facade of the hypostyle hall, with its six splendid Hathor-headed columns connected by low screen walls. On them you will recognize the *sistrum,* the sound of which was believed to dispel sickness and grief. The hall, itself, is a wonderfully harmonious structure. Its capitals bear the face of the lovely goddess on all four sides and support a 49 foot/15 metres-high ceiling decorated with astronomical representations. Among them you will see the scene in which the goddess Nut, enrobed in the waves of the Celestial Ocean, sends the sun out into the world each morning.

You can then go up to the roof to get an overall view of the temple and its surrounds. On the left of the entrance court, among the piles of rubble lying around the temple, you will be able to locate the two *mammisi,* chapels that appeared at the end of the pharaonic era and in which the mysteries of the god's birth were celebrated each year. Between them, you will be able to pick out the ruins of a Coptic church and, closer to you, the brick remains of the sanatorium, which received the people who came here seeking miraculous cures. Turning round, you will then be able to pick out the ruins of a temple dedicated to Isis, situated at the back of the main temple. Finally, on your right, there is a wonderfully preserved sacred lake, where a palm tree has grown. The sanctuary is hidden in the corridors which flank the labyrinth of increasingly dark chambers. Here, too, is a quite extraordinary series of crypts hollowed out of the thickness of the walls, where divine effigies, ceremonial objects and temple treasures were kept. The entrance is very narrow, and there is a wealth of detail provided on the wall just outside, indicating its precise function. The meticulous decoration, which also comprises an endless number of inscriptions all over the temple, is not to all tastes but, for the experts, it has the advantage of illustrating in detail all the ceremonies that took place there. In the carvings on the staircase walls, going up on the west side and descending on the east, you can follow the procession bearing the statue of the goddess up to the temple roof. Here it was carried once a year so that the rays of the rising sun might infuse it with renewed divine energy. The ceremony, hidden from profane eyes by walls built on top of the roof, took place in the kiosk, which is one of the most elegant surviving examples.

After wandering around the ruins, it is not difficult to imagine the great annual procession that accompanied Hathor along the Nile to Idfu, the abode of her husband and then, after 15 days of great rejoicing, returned her to her own domain.

You will then carry on upriver in the direction of Luxor.

Isna★

You begin your southward journey up the river following its broad meandering course between high banks of silt, which then become squeezed between the two rocky crags at **Gebelein.** You then bypass a barrage and stop at a village which, like all the villages of the Nile Valley, is situated along the river's bank. In this little farming community, through which camels often pass to cross over the bridge, you will at first see only a few capitals rising above the level of the street. Then you will suddenly discover an amazing forest of 24 perfectly preserved columns, buried over the years in a depression in the silt; they still support enormous architraves carrying a ceiling 44 feet/13.5 metres high. This is all that remains of the temple built during the Roman period in honor of Khnum, the ram-headed god, and it is quite amazing. Its abundant decoration, predominantly in the form of inscriptions, is of priceless value to archaeologists who are rediscovering, from them, the rituals followed in contemporary festivals.

Your journey continues up the Nile through a pleasant cultivated plain. On the right, 12½ miles/20 kilometres from Isna, a huge brick wall recalls the vanished temple of **Nekhbet,** the tutelary goddess of Upper Egypt. The mountains come down to the river, then recede and rise again and there, standing amid the palm trees and houses of a small village, are the twin towers of a pylon. This is Idfu, your next stop.

Idfu★★

Here, you will discover one of the greatest temples of ancient Egypt, second only to Karnak. Today, it stands cut off from its precinct, the chapel annexes built around it, and its sacred lake, which are all buried beneath the town and its concrete low-income housing. Yet its majestic structures have survived intact. This is the temple of Horus, the solar falcon-god and protector of the pharaohs, and two black granite falcons flank the entrance.

Following pages: the temple of Idfu.

It was built during the Ptolemaic period (327 B.C.) but it remains faithful to the great pharaonic tradition of architecture and it is so well preserved that it helps us to get a better understanding of the buildings that preceded it. Its immense pylon is decorated with the classic scene in which the king is seen sacrificing prisoners. Try and persuade your guide to take you to the top. From there, you will be able to see the layout of the temple.

Beyond the colonnaded forecourt, you will see the imposing structure containing the two hypostyle halls, then the outline of the rectangular block enclosing the chapels radiating around the sanctuary. The whole building is contained within a massive wall, which is connected directly to the pylon and leaves a long narrow passage between it and the temple. It is the archetypal ancient temple. You can follow its structural details from the pylon to the holy of holies as it rises symbolically through a series of chambers that get increasingly smaller and darker as they approach the secret shrine containing the sacred statue of the god. Facing you in the first courtyard, there is a famous crowned statue of Horus. Here, you can walk beneath the colonnades, where you will notice that each capital differs from the one next to it but is repeated on the other side. The wide hypostyle hall that follows has kept the screen walls that shield it from prying eyes. A somewhat unusual effect is achieved by the relative slenderness of the first row of columns. On your right, you may be able to distinguish the library, which has a sort of catalogue of the papyrus scrolls kept in the temple carved on its walls. The second hypostyle hall is less wide, and deeper. There follows next a maze of chambers connected with the temple rites, their decoration indicating their particular functions. In one of them, known as the 'laboratory', scholars found the list of items used in the ceremonies. The sanctuary still contains a superb *naos*, or shrine, cut from a solid block of gray granite and which came from an older temple.

Then go up on to the roof terrace where the ceremony of the 'Union with the Solar Disk' was regularly celebrated. This ceremony exposed the statue of the god to the sun's rays and regenerated the divine impulse within it. The procession accompanying the statue is shown on the walls of the staircase. The whole temple is covered with inscriptions and detailed scenes illustrating the ritual festivals for which it provided the setting. On the way out, pause for a moment by the pylon where, on the base of the inside wall, the most famous of these celebrations can be seen taking place: the marriage in which Horus and Hathor, the goddess of Dendera, were joined together each year. You can see the divine bride's fleet of boats arriving and, for a brief moment, you will be able to relive the glorious events as the priests inside the temple perform the rites in the presence of the pharaoh while, outside, the crowds of curious onlookers wait for the god to welcome the goddess on the landing stage. If you have a moment left before departing, take a walk around the long corridor separating the temple from its enclosure wall.

Beyond Idfu, the river broadens out again to its normal width. The Arabian mountains fade briefly into the distance to make room for a long fertile plain. The valley then narrows once again, its width reduced to little more than that of the Nile itself. The Gebel Silsila, the 'Mountain of the Chain', constricts the river so tightly on the Libyan plateau side that it is claimed a mountain chain once blocked its way at this spot. This is Egypt's oldest and most productive sandstone quarry and it is still being exploited. From here, the river begins to meander. Along the banks the gold of deserted beaches and the green of terraced fields create a patchwork of alternating contrasts. At length, the river enters a vast stretch of territory which it has been possible, with the help of irrigation, to reclaim for the cultivation of sugarcane. This is New Nubia. Its villages bear the names of the ones that were submerged by the waters of the Aswân Dam. You are now in the area of the *wadi* of Kom Ombo. Sacred ruins perched high above a sheer drop command the Nile at the point where it makes a sharp bend. Seldom during your trip has the setting shown a monument off to such perfection.

Kom Ombo★

The ruins of the temple of Kom Ombo rise against the deep blue sky from the sand dunes at the edge of cultivated fields. Dedicated to two deities, the falcon-god Haroeris and the crocodile-god Sobek, it was accordingly laid out along two parallel main axes, corresponding to two temples. You will see its remains as you walk through. The columns of the great hypostyle hall display an astonishing variety. As in all the temples of the Greco-Roman period, the abundance of carved inscriptions may surprise you. Among the reliefs in the outer passage, you will come across a tray covered with surgical instruments, no doubt an allusion to the talents of Sobek the crocodile! You will be left with impressions of a light-colored temple reminiscent of the Acropolis of Athens.

The valley now begins to narrow, and the fields are reduced to small groves of palms which give the scenery the appearance of an oasis. Soon the sandstone rocks will give way to granite. Rows of yellow sand dunes march away toward the west, while to the east the rocks grow dark. The cliffs close in as if to shut off the valley and then suddenly spring apart to enter the majestic rock amphitheater of **Aswân.**

ASWÂN AND NUBIA

Aswân is the site of the first cataract, a stretch of rocks and roiling water that bears no similarity to the broad, straight-channeled, calm Nile you have just sailed up. The unusually harsh terrain here is enclosed by the sands of the Libyan plateau to the west and a brooding amphitheater of hills to the east. The river with its *feluccas* picks its way among the black granite islets, while Elephantine Island, the ancient capital, seems to float upon its surface. People in ancient times thought that land ended there. They also believed that the river's silt-laden floods gushed from a mysterious chasm hidden beneath its rapids at the command of the god Khnum. Today, Aswân still controls the life-giving waters but now by means of a colossal dam. The swirling waters of the past are abating.

Nubia, which the pharaohs were determined to keep under their domination, had two-thirds of its land incorporated within the boundaries of Egypt. In more recent times its people, chased from their villages by the waters of Lake Nasser, have sought asylum in Aswân. The wonderful serenity of its skies has not changed, nor the marvelously benign winter climate and the splendor of its scenery.

Aswân's history or, rather, that of Elephantine Island, is long. At the beginning of the third millennium B.C. it was already a trading center to which desert caravans brought ivory, skins from the Sudanese grasslands and the colored spices that you still sometimes see in huge piles in the markets. It rapidly became a strategic site where the pharaohs kept a garrison and through which their expeditions passed on their way to Nubia and Kush. For 3000 years, Aswân was the site of constant coming and going, as people arrived from Memphis or Thebes to work in the quarries, where they carved the obelisks, huge granite shrines, and the coffins that you have admired during your tour of the Nile Valley. Now Aswân is a delightful, small village inhabited mostly by pure brown-skinned Nubians. It is bound to expand in the future, because the Aswân Dam is here, with its high-tension cables and its promise of development.

PRACTICAL INFORMATION

Getting to Aswân

You can get to Aswân by boat, disembarking along the Corniche, or by train (16 hours from Cairo), arriving at the station in the town center, or by air, landing at an airport that is still under military control 9½ miles/15 kilometres away in the desert near the dam. It is connected to the town by coach.

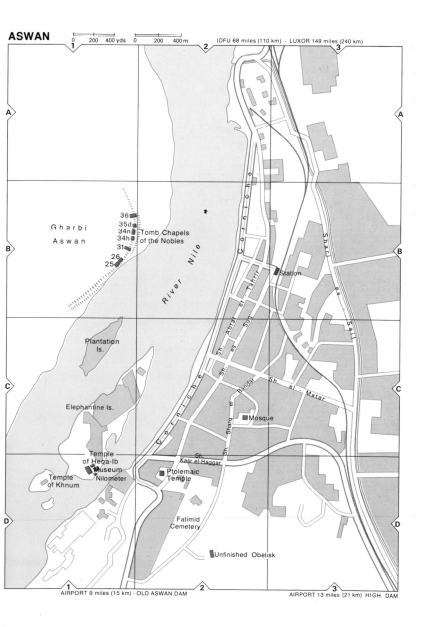

ASWAN

0   200   400 yds   0   200   400 m

IDFU 68 miles (110 km) - LUXOR 149 miles (240 km)

Gharbi Aswan

Tomb Chapels of the Nobles

36
35d
34n
34h
31
26
25

River Nile

Plantation Is.

Elephantine Is.

Station

Sh. Abtal et Tahrir

Sh. es Suq

Shari es Sail

Sh. el - Matar

Bandar

Sharr el

Mosque

Temple of Heqa-Ib
Museum
Nilometer

Temple of Khnum

Sh. Kasr el-Haggar

Ptolemaic Temple

Fatimid Cemetery

Unfinished Obelisk

AIRPORT 9 miles (15 km) - OLD ASWAN DAM

AIRPORT 13 miles (21 km) HIGH DAM

Accommodation and dining

These go together. There is a choice of three excellent holiday hotels: ▲▲▲▲**Aswan Oberoi** (Map p. 143 C–2; tel. 76–28–35; telex 92120). The newest hotel situated on Elephantine Island, it has 150 rooms of the highest standard of comfort. It is an ideal holiday center, despite its somewhat cold exterior. It has a swimming-pool, tennis court, facilities for horseback-riding in the desert, a sports club, two restaurants, one of which is at the top of the tower, a bar, shops and a nightclub. A ferry service links the hotel to the right bank.

▲▲▲▲**New Cataract** (Map p. 143 D–1; tel. 76–73–95; telex 92720) is at the southern end of town overlooking the Nile from a rocky promontory. Recently built, the hotel is extremely comfortable with well-furnished rooms and pleasant service. The swimming-pool overlooks the river in a lovely exotic garden.

▲▲▲**Cataract** (Map p. 143 D–1; tel. 35–76/34–34; telex 92720), next to the *New Cataract*, is a long-established hotel of great charm.

Two recently-built hotels have a full complement of rooms for visitors: ▲▲**Kalabsha** (Map p. 143 D–1; tel. 22-999; telex 92720) has 120 basic but comfortable rooms.

▲▲**Amun** (Map p. 143 D–1; tel. 22-555; telex 92720) is situated on the small island of the same name and connected to the bank by motor-boat.

Also worth mentioning is the ▲▲**Abu Simbel** (Map p. 143 C–2; tel. 22–888; telex 92720). There is a youth hostel on the Corniche (Map p. 143 B–2).

Getting around Aswân

By taxi or *felucca*, either of which can be arranged through your hotel.

Entertainment

The scenery provides the major distraction, and you will never tire of looking at it. At dusk, go to the terrace at the old *Cataract Hotel* to watch the beautiful procession of *feluccas* on the river. You can also attend performances of Nubian dances at the theater on the Corniche.

Shopping

You may not want to buy anything, but you should certainly take a stroll around the **souks** (Map p. 143 C–2) lining the Corniche in the Sudanese bazaar that once brimmed with exotic goods. You are sure to find brightly-colored local basketwork and, like everywhere else, knick-knacks brought in from Cairo.

▬ TRIPS BY FELUCCA

Aswân owes much of its charm to *feluccas*, so you will naturally want to make some trips on the Nile's placid waters. Local boys expertly pilot their craft between the islets, catching the slightest breath of wind to give them motion.

Elephantine Island (Map p. 143 C–1)

Measuring 1640 yards long by 547 yards wide, (1500 by 500 metres), this is the original site of the town. It was here that trading caravans from the Sudan and Nubia ended their journeys during the third millennium B.C., and it was probably one of the first customs posts in the world. It was also from here that expeditions were mounted into the south by the pharaohs. Today, it is a garden filled with palm trees into which two Nubian villages are still tucked, unfortunately overshadowed by the heavy outline of the *Aswân Oberoi* tower to the north. A number of relics from the past are assembled in a little four-roomed **museum** (Map p. 143 D–1) here, which is open from 9 am to 2 pm every day except public holidays.

A short distance away, amid the stones of a quay that some people ascribe to pharaonic times, you will find the famous **Nilometer**, about which the Greek geographer Strabo wrote around the time of Christ. It allowed experts to forecast the time and size of impending floods. Unfortunately, it is now in a badly ruined state. A staircase of 90 steps descends into the Nile. On it, you can read the height of the greatest floods. Nearby, you will be able to identify the ruins of the Ptolemaic **temple of Khnum,** the god of floods, and a number of sarcophagi which once contained the rams that were sacred to the temple.

Plantation Island (Map p. 143 C–1)

Once known as **Kitchener Island,** this is a very short distance away by boat. It is a botanic garden where all kinds of tropical Asian and African species grow together. Enjoy a stop there for a while amid the symphony of colors, scents and bird songs as you drink a glass of *karkadé* at the rest-house. After that, you can go on into the desert on the left bank.

▬ THE AREA AROUND ASWÂN

The rock-cut tombs of the nobles of Elephantine★
(Map p. 143 B–1)

These are arranged in tiers up a hillside and are difficult to reach because the sand has covered the steps leading up to them. If you have the energy, climb to the top of the hill where the adventurers who opened up the African trade routes at the beginning of the third millennium B.C. lie in eternal rest. According to the inscriptions, one of them discovered the pygmies. From the height of their tombs you will enjoy an extremely beautiful panoramic view over the Nile, the town, the lush green islands, the black rocks of the cataract and the straight line of the dam.

The mausoleum of the Aga Khan

The mausoleum contains the tomb of the Aga Khan (1877–1957), the supreme religious leader of an Ismaili Muslim sect comprising about four million believers, mainly in Pakistan. It commands the desert bank of the Nile, and the journey to it, first by *felucca* then by camel if you wish, has a certain picturesque charm. Within a 20-minute walk from here across the sand, you can reach the impressive ruins, flanked by towers and lookout turrets, of one of the oldest Christian monasteries, the **monastery of St. Simeon.** It is an experience not to be missed.

Seheil Island

Allow three or four hours for the round trip to visit the island. Fix the price before embarking and remember to bargain! This lovely excursion will take you away from tourists into the maze of rocks where, it is said, the god Khnum concealed the mysterious chasm containing the river's precious silt. The island itself once commanded the crossing over the cataract. Sesostris III (1878–1843 B.C.) had a canal built along the bank to permit his little fleet of ships to sail on to Nubia and the mysterious land of Kush. Along the way you will notice the inscriptions left by the kings and explorers who, over the ages, ventured into these parts between the river's submerged black reefs. They cover the rocks that lie around the island to the south. Climb over them and look down over the cataract. Notice the carved stele nearby, the 'Famine Stele', with its apocryphal inscription telling of the homage paid by King Zoser (*c.* 2700 B.C.) to the god Khnum to entreat him to bring to an end seven years of drought.

The unfinished obelisk (Map p. 143 D–2)

We know that, from the beginning of the third millennium B.C., Aswân granite provided the outer casing for pyramids and, because of its durability

Nubian village at Aswân.

it remained the favorite material for temple obelisks and sarcophagi until the Roman period. Throughout the whole region, therefore — on the islands and among the mountains to the east — signs of quarries have been found that were all the more numerous because there were highly valued crystalline rocks, as well as the famous granite, hidden around Aswân. Less than a mile from the town you will see an **unfinished obelisk** 138 feet/42 metres long, the cutting of which was probably stopped when

Return from fishing.

a crack was discovered in the granite. Note the regularly spaced slots cut into the rocks round about. They show the method used by the Egyptians to detach the blocks they needed. After marking out the shape, the stonecutter inserted into the slots wooden wedges which, when wet, swelled and split the stone. When the work was completed, the polished blocks were gently slid down sloping ramps to the river bank — or rather, onto grounded rafts which rising floodwater would then set afloat.

A few years ago, a sculptor attempted to detach a carved head of a pharaoh from a quarry using dolorite hammers, wooden wedges and flints — and he succeeded.

THE DAMS

To visit the high dam and the temples of Kalabsha, visitors who are not members of an organized tour must first get permission from the police.

When you set off toward the south from Aswân, you will first pass the old Fatimid cemetery on the left. On the hill to the right, cenotaphs were erected in memory of the most revered holy men of Islam. After another 3 miles/5 kilometres, the road reaches the **old dam.** Nearly 1½ miles/2 kilometres long, it was built in 1898 using granite blocks from nearby quarries. Its height was raised in 1907, and it was strengthened again between 1929 and 1934, in the process, submerging Nubia for 183 miles/295 kilometres. However, it soon proved to be inadequate. Today, it provides a pleasant walkway through the rocks of the **cataract,** the water of which, lying placid and still above the dam and a raging torrent below, now operates an electric power station. The road then climbs the cliffs commanding the left bank of the river and crosses a stretch of desert as far as the small community created at the time of the construction of the high dam. It is signposted some distance ahead by the huge concrete lotus flower commemorating its inauguration.

The high dam
The **Sadd el-Ali,** the Egyptian name for the high dam at Aswân, is a colossal undertaking and one of the most impressive of its kind in the world. The statistics speak for themselves. Measuring 1508 million cubic feet/42.7 million cubic metres, its volume is 16 times that of the Great Pyramid and more than half that of the earth removed to dig the Suez Canal. It is 590 feet/180 metres wide at the base and 131 feet/40 metres wide at the top, 11,815 feet/3600 metres long and 364 feet/111 metres high. The artificial lake it has created has a length of 310½ miles/500 kilometres, of which 93 miles/150 kilometres lies in the Sudan. Its width varies between 6 and 18½ miles (10 and 30 kilometres). It retains 5545 billion cubic feet/157 billion cubic metres of water, thus ranking second in the world after the Zambezi Dam. Dimensions such as these are enough to dumbfound you. They certainly ensure that the water of the Nile can be stored up, whatever the size of the annual flood and that the harvests can be saved from the age-old uncertainties of the past. They can best be accounted for by the dramatic size of the problems presented to the Egyptian government by the unrestrained growth in population, increasing by 800,000 people a year in a country that is 96 percent desert. For President Nasser, whose name is still associated with this achievement, the problem was twofold. In addition to providing desperately needed irrigation of farmland, particularly the rice fields, and continuing to expand areas of cultivation, employment had to be created for the extra rural population. The dam was meant to provide what new industrial development had always lacked — a source of energy. At the right-hand end of the dam you will see a diversion channel supplying a power station equipped with 12 turbines. Electricity output is now 2.1 million kilowatts per hour.

The objective of the **Aswân Dam** was, in short, to set the Egyptian people on the road to modernization. It was a revolutionary idea but Egypt could not achieve it alone. It is well known that the United States, like other western nations, refused to participate financially in the project and that the Soviet Union took on the responsibility. Preliminary studies were made in 1955. Among the problems which had to be overcome was the piling up of sediments over 656 feet/200 metres thick above the cataract, which made it impossible to anchor an arch dam. Therefore, thinking turned to a gravity dam. Work on the site began in 1960. In 1964, a ceremony was held to mark the first flow of water from the now permanently blocked Nile down the diversion channel. At the end of 1972, when the filling of the lake had been completed, the dam was inaugurated amid great pomp by President Sadat and Soviet President Podgorny.

The time to draw up a first balance-sheet appraisal of the dam has now arrived. The high-tension cables that cross the landscape and the various industrial complexes along the Nile Valley can be entered broadly among the positive results of the scheme. So, too, can the definite stabilization of the level of the river, which ensures it is navigable all the time and, as a result, the tourist cruise-boats are the first to benefit. However, the debit side of the balance-sheet is continuing to grow. It was known that the sacrifice of Lower Nubia, with the displacement of 60,000 of its inhabitants, would create serious human problems. People around the world are also aware of the tremendous effort made by UNESCO to save part of its artistic heritage by resiting, among others, the temples of Abu Simbel, but what we are discovering today are the ecological consequences of this colossal enterprise. Fertile silt is now accumulating behind the dam, while the farmers are forced to buy chemical fertilizers. There is an irreplaceable loss by evaporation of part of the water in the lake, which is exposed to the sun over too large an area. A change in the climate has ensued: clouds now appear in the sky over Aswân where, for the first time in history, rain has fallen, throwing the local people into a panic. There is also an increase in the salt content of the soil, which is the outcome of excessive irrigation and results in crops being scorched and the foundations of ancient temples being undermined. Finally, there is the change in the fauna of the delta, which no longer receives a flow of silty fresh water and is being invaded by species from the Red Sea that are ruining the fishermen. Perhaps it is also due to the Aswân Dam that sharks have appeared in the Mediterranean.

When you leave the dam, you will follow the right bank back to town. On the way, you will see a huge unfinished statue of Osiris in the sand. You will then go round the **Kima** industrial complex, which uses electricity from the dam to produce the nitrogenous fertilizers now needed by the farmers.

If you are not going on to Abu Simbel, you will, perhaps, have time before leaving Aswân, to visit two sacred buildings that were saved from the rising waters of the dam.

▬ *THE RESITED TEMPLES*

The temple of Philae★★

On the island of Philae, where it was built, you will no longer see the temple begun there by the last pharaohs (the 30th dynasty) and finished by the Romans. Situated between the two dams, it was already flooded for six months of the year by the rising water of the first dam, when the construction of the second one condemned it to vanish forever. The Egyptian government was galvanized into action and decided to save the complex, which was one of the last pharaonic temples 'in operation'. We know that the cult of Isis attracted pilgrims there from Nubia and Greece until the middle of the 5th century A.D. The **temple** was, therefore, resited with the assistance of UNESCO. Its buildings were first surrounded by a coffer dam 49 feet/15 metres high and 6½ feet/2 metres wide which permitted them to be kept dry. Then, following techniques tried out at Abu Simbel, they were dismantled, each of the stones being carefully numbered, and finally rebuilt on the nearby small island of **Agilka,** where the ground was landscaped to provide the same surroundings they had had where they were originally built. This colossal operation, begun in 1972, was completed in 1980, and a tour of the temple is now one of the most romantic in Egypt. From a cove you will take the motor-boat which waits for visitors there and speeds you across the water toward the shimmering temple pylons that dominate the landscape. Your first stop will be at the

kiosk of Nectanebo, the columns of which stand above the water at the southern end of the island. Dating from the 4th century B.C., they are the oldest on the site. They stand before a *dromos*, or sacred avenue, which is marked out by two colonnades. The one on the left is completely covered with scenes of offerings inscribed with the cartouches of Augustus, Tiberius, Claudius and Nero, while the one on the right remains unfinished. Go along the right-hand side to a small stone door, on which you will see a row of Greek characters accompanying a hieroglyphic inscription. The **first pylon** that now rises before you is 59 feet/18 metres high and 148 feet/45 metres wide. Its surfaces are decorated with scenes of prisoners being massacred. The king depicted is Ptolemy Auletes, the father of the celebrated Cleopatra. The scenes above the entrance date back to the 4th century B.C. As you pass through, note the inscription on your left recording a visit by Napoleon's expedition. In the great court of the temple, you will observe the harmonious blend of centuries that makes up the special charm of Philae. On the right, a colonnade opens on to six small rooms that must have made up the sacristy. Begun 50 years before the birth of Christ, these structures were only completed under Tiberius in about A.D. 25. Facing them is the *mammisi*, or birth-house, with its row of three small chambers and preceding *pronaos*. It was built in the middle of the 3rd century B.C., while the scenes on its walls, depicting the childhood of the god Horus from the time of his birth, were not finished until the middle of the 1st century A.D. Above the exterior facade you will notice two bilingual inscriptions, one of which reproduces the text of the Rosetta Stone, which enabled hieroglyphic script to be deciphered.

The **second pylon,** which is higher than the first, is of the same period, and on it you will find scenes illustrating the massacre of prisoners. A huge slab of granite pierces the right-hand tower. It has been sawn off and bears an inscription of the 2nd century B.C.

Go up a few steps into the *pronaos*, the front part of the temple, which was transformed into a church in the 6th century A.D. Today it appears as it was originally designed. Its columns still preserve traces of color, and the decoration covering them and extending over the whole building employs all the classic Egyptian themes, from the symbolic vulture, the solar bark and astronomical ceiling decorations to mythological compositions on the walls.

As you move on from the *pronaos* toward the *naos*, or sanctuary, you will go back in time from the 2nd to the 3rd century B.C. The 12 rooms and crypt here are decorated with scenes of various ceremonies. Note the king burning incense and making libations in the offerings chamber on the right. Still surviving in the darkness of the sanctuary is a granite shrine.

Go out next through the left-hand side of the temple to go up to the **funerary temple of Osiris,** or rather what remains of it. The decorations illustrate the rites associated with the cult of the god. Towards the river on the right, there is a Roman gateway rising above the scenery. It marked the beginning of the path taken by pilgrims since the time when the Greek pharaohs and after them, the Romans, came to call on the Egyptian gods. Nearby is the little **temple of Hathor,** which was built in the 2nd century B.C. and completed under Augustus. In its reliefs, the god Bes can be seen playing various musical instruments, especially the harp. You will then come to the tall columns of the great **kiosk of Trajan,** which will captivate you with its elegance, even though it has lost its wooden roof. Inside, on the wall to the right, the emperor is seen performing the offering rites before Isis and Horus in one part, and before Isis and Osiris in another. Was the kiosk a landing-stage? Or was it a station chapel where the necessary ceremonies were performed so that Isis could leave her island and find it again? Leaving such speculation aside, your most lasting memory will be of the beauty of Philae and the love-story to which its temple was dedicated.

Abu Simbel, temple of Ramesses II.

The three temples of Kalabsha

Situated above the Aswân Dam on the left bank of the lake, the three temples of Kalabsha are within easy reach; it is a trip of about an hour and a half. The **temple of Mandulis,** one of the largest in Nubia, was moved from its original site with West German money. It was already a Roman reconstruction of a New Kingdom temple. From the roof, the view extends over the lake, the dam and the surrounding desert. Of the little **kiosk of Kirtasi,** only four columns remain, surmounted with palm capitals and connected by screen walls and a doorway with two Hathoric pillars. To the northwest, a road leads to the little rock-cut temple of **Beit el-Wali.**

▬ *ABU SIMBEL★★★*

The trip to **Abu Simbel,** which takes you in the direction of the second cataract in African territory along Lake Nasser, will be one of the highlights of your stay in Aswân and an opportunity to renew your acquaintance with the splendor of classical Egypt.

Getting there

Situated 174 miles/280 kilometres from Aswân, the site is connected to the town by a regular air service which allows you to leave early in the morning and to be back for lunch. It is also possible to spend the night at the site at the *Nefertari Hotel* by Lake Nasser (reservations through the *New Cataract Hotel* in Aswân), but a seat on the return flight is not certain until the last minute. The extraordinary beauty of the temples in the moonlight, and particularly at sunrise, when the sun's rays rise over the Arabian mountains and penetrate the interior of the great temple, is worth the risk of the extra wait for a flight.

The salvage operation

What you will see at **Abu Simbel** is quite magnificent. There is a virtually intact complex of rock-cut temples set in pink sandstone and dedicated to Ramesses II and Queen Nefertari. The whole complex, however, was very close to disappearing forever beneath the waters of the dam. Indeed, only 20 years ago, scholars alone were aware of the archaeological importance of Lower Nubia. UNESCO had to mount an intense publicity campaign to convince the world's better-off nations to participate in saving monuments that had been built by the pharaohs.

Following a survey, 14 Nubian temples were dismantled in order to be rebuilt away from the danger zone and, although a large number of them are still waiting in crates for the funds needed to complete the operation, **Abu Simbel** stands above Lake Nasser today as a symbol of what can be achieved through international co-operation.

The salvage operation was an undertaking of colossal dimensions, and was completed in six stages:
1. Uncovering the temples by removing the hills lying above them: 98 feet/30 metres above the great temple, 131 feet/40 metres above the small one; excavation of these hills down to 263 feet/80 metres above the roofs of the temples.
2. Construction of a coffer dam 82 feet/25 metres high to hold back the rising water during the removal operations.
3. Cutting of the two temples into 1036 blocks, some of which weighed 33 tons/30 tonnes. This presented some difficulties, because the fragility of the Abu Simbel sandstone was such that it was necessary to treat it so that it would not crumble and sometimes, the best way to avoid this was to do the cutting by hand.
4. Numbering and removing the blocks (12,650 tons/11,500 tonnes from the great temple, 3850 tons/3500 tonnes from the small one).
5. Re-erection of the temples by fixing their blocks on to a concrete superstructure, keeping their respective orientation and positions.

6. Restoration, as faithful as possible, of the original outer covering of rock by the construction of concrete vaults designed to support a casing of rock similar to that which once covered the temples.

Begun at the end of 1963, the operations led to the placing of the first stone of Abu Simbel on the new site in January 1966. The inauguration ceremony took place on September 22, 1968 but the final completion work was not finished until 1972.

This was a long time, but you will not be thinking about that as you look down from the aircraft at the **four colossal figures** of Ramesses II cut into the rock in front of the **great temple.** When you have flown over the artificial lake from which only small desert islands emerge, these statues take on a surprisingly human grandeur.

The visit to the temples

These four giant figures sit in the burning sun at a bend in the rocky road, looking out over the immense stretch of water. One of them is broken off above the knees. Its body and head lie on the ground. The other three sit quietly, their heads covered with the double crown resting on top of the *nemes* headcloth, and they are smiling. The royal cartouche is repeated on the pectoral and arms. Prisoners appear on the sides of their seats. To left and right of each statue, there are standing figures of the pharaoh's daughters, wife and mother, treated with more realistic human proportions but not even reaching as high as the king's knee. For those who like precise details, the height of the large statues from the top of the crown to the sole of the feet is about 66 feet/20 metres; the brow measures 2 feet/0.59 metres, the nose 3 feet, 3 inches/0.98 metres; the ears, 3 feet, 6 inches/1.06 metres; the eyes, 2 feet, 9 inches/0.84 metres; and the mouth 3 feet, 8 inches/1.1 metres. The breadth of the face from ear to ear is 13 feet, 7 inches/4.17 metres, the hands, 8 feet, 7 inches/2.64 metres. Even more striking than these dimensions are the expression on the faces, the perfect proportions and the whole arrangement of the figures. You can study this as you climb the few steps up to the gently sloping terrace on which they stand behind a balustrade. Along the base of the balustrade, there are scenes showing, on the left-hand side, Africans kneeling before an offerings table and extending their hands toward the temple entrance and, on the other side, Asian prisoners. The facade displays extreme simplicity of line. Along the top, there is a band of hieroglyphs surmounted by a cornice and a frieze of 20 seated baboons. In a niche above the entrance, stands a large statue of the god Ra, the sun-god with the head of a hawk. The ritual scenes flanking the entrance are treated with great attention to detail, as are the offering scenes on the door lintel.

You may wish to linger awhile here but decorations of extraordinary beauty await you inside. You will not be able to see them right away in the darkness of the hypostyle hall, where you will be immediately struck by the size of the eight Osiride pillars. The colossal figures attached to them bear the features of Ramesses and support a 33-foot/10-metre high ceiling decorated with royal inscriptions and vultures, their wings outstretched. The sides of the pillars are carved with offering scenes. When your eyes become accustomed to the dark, you will be able to gradually pick out the epic story of the pharaoh's military campaigns illustrated in a series of more or less consecutive scenes on the two walls facing each other across the chamber. The whole composition is of great perfection.

The various phases of the battle fought by Ramesses against the Hittites at Kadesh are depicted on the right. The action is divided into two sections. In the lower register, there is a series of three pictures. First: the king, seated on his throne, holds a council of war with his officers; note his chariot and his guard, and spies being beaten to force confessions out of them. Second: the Egyptian camp, surrounded by a stockade of shields, with loose horses, soldiers going about their billet and cook-house duties and on water fatigues. Third: the departure of the troops of infantry and chariots. The upper register is devoted to the battle itself. In the center is Kadesh, surrounded by the River Orontes; on the left, the king, mounted on his chariot, decimates his enemies, who had led him into an ambush; and much of the lower part is filled with a cavalry battle. On the right, you see the end of the battle; the king is standing in his chariot presiding over the arrival of a line of prisoners and the counting of the hands and genital organs cut off. The opposite wall (on your left) is also divided into two panels. The upper register consists of five offering scenes in which the king appears in the presence of different deities. The lower register is marvelous. In the center, the king is engaged in hand-to-hand fighting with a Hittite, whom he seizes with one hand while brandishing his lance in the other. On the left, you can see an attack on a Syrian fortress; the king, followed by three of his sons, charges at the head of his troops. There is a good deal of violent movement. To make it more expressive, the sculptor has had no qualms about correcting the line of the king's arm and bow.

The entrance to the **vestibule** which follows is flanked by two symmetrical scenes in which the deified king leads a batch of prisoners before a group of three gods. This smaller chamber is supported by four thick square pillars decorated with two-figure scenes showing the king with different deities. Note the sacred boat being carried along on the walls.

Three doors in the rear wall lead into a **third chamber,** which, as in all other temples, is not so high or broad. Then three more doors aligned directly behind them open into the **sanctuary** itself. In the center, there is an altar and, at the rear, statues of the king and three gods (among them Amun-Ra) are cut into the rock.

The **chapels** are of no more interest than the eight rooms arranged on each side of the hypostyle hall. Narrow and low, they were never completed and they served as storerooms for objects connected with the cult.

Before leaving the temple, take another glance at the decoration of the hypostyle hall and the walls on each side of the exit, where you will see the king sacrificing prisoners to the god Amun-Ra. His daughters, on the left, are presenting him with *sistra* and his sons, on the right, are holding standards in one hand and making a gesture of worship with the other. Outside, behind the mud-brick balustrade enclosing the forecourt, a door opening into the rock will enable you to go inside the mountain which has been reassembled around the temple above a huge concrete vault. Here you can appreciate the tremendous achievement of the salvage operation.

The **temple of Hathor,** some 55 yards/50 metres away, is on a more modest scale. Even so, **six colossal statues** are cut into the rock forming the facade, and are set in deep recesses between seven inclined buttresses. They stand 33 feet/10 metres high but the whole arrangement is so harmonious that you forget its dimensions. This is a temple dedicated to Hathor, the goddess of happiness and love who, here, takes on the attributes of Queen Nefertari. Indeed, it is the queen's image, in the goddess's clothes, that dominates the whole facade. It stands between two colossal statues bearing the features of Ramesses II on each side of the entrance. You will also notice the usual statues of the pharaoh's sons that reach up to the height of his knees and statues of the royal princesses around the feet of the queen. With its symmetrical design arranged around a powerful central buttress, the facade displays great charm, for all its severity. There is, too, a whimsical touch for modern visitors: the variety of headgear worn by the king. In fact, each had a precise theological significance at that time.

The inside of the temple is very simple. The hypostyle hall is almost intimate in size. It is formed by six Hathor-headed pillars arranged in two rows and bearing the face of the lovely goddess with cow's ears nearly 10 feet/3 metres above the ground. The two principal walls of the chamber are decorated with scenes of offerings, in which the king appears three times as the main figure, the queen once. The rear wall, divided by three doors, is entirely given up to the queen. Here, her captivating image can be seen paying homage to the goddess Mut on one side, and to Hathor on the other. The vestibule that follows, which is flanked by two chambers of no particular interest, opens into the sanctuary, from the back of which the divine cow emerges from the rock toward you between two Hathor-headed pillars.

You will, perhaps, remain for a moment in this cool, hospitable place and imagine the goddess-queen, but on the way out of the temple, note the king slaughtering a prisoner in the presence of his wife before Amun-Ra!

Before you get back into the bus, you can see historic stelae from the time of Ramesses carved on rocks to the north of the temple and, with a little luck, find some refreshments there.

ALEXANDRIA

A visit to Alexandria is the natural and traditional way to end a journey along the Nile Valley because the founding of this city by Alexander the Great in 330 B.C. brought to an end the centuries-old course of pharaonic civilization. Indeed, the new capital was destined to become one of the most important commercial and cultural centers. The Ancients were not mistaken when, far from linking the city with Egypt, they called it 'Alexandria ad Egyptum' — Alexandria on the way to Egypt.

Few vestiges remain of the outstandingly brilliant history of this port which, until the end of the 15th century, was one of the major points of contact between the Middle East and the Mediterranean. There is a marvelous museum, but you will find no trace of the library that drew all those Greek scholars and learned men, nor of the lighthouse that was one of the Seven Wonders of the World. By the same token, the few remnants of the Arab era will hardly conjure up for you the busy medieval port from which Far Eastern spices, precious woods and ivories from Africa and other treasures were sent off to Venice. What you will find in Alexandria is a bustling modern city of two million inhabitants which, with its port and docks and its warehouses and great shipping companies, is still Egypt's business center, It is directing its future toward industrial development and linking its fortunes with those of the Arab world in general.

▬ THE JOURNEY TO ALEXANDRIA

The distance between Alexandria and Cairo is about 139 miles/225 kilometres, a distance you can cover in three hours, leaving, if need be, in the morning and returning the same evening. That would, however, be a pity, because the two possible routes are both interesting and worth covering during the daytime.

The desert route

A regular coach service from Cairo (booking office and departure point in Midan el-Tahrir — Map pp. 66–67 C–2 tel. 70-651) provides hourly connections to Midan Saad Zaghlul (Map pp. 158–159 B–4) in the center of

Alexandria (tel. 80–96–85) and vice-versa. The journey takes three hours, with a halfway stop at the rest-house at Wadi el-Natrun.

The main interest of this route is that it passes the **Wadi el-Natrun,** a once-barren valley where there is a string of salt lakes that leave deposits of precious natron (sodium carbonate) along their shores during the summer months, and where some 50 monasteries sprang up in the 4th century A.D. during the spiritual upsurge that drew contemporary Christians to the monastic life. There are four of these monasteries left today. You will be able to hire a taxi at the rest-house to pay a visit to the most important one, the **monastery of St. Macarius.** The trip takes a little over an hour and allows you to continue your journey to Alexandria by the next coach. From a distance you will be struck by the size of the monastery, which covers nearly 10 acres/4 hectares, and by the height of its windowless walls which, although modern, have machicolations and a tightly closed drawbridge. This is, in fact, a fortress. Inside, standing beside two fairly old churches, you will still find the *qasr*, the keep found in desert monasteries that allowed the monks, even until quite recently, to keep an eye on the bedouins and to take cover from their raids. All the monasteries in this region resemble each other. You will come into Alexandria via **Lake Maryut,** which was once famous for its sparkling water and its fish. An industrial zone is now being developed around the lake.

The delta route

You should make this journey by train because the road is dangerous. The trip takes two and a half hours by express train, which has air conditioning and sleeper-cars, and three hours by other fast trains. Avoid the trains with stops, as these are very hot. The station in Cairo is in Midan Ramses, (Map pp. 66–67 B–3; tel. 58–458). There are several trains every day. The station in Alexandria is in Midan el-Gumhuriya; (Republic Square, Map pp. 158–159 C–5; tel. 23 207) in the city center. You should make the trip by day, because the scenery is very striking. The train passes through a tranquil setting of lush green countryside, traversed by *feluccas* that glide by along invisible canals between the cultivated fields and palm trees. Nearly a third of Egypt's population lives here in small villages dominated by the familiar mosque, and it is hard to believe that the delta has known great capital cities, such as Sais and Tanis. Today, camels are no longer laden with bales passing through the cotton fields, nor are young urchins goading buffaloes into the meadows when the beasts are not wallowing in the water.

Rather than the splendors of the past, it is the muddy delta marshlands, rich in bird life, which are of interest here. Until the arrival of the Greeks, these were the best defense pharaonic Egypt had against incursions from the Mediterranean and, at the dawn of history, they enabled Isis to shelter her son Horus from Seth, the god of evil and the slayer of Osiris.

▬ *YOUR STAY IN ALEXANDRIA*

Accommodation and dining

Intended for affluent visitors, the city's three leading hotels (Cecil, Windsor, Metropole) are very expensive. The most famous (Cecil) includes a casino and nightclub.

Within the city itself there is a choice among:
Two first-class hotels:
▲▲▲▲**Cecil** (Map pp. 158-159 B–4; tel. 80–75–32; telex 54358), 16 Midan Saad Zaghlul.
▲▲▲▲**Windsor** (Map pp. 158–159 B–4; tel. 80–87–00), 17 Shari el-Shuhada.

A second-class hotel:
▲▲▲**Metropole** (Map pp. 158–159 B–4; tel. 21–467; telex 43350), 52 Shari Saad Zaghlul.

Two third-class hotels:
▲**Le Roy** (Map pp. 158–159 C–4; tel. 80–95–10), 25 Shari Talaat Harb.

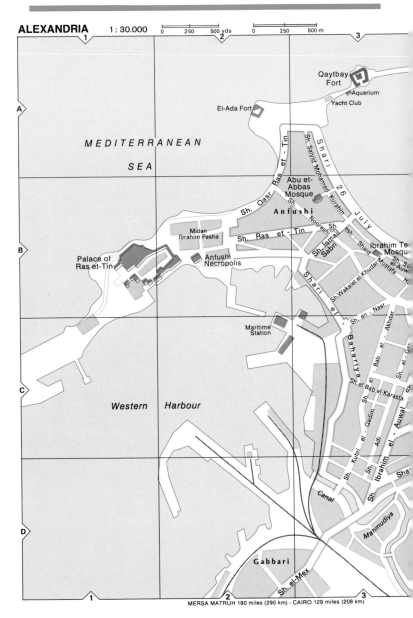

ALEXANDRIA 1 : 30.000

MERSA MATRUH 180 miles (290 km) - CAIRO 129 miles (208 km)

▲**Capri** (Map above B–4; tel. 80–93–10), Midan Saad Zaghlul.

The **youth hostel** (Map above A–6; tel. 75–596) is at 13 Shari Port Said.

On the Corniche, there are:
Two first-class hotels:
▲▲▲▲**San Stefano** (tel. 63–580; telex 54201), el-Guesh Avenue at San Stefano.

▲▲▲▲**Beau Rivage** (tel. 62–187; telex 92355), 434 el-Guesh Avenue.

One second-class hotel:
▲▲▲**San Giovanni** (tel. 84–09–84; telex 54213), 205 el-Guesh Avenue at Stanley.

In the Montazah Gardens, about 24 miles/15 kilometres from the city:

▲▲▲▲**Alexandria** (tel. 96–85–50; telex 54706), belonging to the Sheraton chain.

▲▲▲▲**Palestine** (tel. 86–17–99; telex 54027), worthy of the wealthiest of emirs.

▲▲▲▲**Salamlek** (tel. 86–54–01; telex 65813), occupying a former royal pavilion.

▲▲▲▲**Maamoura Palace** (tel. 86–54–01; telex 67107), on the beautiful beach of the same name just beyond the Montazah Gardens.

Restaurants include, in addition to those in the hotels listed in the city center:

Santa Lucia (Map pp. 158–159 B–4; tel 24–240), 40 Shari Safiya Zaghlul, considered the best restaurant in Alexandria.

Union (Map pp. 158–159 B–4; tel. 80–53–13), 1 Shari el Bursa el Kadima.

El Ikhlas (Map pp. 158–159 B–5; tel. 23–571), 49 Shari Safiya Zaghlul, famous·for its Middle Eastern cuisine.

Pastroudis (Map pp. 158–159 B–5; tel. 29–609), 39 Shari Gamal Abd en-Nasser, which also makes pastries.

Fish and seafood restaurants along the Corniche around Midan Saad Zaghlul must also be mentioned, notably the following:

Nassar (tel. 80–53–70), 145 Shari 26 July.

Darwish (tel. 28–938), near Midan Saad Zaghlul.

Useful addresses

Passport office (Map pp. 158–159 B–4; tel. 80–86–99), 28 Shari Talaat Harb.

Tourist information office (Map pp. 158–159 B–4; tel. 80–79–85), Midan Saad Zaghlul.

United Kingdom Consulate (Map pp. 158–159 B–5; tel 47–166), 3 Shari Mina.

United States consulate (Map pp. 158–159 B–5; tel. 80–19–11), 110 Shari Gamal Abd en-Nasser.

▬ *A TOUR OF THE CITY*

A sample day spent in Alexandria might include, for example, a tour of the city, with visits to the museum and the Roman amphitheater, ending with dinner at one of the beach resorts. The tour alone will need two hours by taxi, because distances are great. Leaving from Midan Saad Zaghlul (Map pp. 158–159 B–4), which is considered to be the center of the modern city, you will come immediately on to the Corniche which, under the name of Shari 26 July, runs for 2 miles/3 kilometres around the shore of the ancient eastern harbor — the *portus magnus* — which is no longer used. Leaving Silsila Point to the east, you should now make for **Fort Qaytbay** (Map pp. 158–159 A–3), which was built by the Arabs on the island of Pharos in the 15th century, the site of the celebrated ancient lighthouse. On the way, you can visit the interesting **aquarium** of the Hydrobiological Institute (*visit: daily 9 am – 5 pm; admission charge*) to see fishes from the Nile and Red Sea. After passing through the residential district to the west, you will come to the **Ras et-Tin Palace** (Map pp. 158–159 B–1) at the end of the esplanade, one of the oldest royal residences in Egypt. Today, it is reserved for the use of the country's official guests. Behind it, in the background, you will see the modern port. In a small enclosed park off the square, you can visit the Ptolemaic **Anfushi Necropolis** (Map pp. 158–159 B–2).

You should then ask your taxi driver to take you to 'Pompey's Pillar' (Map pp. 158–159 D–4), which is, in fact, dedicated to Diocletian and must have once been part of the portico of the ancient Serapeum. Its beautiful red granite shaft now stands in the midst of an enclosure containing a collection of Roman ruins (*visit: daily 9 am to 5 pm; admission charge*).

Return to the city center via the **catacombs of Kom esh-Shuqafa** (Map pp. 158–159 D–4), decorated in a strange mixture of Greco-Roman styles and Egyptian art. You can then end your tour at the Roman amphitheater, which was discovered in 1963 and now lies in a lovely garden.

The Greco-Roman Museum (Map pp. 158-159 B–5)

Visit: daily 9 am – 4 pm, 3 pm on public holidays; closed Fridays 11.15 am – 1.15 pm in summer, 12 – 2 pm in winter. Taking photographs is prohibited. Entrance charge.

Situated in a quiet little street just a few steps from the city center, the museum offers an escape from all the noise and bustle and immerses you in the refined culture of Alexandrian society at the beginning of the Christian era. This refinement is demonstrated in works that take Greek and Egyptian themes but interpret them in a style that displays considerable charm.

From a strictly chronological point of view, a visit to the Alexandria Museum should be interposed between visits to the Egyptian Museum and the Coptic Museum in Cairo. The first rooms contain a mixture of Greek and Egyptian objects which you pass by on the left. In **room 7** you will find typical objects of the pharaonic era; **room 8,** sarcophagi; **room 9,** extremely interesting relics of the 2nd century B.C. from El Fayyum; **room 10,** a fine collection of objects ranging from a group of vessels from the beginning of the third millennium B.C. to funerary masks of the Roman era.

The Greco-Roman collections effectively begin in **room 11,** with large sculptures, mosaics, architectural elements and vases. In **room 12,** on the right at the back, near a head of Julius Caesar, there is an extremely lifelike yellow limestone head of a woman, her hair partly covered by a veil. **Room 15** is mostly taken up by a painted wall from a tomb, on which you will see a *sakia,* the wheel turned by two oxen which is still used today to raise water from wells in the fields. In **room 16,** note the marble forearm clutching a sphere; it is an anatomical study. Then pause by the glass cases displaying small sculptures, heads and statuettes; it is in these that Alexandrian art attains its greatest charm. Do not miss the headless marble figure of Dionysos. In **room 17,** a white marble sarcophagus features a relief of Ariadne, surprised while sleeping on Naxos by Dionysos and his retinue. In **rooms 18** and **18a,** you will see genuine Tanagra objects (made in the village of Tanagra, in Greece), including grotesque figurines and all kinds of realistic statuettes, such as the very attractive richly clad female musicians and dancers. In **room 22** there is a fine collection of jewelry and gold and silver objects.

Return through the **garden,** where a number of large items and reconstructions are assembled. Before leaving the museum, go through the vestibule on the left into **room 1,** which contains a collection of objects particularly textiles from the great monasteries of the region.

Lying some 218 yards/200 metres from the museum exit to the northeast are the beautiful **Shallalat Gardens,** which will enable you to rest for a while.

The beaches of Alexandria

Alexandria's celebrated beaches stretch eastward along the coast from the old harbor, many with evocative names: Ibrahimia, Cleopatra and Camp Shizar (Caesar's Camp). It is here, more than anywhere else, that you will find the luxurious setting associated with the elegant, sensual and cosmopolitan Alexandria of the inter-war years. Today, public housing developments are gradually taking over the land, yet the area retains its charm. You might have dinner here but, if you have friends or a car, you will probably prefer to go on to the **Montazah Gardens, Maamoura Beach,** or the small village of **Abukir** (15 miles/24 kilometres) to dine on fish and seafood at the *Zephyrion* restaurant (tel: 86–07–58). You will then be a very long way indeed from the world of the pharaohs.

BIBLIOGRAPHY

Badawy, A.: *Coptic Art and Archeology: The Art of the Christian Egyptians from the Late Antique to the Middle Ages* (M.I.T. Press, Cambridge, Massachussets, 1978)

Blue Guide: *Egypt* (Ernest Benn, London, 1984)

Carter, Howard: *The Tomb of Tutankhamen* (Pygmalion, London, 1978)

David, A.R.: *The Egyptian Kingdoms* (Phaidon, London, 1975)

Durrell, Lawrence: *The Alexandria Quartet: Justine, Balthazar, Mount Olive, Clea* (Faber and Faber, London 1963)

Edwards, Amelia, B.: *A Thousand Miles Up the Nile* (Century, London, 1982)

Edwards, I.E.S.: *Tutankhaman: His Tomb and its Treasures* (Victor Gollancz Ltd, London, 1979)

Forster, E.M.: *Alexandria: A History and Guide* (Michael Haaq Ltd, London, 1982)

Frankfort, H.: *Ancient Egyptian Religion: An Interpretation* (Harper and Row, New York, 1961)

Golding, W.: *An Egyptian Journal* (Faber and Faber, London, 1985)

Holt, P.M.: *Studies in the History of the Near East* (F. Cass, London, 1973)

Hoving, T.: *Tutankhamon: The Untold Story* (Hamish Hamilton, London, 1978)

Ivimy, J.: *The Sphinx and the Megaliths* (Turnstone, London, 1974)

Johnson, A.C.: *Egypt and the Roman Empire* (University of Michigan Press, 1951)

Kay, S.: *The Egyptians: How They Live and Work* (David and Charles, Vancouver, 1975)

Lord Kinross: *Between Two Seas, the Creation of the Suez Canal* (John Murray, London, 1968)

Lane, E.W.: *An Account of the Manners and Customs of the Modern Egyptians* (Dover Publications, New York, 1973)

Lane, Poole S.: *A History of Egypt in the Middle Ages* (Methuen, London, 1901)

Little, T.: *Modern Egypt* (Ernest Benn, London, 1967)

Lloyd, C.: *The Nile Campaign: Nelson and Napoleon in Egypt* (Barnes and Noble, New York, 1973)

McGrath, N.: *Frommer's Dollarwise Guide to Egypt* (Simon and Schuster, New York, 1986)

Moorehead, A.: *The White Nile* (Penguin, London, 1984)

Parker, R.: *A Practical Guide to the Islamic Monuments of Cairo* (AUC Press, Cairo, 1973)

Tompkins, P.: *Secrets of the Great Pyramids* (Harper and Row, San Francisco, 1971)

Vatikiotis: *Egypt since the Revolution* (G. Allen and Unwin, London, 1968)

▬▬ INDEX

Places and sites

When a place or site listed here also appears on one of the maps, the page number of the map is in **bold type.**

Printed in Singapore by Tien Wah Press
Dépôt légal: 3801-1-1987
ISBN 0-13-331299-2